Exploring in Security

This book builds a key clinical bridge between attachment theory and psychoanalysis, deploying Holmes' unique capacity to weld empirical evidence, psychoanalytic theory and consulting room experience into a coherent and convincing whole. Starting from the theory–practice gap in psychoanalytic psychotherapy, the book demonstrates how attachment theory can help practitioners better understand what they intuitively do in the consulting room, how this benefits clients and informs evidence-based practice.

Divided into two parts, theory and practice, *Exploring in Security* discusses the concept of mentalising and considers three components of effective therapy – the therapeutic relationship, meaning making and change promotion – from both attachment and psychoanalytic perspectives. The second part of the book applies attachment theory to a number of clinical situations including:

- working with borderline clients
- suicide and deliberate self-harm
- sex and sexuality
- dreams
- ending therapy.

Throughout the book theoretical discussion is vividly illustrated with clinical material, personal experience and examples from literature and film, making this an accessible yet authoritative text for psychotherapy practitioners at all levels, including psychoanalysts, psychiatrists, clinical psychologists, mental health nurses and counsellors.

Jeremy Holmes is a Psychiatrist and Psychoanalytic Psychotherapist and Visiting Professor at the University of Exeter, UK. He has published prolifically in the field of Attachment Theory and psychoanalytic psychotherapy. Now retired from the NHS, he co-runs the postgraduate degree and qualifying course in psychodynamic psychotherapy at Exeter University, and has a small private practice. In 2009 he received the prestigious Bowlby-Ainsworth Award for his contributions to the field of attachment.

Exploring in Security

Towards an attachment-informed psychoanalytic psychotherapy

Jeremy Holmes

Routledge
Taylor & Francis Group

LONDON AND NEW YORK

First published 2010
by Routledge
27 Church Road, Hove, East Sussex BN3 2FA

Simultaneously published in the USA and Canada
by Routledge
711 Third Avenue, New York NY 10017

*Routledge is an imprint of the Taylor & Francis Group,
an Informa business*

© 2010 Jeremy Holmes

Typeset in Times by
RefineCatch Limited, Bungay, Suffolk
Paperback cover design and illustration by Andrew Ward

British Library Cataloguing in Publication Data
A catalogue record for this book is available from the British Library

Library of Congress Cataloging-in-Publication Data
Holmes, Jeremy.
    Exploring in security : towards an attachment-informed
    psychoanalytic psychotherapy / Jeremy Holmes.
        p. cm.
    Includes bibliographical references and index.
    1. Attachment behavior.   2. Security (Psychology).
    3. Psychoanalysis.   4. Psychotherapy.   I. Title.
    RC455.4.A84H654 2009
    616.89'17—dc22   2009020060

ISBN: 978–0–415–55414–5 (hbk)
ISBN: 978–0–415–55415–2 (pbk)

For Reuben and Ilya

Contents

Preface

For followers of attachment, the past decade has been an exciting one, with many significant theoretical and empirical advances. A number of seminal volumes have been published summarising the latest research and clinical applications (Cassidy and Shaver 2008; Wallin 2007; Fonagy et al. 2002; Brisch 2002; Carter et al. 2005; Obegi and Berant 2008). In particular, the concept of mentalising (to be fully expounded in Chapter 2) has come to the fore, with far-reaching ramifications for psychotherapy generally (Allen 2008). At the same time psychoanalysis has undergone a period of soul-searching, out of which have emerged new approaches to: its evidence basis (Leichsenring and Rabung 2008); links with neuroscience (Zeki 2008); scientific status (Wallerstein 2009); competency assessment (Tuckett et al. 2008; Roth and Lemma 2008); and modifications for working with difficult clients (Bateman and Fonagy 2008). The aim of this book is to weld together these new attachment and psychoanalytic ideas in the service of improving everyday psychotherapeutic practice.

The book's title reflects one of the simple yet profound ideas attachment has brought to our discipline: the mutual incompatibility of insecurity and exploration. This leads to the paradox, whose unravelling is central to the business of psychotherapy, that until safety prevails, care-seeking people – i.e. a 'patient' or 'client' – cannot begin to explore themselves, their life situation and their feelings; yet it is that very insecurity that brings them for help. As one client said in response to the annunciation of Freud's (1912) 'fundamental rule' – 'say whatever comes into your mind, however irrelevant, embarrassing or impolite' – 'if I could do that I wouldn't need to be here in the first place'. The task of therapy is both to *explore insecurity*, its origins and ramifications, and to provide a space where a person can *explore in security*. Much psychoanalytic practice, to which the clinical part of the book is devoted, consists of working with that dialectic.

For my subtitle I am indebted to Arietta Slade's elegant formulation (2008, p. 763):

> attachment theory and research have the potential to enrich (rather than

dictate) a therapist's understanding ... Understanding the nature and dynamics of attachment informs, rather than defines, intervention and clinical thinking.

In the spirit of that gloss, what is presented here is a particular angle on psychoanalytic work, imbued with attachment ideas but still broadly within the psychoanalytic framework, especially the more relational, independent stream. Setting up a psychoanalytic psychotherapy training *de novo* over the past five years has brought home to me the need for greater focus than is traditional on the 'infrastructure' of psychoanalytic technique, and how it relates to the theoretical superstructure.

Freud's papers on technique (Freud 1911–1915), although still indispensable, are now a century old. Attachment theory, with its primary interest in the vicissitudes of intimate relationships, has a vital contribution to understanding the health-promoting (and, sadly, sometimes health-diminishing) aspects of the therapist–patient relationship. Recent attempts by the UK Department of Health (Roth and Lemma 2008) to look behind professional titles at psychotherapeutic competencies (including psychoanalytic competencies) – what therapists actually do and say with their clients in the consulting room – is consistent with this project.

Psychotherapy as art, craft or profession

Psychotherapists enjoy debating whether what their discipline is an art or a science (Holmes 1992) – a discarded title for this book was *What Do Psychotherapists Do All Day?*. It is perhaps best seen as a craft (cf. Sennett 2008), drawing on both art and science but distinguishable from both.

Craftsmanship/craftswomanship has a number of features relevant to psychotherapy. First, a craft is something that cannot be learned from books alone – as anyone who has tried to master skiing, carpentry or playing a musical instrument will attest. Second, acquiring a craft invariably involves apprenticeship – watching and practicing under the tutelage or supervision of a 'master'. Third, unlike science or art, at least as they are constituted in capitalist societies, craft is largely non-competitive. We admire master-gardeners or chefs, try to emulate and learn from them, but that does not diminish the value of our own horticultural or culinary efforts, however modest. It is to everyone to cultivate their garden or kitchen to the best of their ability and resources. Similarly, each psychotherapist–patient relationship has its own unique quality deserving of honour, however much it differs from or falls short of the ways in which the psychoanalytic pantheon perform. Fourth, professional craftspeople typically form relatively homogeneous communities, or guilds, of varying degrees of esotericism, with their own rites of passage (initiation, graduation, admission to senior status, etc.) values, ethics and traditional practices. Finally, in its modern usage, the related word 'crafty' implies subtlety, finesse and skilfulness, and occasionally a degree of showmanship or benign deceit.

The etymology of the craft/profession dichotomy neatly captures the public and private faces of psychotherapy. The Anglo-Saxon, monosyllabic 'craft' derives from the Germanic word for power, ability or skill. The Latinate 'pro-fession' comes from the open declaration of faith required of Church supplicants. Many modern professions evolved out of crafts, just as the professions themselves were modelled on ecclesiastical hierarchies. In Britain, nineteenth-century barber-surgeons, no less than Harley Street grandees, became, by an 1858 Act of Parliament, 'doctors' – their craftsmanship as bone-setters and herbalists being transmuted, via the 'grandfather clause', into a common 'medical profession'. Medical men (as they then all were), while retaining many of the autonomous features associated with a craft, were now subject to, but also protected and dignified by, a degree of state regulation, especially of the qualification procedures enabling practitioners to call themselves doctors. The parallels with the establishment of a state-regulated psychotherapy profession are striking.

A century later, following a series of medical scandals, postgraduation medical practice in the UK and throughout the world is now increasingly exposed to public view and external scrutiny. This further twist implies a degree of *de*-professionalisation as medical work is broken down into a series of technical procedures that can be defined, operationalised and performed semi-impersonally – in the case of medical robotics literally so. Many feel that vital ingredients have been lost in the process – the uniqueness of the doctor–patient relationship; holistic approaches encompassing the physical, emotional and spiritual aspects of personhood; continuing scrutiny and care through the life-cycle; the doctor's role as witness to perennial existential themes of conception, birth, growth and development, sexuality, trauma, illness, death and renewal.

Psychotherapy is a natural home for what has been lost in this process of societal splitting and repression. But being thus thrust into a public role puts psychotherapy in a bind. On one hand it needs to remain true to itself as the champion of the individual life story and the healing potential of human relationships. On the other, in moving from cottage-industry craft to profession, it aspires to the advantages of public recognition, access to state funding ('taxpayers' money') and the credence that confers. Medicine provides the inescapable template. Respectability for 'professions allied to medicine' requires conforming to medicine's values and procedures. Cognitive behavioural therapy (CBT) has successfully accommodated to this 'medical model'. CBT's repute is as an 'evidence-based treatment', equivalent to a good drug, for psychological 'disorders', while remaining committed to the co-constructedness of the therapeutic relationship.

This in turn has led to further splitting and projection within psychotherapy. As CBT becomes increasingly standardised and packaged, the unconscious as a locus where all that is unacceptable, inexpressible and shameful is located may be 'Othered', seen as irrelevant to the process of 'treatment'. Long-term struggle with pain and suffering is jettisoned in favour of superficial solutions, with ever-present risk of relapse. The distortions of a life-trajectory associated with trauma and neglect that contribute to the formation of 'character' are overlooked, or seen as unreachable or irremediable. This remains the province of psychoanalytic psychotherapy.

A wider aim of this book, therefore – beyond initiating a conversation with colleagues about meeting points between psychoanalysis and attachment – is to begin to develop a framework for thinking about the role of psychoanalysis with the psychotherapeutic community. It can be seen as a contribution to the 'common language for psychotherapies' debate (see Holmes and Bateman 2002), exploring the implicit 'language of thought' (Cheney and Seyfarth 2007), which underlies the psychoanalytic school and dialect that happens to be any given practitioner's particular vernacular.

The book's methodology and structure

The provenance of this book is a combination of theoretical synthesis and consulting room conjecture typical of the psychoanalytic approach. It draws on relevant research wherever possible. As well as psychoanalysis and attachment theory, the influence of theories and findings from primate ethology, child developmental research and, occasionally, neuroscience will be evident. A prime aim is to suggest that attachment thinking can help and guide psychoanalytic work, but what goes on in the consulting room can never be fully captured by any theoretical model, however well grounded. The therapist brings an implicit ethic to the therapeutic relationship whose components include: respect, attention, validation, reticence, spontaneity, trust, valuation of the articulation of emotional truths, boundedness, and acknowledgement of mistakes and the necessity for repair when they occur. Attachment can help theorise some of those ingredients, but in the end the therapist and patient are on their own with their relationship and the human qualities they bring to it. Part of the genius of psychoanalytic psychotherapy is to set constraints on a relationship and then work with the creativity and the limitations that flow from those constraints.

Acknowledging both theoretical bedrock and mysteriousness, the methodology of this book could be seen as 'vignette and counterpoint'. The word 'vignette' comes from the French word *vigne*, and was originally a decorative embellishment of grapes and vine leaves used to fill in blank spaces between the printed matter in books. From there it has come to mean an illustrative miniature story that, like a parable or fable, conveys some wider truth.

The vignette is particularly relevant to psychotherapy, partly because psychotherapists have from the outset relied on case histories to communicate and underpin their theories. Psychotherapy is specifically concerned with the unspoken truths, the 'blank spaces' between the official text of people's lives. Helping to fill in those psychic spaces is a prime psychoanalytic task.

Nevertheless, for methodological, theoretical and ethical reasons, the 'case history' method is intrinsically problematic. Methodologically, there can be no guarantee that the reported stories and conversations are accurate – the intrinsic messiness of the consultation is easily glossed and polished in the telling. Clinical material is always open to a number of interpretations. My contention here is that the attachment 'lens' offers a useful addition to therapeutic discourse. I shall also argue that attachment provides a wider theoretical justification for the 'polysemy' – the 'many meaning-ness' – of psychoanalytic theorising. There is also the intractable problem of confidentiality, which can be tackled in a number of ways including 'thick disguise'; pure (if there can be such a thing) fiction; composite cases; asking permission (Gabbard 2000); and using already published material.

The book is divided into two parts. Part I lays out the theoretical and evidential background to attachment-informed psychoanalytic psychotherapy. After an introductory chapter, I embark on the book's main theme: mentalising as a meta-concept and its implications for therapeutic work. The succeeding three chapters are devoted to the three principal components of all effective therapies – forming a therapeutic relationship, meaning-making and promoting change – as they apply to the attachment-informed approach advocated here. I continue in Chapters 6 and 7 by expounding two further key concepts: empowerment and rupture/repair. Chapter 8, a transitional point, draws an analogy between psychotherapy and poesis.

Part II – 'Practice' – picks up these theoretical ideas and applies them to a variety of clinical themes: sex and sexuality, working with complex and disturbed cases, suicide, dreaming and termination. Throughout, the aim is to bring together theory, relevant research and consulting room experience. The tone changes here, being more personal, and in places has a valedictory feel, marking my retirement from psychiatric practice and move to part-time psychotherapist and teacher. Given my psychiatric background, some of the cases described may seem beyond the scope of normal office psychotherapy.

General psychotherapeutic practice

Psychoanalytic theorising can be strangely de-contextualised. Money, class, gender, ethnicity and social context are, with honourable exceptions (Dalal 2002; Ruiz et al. 2005) driven to the periphery of what is sometimes presented as an abstract, universalised, psychoanalytic space. Since I adhere to the systemic (and Marxist) view that 'material conditions' – i.e. context – determine consciousness, mention should be made of the work setting out of which this book arises, and which forms the basis for the fictionalised clinical stories that illustrate the theoretical arguments of this book, to whose originals I am deeply grateful.

I define my practice, both in the public and private sectors, as 'general psychotherapy' analogous in medicine to 'general practice': i.e. an open access, non-highly-specialised, all-comers form of work.

General psychotherapy practice as I see it implies a particular approach to diagnosis, duration of treatment, technique and frequency. It includes:

- working with a range of clients (I use the terms 'client' and 'patient' interchangeably throughout; similarly he/she), from high-functioning people with relationship difficulties to those with major mental illnesses
- therapy of varying duration, from brief to intermediate (up to a year) to long-term (my current record is 22 years)
- striking a balance between interpretive and supportive approaches
- using predominantly psychoanalytic technique but borrowing occasionally from other disciplines such as psychodrama-influenced role-play, and CBT-style challenge and homework
- seeing most clients weekly; a few twice-weekly; some, especially towards the end of therapy, less frequently
- working predominantly with individuals, but occasionally couples and families
- in isolated instances combining drug prescription and psychotherapy.

I believe that this type of practice is not so far removed from the psychoanalytic psychotherapy norm. Whether general conclusions can be drawn from the particular attachment-informed theoretical and practical approach explored in what follows is for the reader to decide.

Acknowledgements

My primary debt is to the unofficial grouping or 'guild' of colleagues, centred mainly on the Anna Freud Centre in London but also in affiliated centres in the USA, who have been my intellectual inspiration and comfort over the past few years. The common theme of this group is a fundamental allegiance to psychoanalysis but also, with the help of attachment theory and research, a wish to subject it to empirical and theoretical scrutiny. Without the outstanding contributions of Peter Fonagy and Mary Target (1997, 2000, 2005, 2007), Anthony Bateman (Bateman and Fonagy 2004, 2008), John Allen (2006, 2008), Arietta Slade (2005, 2008), Howard and Miriam Steele (2008), Jeremy Safran (Safran and Muran 2000) and Morris Eagle (Eagle 2007; Eagle and Wolitzky 2008), this volume would not have been possible.

This book is the fruit of several years of reading, thinking, lecturing and writing. I am grateful to the students, colleagues, institutions and journals with whom and which I have shared my ideas in their preliminary form, and that have helped improve and amend them and stimulated their further development. Especially important has been the academic programme in psychological therapies at the University of Exeter, and my students and colleagues there, especially Eugene Mullan and Richard and Sue Mizen. Others include The Australian and New Zealand College of Psychiatrists, The Guild of Psychotherapists, The Westminster Pastoral Foundation, The Bath Centre for Psychotherapy and Counselling, Konrad Michel and The Aeschi Foundation Switzerland, Teresa Chan and Irene Kam in Hong Kong, Evrynomi Avdi in Thessaloniki, Kristin White in Berlin, The Salt Lake City Children's Center, and the City University in New York.

Many colleagues, friends and family members have directly or indirectly influenced, supported, stimulated, tolerated and contributed to the process that underpins the sanity-forging and sanity-disrupting processes involved in making a book. I would especially like to thank Jon Allen, Anthony Bateman, Sidney Bloch, Kath Buckell, Errolyn Bruce, Andrew and Penny Elder, Peter Fonagy, Sebastian Kraemer, Richard Lindley, Louiza and Chris Pearson, Robert and Lorraine Tollemache, Nic Sarra, Arietta Slade, Mary Target, Paul Zeal, and (as always) Ros, Jacob, Matthew, Lydia and Josh Holmes.

I thank the Society of Authors and the Henry Reed Estate for permission to use 'Naming of Parts', from *New Oxford Book of English Verse*, edited by H. Gardener (1972), Oxford: Oxford University Press.

The poem 'Dinner with My Mother' from *Dock Leaves* © Hugo Williams, 1994 is reproduced by permission of Faber and Faber Ltd.

A number of the chapters here have had previous incarnations as articles or book chapters, as follows.

- Chapter 2: (2006) Mentalising from a psychoanalytic perspective: What's new? In J. Allen and P. Fonagy (Eds.), *Mentalisation*. Chichester, UK: Wiley.
- Chapter 8: (2008b) Mentalisation and metaphor in poetry and psychotherapy. *Advances in Psychiatric Treatment*, *14*, 167–171.
- Chapter 9: (2007) Sense and sensuality: Hedonic intersubjectivity and the erotic imagination. In D. Diamond, S. Blatt, and J. Lichtenberg (Eds.), *Attachment & sexuality*. New York: Analytic Press.
- Chapter 10: (2003) Borderline personality disorder and the search for meaning – an attachment perspective. *Australian and New Zealand Journal of Psychiatry*, *37*, 524–532.

Part I

Principles

Chapter I

Assuming

Any activity, whether intellectual or practical, is informed by an ideology: a set of more or less conscious underlying guiding beliefs and principles. These taken-for-granted facts and theories form the seedbed from which new ideas arise, but, if unexamined, also trammel creative thought. The aim of this preliminary chapter is to foreground this book's basic assumptions, clearing the ground for what follows. I start with a brief orientation for those unfamiliar with attachment theory (and an update for the initiated), followed by a summary of the particular psychoanalytic perspective adopted.

A very brief history of attachment theory

Since its inception nearly half a century ago, attachment theory's history, especially as it has developed in the UK, can be divided into three main phases (for a comprehensive account, see Cassidy and Shaver 2008). The starting point for Bowlby (in the UK) and Ainsworth (first in Uganda and then in Baltimore, USA) was the 'obvious' fact, somehow overlooked by psychological theorists, that individuals of whatever age, when threatened, ill, tired or vulnerable, seek proximity to a wiser, stronger 'secure base' for protection, and that until these attachment needs are assuaged, other motivational forces – sex, exploration, etc. – are in abeyance. In children, or severely stressed adults, physical proximity is sought. Where stress is less, or the subject is mature, vocal (e.g. cell-phone) or visual (e.g. through a photo) contact may suffice.

Ainsworth's Strange Situation enabled researchers observing reactions to a brief separation from care-givers to classify young toddlers into two overall categories: securely and insecurely attached. The latter were then further subdivided into two main patterns, now conveniently known as the deactivating (formerly avoidant) and hyperactivating (formerly ambivalent) pattern. The new nomenclature derives from the US-based self-report strand of attachment research, studying young adults and their romantic relationships (Mikulincer and Shaver 2008). Longitudinal studies have subsequently shown that these patterns remain relatively stable through childhood and adolescence, although children can move from secure to insecure and vice versa under defined circumstances (e.g. mother becomes depressed – secure to insecure; mother's circumstances improve or she receives psychotherapy – insecure to secure).

Phase 2 of attachment theory's history, sometimes described as a 'move to the level of representation', was initiated by Mary Main and her co-workers at Berkeley, California (Main 1995). This refers to a shift from Bowlby and Ainsworth's ethologically influenced accounts of attachment *behaviours* in children and their parents to Main and Solomon's Adult Attachment Interview (AAI), which classifies adult's verbal *descriptions* of their childhood experiences of attachment, loss and trauma. The AAI taps into the respondent's narrative style, as a manifestation of how relationships are experienced, thought about, verbalised – 'represented' – in the subject's mind.

In another of her inspired contributions Main and co-workers also identified a third category of insecure attachment – 'insecure disorganised' – which is particularly associated with high levels of stress and disturbance, both in children so classified and in their care-givers (Lyons-Ruth and Jacobvitz 2008).

Phase 3 starts around the 1990s with a series of experimental, theoretical and clinical studies associated initially with Peter Fonagy and Miriam and Howard Steele at University College London. Using the AAI, they prospectively linked parents-to-be's 'state of mind with respect to attachment' with the subsequent attachment classification of their infants in the Strange Situation (Fonagy et al. 2002). Their 'reflexive function' subscale refers to the care-giver's ability to 'think about thinking': (a) to see their own thoughts and those of their infants for what they are, not necessarily accurate representations of reality, and (b) to comprehend others as autonomous beings whose emotional arousal is motivated by desires, wishes and projects, reflecting an 'inner' sentient Self. Parents' capacity to reflect on their own and their infant's mental states was strongly linked to security of attachment in their offspring. Attachment security or insecurity is thereby transmitted down the generations.

Experimentally measurable 'reflexive function' then formed the core of what, by the turn of the century, had become the guiding theoretical concept of this group – 'mentalising' (Allen and Fonagy 2006; Allen et al. 2008). Mentalising refers to the ability to reflect on thinking and thereby to grasp the perspectival nature of thought, and the experiential ground from which it arises. Portmanteau definitions of mentalising include: 'the ability to see oneself from the outside, and others from the inside', and 'thinking about feelings, and feeling about thinkings'.

Fonagy, Target, Gergely and their collaborators (Fonagy et al. 2002) see mentalising as a developmentally acquired skill, emerging in the first five years of life, gradually elaborated throughout the psychological life-cycle. They contrast mentalising with 'pre-mentalising' states of mind such as, in their terms, 'pretend' and 'equivalence' modes of thinking that developmentally precede it, and that may persist in psychopathology. In the former the individual withdraws from reality into a world of subjective desire and play; in the latter the thought–reality gap is obliterated, and the way the world is is assumed to be identical with, i.e. 'equivalent' to, the way one feels about it. Some may see in the contrast between mentalising and pre-mentalising modes of thought echoes of the Kleinian dichotomy of depressive and paranoid-schizoid positions. Whether the attachment perspective usefully adds to that dichotomy will be extensively discussed in Chapter 2.

The clinical impetus behind the elaboration of mentalising comes from trying to understand and help people suffering from borderline personality disorder (BPD), for whom 'standard' treatment approaches have had, at best, only modest success. There is now accumulating evidence for the effectiveness of mentalisation-based therapy (MBT) in improving the prognosis and life-course of BPD sufferers (Bateman and Fonagy 2008). Other specialised therapies such as transference-focused therapy and dialectical behavioural therapy have also shown good results.

An attachment-informed psychoanalytic credo

How do these attachment ideas link with the psychoanalytic viewpoint that is this book's conjoined theme? A fundamental bridge between the two disciplines is modern evolutionary theory. Freud was a Darwinian (Sulloway 1980), seeing beneath the veneer of civilisation the mind's earlier phylogenetic inheritance; emphasising adaptation as a mark of psychological health; and pointing to the necessary compromises that such contradictions entail.

Neo-Darwinism also underpins the science of ethology, one of attachment theory's roots. Ethology shows that our near relatives such as baboons, living in close social groups, have a deep grasp of social relationships (Cheney and Seyfarth 2007; Suomi 2008). Non-human primates, if they are to flourish, must understand dominance hierarchies, social rank, sexual mores, security relationships, child-care arrangements and feeding precedence. Despite a limited and largely stereotyped *expressive* repertoire, non-human primates' *receptive* 'language of thought' is manifest in subtle and varied behavioural ways – how they approach one another, whom they approach, how they react to threat, and in their feeding behaviours and mating preferences. Social relations, even though verbally inaccessible, are thus firmly represented in the primate mind. The psychoanalytic approach to infant observation (*infans = without speech*) similarly reconstructs a pre-verbal child's 'language of thought' from observations of social context and behaviour, facial expression and affective communication. Psychoanalysis' primary domain is this language of thought, and the capacity to give it voice.

Freud's first great discovery, a theoretical one, was that in any intimate human relationship, two simultaneous 'conversations' are in play: conscious and unconscious, or verbal and non-verbal (Freud 1911). In 'normal life' the non-verbal, biologically salient, aspects of communication are concealed or repressed. Telephoning a friend, I assume that I am just telephoning a friend – not counting on her to protect or feed me, wondering whether we might go to bed together or form an alliance against a stronger competitor. This leads us to the fundamental paradox with which psychoanalysis is concerned. On one hand, to become conscious of the sexual, competitive, hierarchical, security-seeking aspects of interaction is inherently disturbing. On the other, *not* to be aware of this domain means running the risk of sleepwalking into and through relationships, driven by forces of which one is largely unaware.

In order to think about this dilemma – to be aware is to suffer, and yet *not* to be aware may lead to even greater suffering in the long run – security is essential. Anxiety is the enemy of mentalising. An attachment figure is required to whom we can turn, and the more secure that attachment, the more capable we will be of exploring our true nature.

For Bowlby, attachment and love were synonymous. The secure base is his 'good object'. A secure base-provider is accessible when needed and is uniquely capable of understanding the care-seeker. To be a good object one has to be able to put oneself in another's shoes and to comprehend the nature of their experience. A secure base is there to carry one over the cracks and fissures – 'ruptures' – in human relationships. The secure base/good object is able to withstand the protest that separation evokes, while continuing to hold the loved one in mind.

Freud's second great invention, a practical one, was that of the consulting room and the couch. The analytic relationship is an *in vitro* experiment in intimacy. The consulting room is a place in which the language of thought begins to be articulated – fear formulated, desire described, sorrow given words. The analyst is an attachment figure who provides the security needed for insecurity to be explored. Insecurity is precisely that which the analyst's presence evokes – desire, rivalry, fear of rejection, humiliation, neglect, exploitation, and so on. What begins as 'transference' – unarticulated non-verbal relational resonance – ends up as 'insight', the ability to read one's own 'language of thought' and that of others. In phantasy the analyst is the 'one supposed to know' (Zizek 2006), the expert on the 'unthought known' (Bollas 1987). As therapy proceeds the analyst disavows this, and, like an allergist, gradually helps the patient to expose themselves to manageable bits of their unconscious shames and fears.

Theory and practice in psychoanalytic psychotherapy

I justify this book on the grounds that there is a *theory–practice gap in psychoanalytic psychotherapy* (cf. Canestri 2006). As Fonagy elegantly puts it (Fonagy 2006a, p. 76), 'clinical technique is not logically entailed in psychoanalytic theory'. Psychoanalytic therapy cannot be assembled from its theory in the way that a furniture flatpack arises effortlessly out of its instruction diagram (usually in my case with one or two screws loose!).

What goes on in sessions – verbally, non-verbally, interactionally, physiologically, consciously and unconsciously – is at best only partially captured by avowed theoretical positions. There is a need for a developmental-based, empirically underpinned meta-theory with which to study the minutiae of therapist–patient interaction. The contention of this book is that attachment theory can contribute to such a heuristic, with its clear account of what is and is not helpful in therapeutic relationships.

O'Neill (2008) usefully takes up Donnet's (2001) notion of the psychoanalytic 'site'. A 'site' is a geographical metaphor referring to the constellation of procedures, together with their theoretical underpinning, which constitutes the essence, location or 'place' of a particular cultural phenomenon.

Within psychoanalysis there are fierce debates about what constitutes 'proper' analysis. Given the plurality of theories and practices, the search for a 'common ground' has also proved elusive, seen as essential to psychoanalysis' survival by some (Wallerstein 1990), an elusive chimera by others (Green 2005). In Tuckett et al.'s (2008) European Psychoanalysis project, analysts from different cultural, linguistic and psychoanalytic backgrounds examine one another's work. They show how challenging it is for psychoanalysts from divergent traditions and nationalities to respect as valid 'psychoanalysis' methods of working that differ from their own. Faced with uncertainty, analytic charisma and arbitrary authority – and sometimes subtle contempt and denigration – replace exploration and open debate.

Tuckett et al. (2008) develop a framework attempting to understand and theorise what psychoanalysts actually do – as opposed to what they say, or think, they do. They classify psychoanalytic interventions in five broad categories:

1   'housekeeping' remarks aimed mainly at maintaining the basic setting (e.g. 'reminding you that I shall be away next week')
2   brief 'unsaturated'/'polysemic' (i.e. ambiguous) comments that further the analytic process (e.g. 'walls!', 'a mouth without teeth?'!)
3   questions and clarifications
4   various forms of interpretive comment either on the here-and-now relationship with the analyst or forging links between present and past
5   spontaneous 'mistakes' (possibly induced enactments) on the part of the analyst – e.g. inappropriately reassuring comments – whose later exploration may bear analytic fruit.

Using a related but simplified classification (Castonguay and Beutler 2006), in what follows I shall be guided by a tripartite division of psychoanalytic interactions. After an extended discussion of mentalising, these are expanded, expounded, and explained in the three chapters that follow (cf. Holmes 2008a).

1   A *therapeutic relationship* with the following properties: (a) intensity; (b) 'contingency' in that the analyst is primarily responsive to the client's initiatives; (c) a 'secure base' in which the client sees the therapist as able to contain and assuage her anxieties, however overwhelming; (d) once assuaged, enlivenment and 'companionable interaction' follow; (e) one that is continuously self-monitoring and self-repairing.

2   A primary task of *meaning-making* in which analyst and client begin to make sense of problematic or symptomatic experiences and behaviours. The primary data for this sense-making process are: (a) free association in which the 'material' brought to the session by the client is analysed as much for its relationship to the client's inner world as for its manifest content; (b) dreams; (c) language, in which words are seen as manifestations of chains of unconscious meanings; (d) the therapeutic relationship itself, i.e. transference feelings and enactments evoked by the therapeutic process; (e) patterns in the client's developmental history, in which the long-term implications of infantile and childhood trauma are explored.

3   *Therapeutic action* or change, brought about by inducing tension or a 'benign bind' that: (a) helps promote the client's capacity to think about his own feelings and actions and those of others; (b) helps the client to reintegrate repressed, disowned or projected affects or parts of the self with resulting greater sense of vitality, efficacy and 'real-ness'; (c) enhances emotional articulacy, including mourning and processing past losses and traumata; (d) replaces rigidity and transference-driven repetitiousness with more creative, fluid, interpersonal and narrative capacities.

Darwin showed incontrovertibly (but not uncontroversially) that evolution by natural selection was the best possible explanation for the origin of species, but until the advent of genetics he was in the dark as to its underlying 'mechanism of action'. Similarly, we know for sure that psychoanalytic psychotherapy 'works' (see Chapter 5), but we do not know *how* or *what is it about it* that produces change – therapeutic charisma, accurate interpretation, secure attachment, instillation of mentalising capacity, or some as yet unarticulated factor. The aim of this book is to explore how attachment theory can help towards a better understanding of this elusive DNA of our discipline.

Chapter 2

Mentalising

When I first encountered the term 'mentalising' I found it off-putting, with its abstract pseudo-technical ring, and wondered if this was not yet another example of Molière's bourgeois gentleman discovering that he had been speaking prose all his life. I have come round to the view that mentalising captures a crucial aspect of psychological health, and psychotherapists' efforts to promote it. The aim of this chapter is to take the reader on a similar intellectual journey.

As stated in the previous chapter, the term, and its related noun *mentalisation*, were introduced to the Anglo-Saxon world by Fonagy, Target, Gergely, Bateman (Bateman and Fonagy 2004, 2008; Fonagy et al. 2002) and Allen (2006, 2008) as part of a project aiming to improve the treatment of people suffering from borderline personality disorder. But mentalising can be seen as a much wider theme permeating psychotherapy generally. In what follows I shall track its definition, phenomenology, intellectual roots and clinical applications.

Bollas (2007) states that the greater the number of theoretical approaches available to the analyst, the better equipped she is to respond to the variety of experiences she meets in the consulting room. Bion (1962, p. 88), by contrast, states that 'psycho-analytic virtue lies not in the number of theories the psychoanalyst can command but the minimum number with which he can meet any contingency'. In this chapter we shall look at whether mentalising passes this stringent Bionic parsimony test, offering a useful and genuinely new perspective on our work.

Definition

Neither mentalising nor mentalisation is to be found in the *Shorter Oxford English Dictionary* or *Chambers Dictionary*; nor do they appear in Rycroft's (1995) or Laplanche and Pontalis' (1973) psychoanalytic thesauruses. Bateman and Fonagy (2004, p. xxi) define mentalising as 'the *mental process* by which an individual implicitly and explicitly *interprets* the actions of himself and others as *meaningful* on the basis of *intentional mental states* such as personal desires, needs, feelings, beliefs and reasons' (emphasis added).

This definition suggests several interrelated aspects of the concept. Mentalising is 'meta-cognitive', in the sense that it refers to the capacity for *interpretation* of thoughts and actions – to think about thinking, to be 'mind-minded' (Meins 1999). Nevertheless, mentalising is not primarily an intellectual or rational phenomenon. Full-blown explicit mentalising is a three-stage process. Firstly, it is *experiential* in the sense that its starting point is an 'automatic' affective response – a 'thought' often accompanied by somatic sensations and/or images. This is followed, secondly, by *awareness* or 'noticing' what one is thinking and feeling. Thirdly, and only in explicit as opposed to implicit mentalising, there is *thinking* about what one has caught oneself thinking about.

In implicit mentalising these processes also occur, but below the surface of awareness. People manage to walk down the street mostly without bumping into one another. The mind 'computes' others' trajectory and intentions and one's own to guarantee safe passage. Only when this goes wrong does the process need to become explicit and conscious – when walker A goes right at exactly the moment walker B coming in the opposite direction thinks she is going left, and they all but bump into one another, often with an moment of acknowledgment and mutual amusement.

Next, mentalising is concerned with the *meanings* that we attribute to our own and others' actions – that is, to the *implicit or explicit* hypotheses we use to understand why we, or another, might have thought or done such and such a thing. This links with a third aspect, which picks up on mentalising as a key attribute of *persons*, as opposed to the inanimate world. Implicit in mentalising is Dennett's (1987) *intentional stance* – the capacity to have projects, desires and wishes. Mentalising is related to empathy in that it implies the ability to put oneself in another's shoes – to see the other as a sentient person, as opposed to a 'thing'. Finally, mentalising is not a fixed property of mind, but a *process*, or skill, that may be present or absent to greater or lesser degrees.

The Fonagy–Target model of mentalisation arises out of research using the Adult Attachment Interview (AAI) (Fonagy et al. 1997). The 'reflective function' subscale provides an operationalised quantitative measure of the capacity for mentalising. Transcripts of AAI are rated using a number of criteria listed below (Bateman and Fonagy 2004, p. 75), with my examples interpolated:

- awareness of the nature of mental states (*'sometimes I wonder if I'm just making all this up'*)
- explicit efforts to tease out the mental states underlying behaviour (*'I suppose my mother was pretty stressed at the time and didn't have much space to think about us children'*)
- recognition of the developmental aspects of mental states (*'I was so*

young at the time I didn't realise that the things my step-dad asked me to do weren't quite normal')

- showing awareness of mental states in relation to the interviewer (*'being here means I'm on my best behaviour, but inside I feel pretty churned up and confused'*).

The phenomenology of mentalising

Before considering the theoretical background to mentalising, here are some examples of how it can be used to understand both everyday and clinical phenomena.

Mary and Elizabeth: The emergence of mentalisation in the face of traumatic loss

Mary, aged 85, had been married to John, 90, for 65 years. Following a fall, and hip fracture, John became bedridden. He was admitted to hospital and was very ill. Mary lived alone but was in close contact with her daughter, Elizabeth, by telephone. When Elizabeth phoned about her father's progress, Mary said: 'Dad's not himself today. It must be those tablets the doctors are giving him'. The next day the phone message was: 'The doctors seem to think that John is not at all well'. Elizabeth, who lived some distance away, decided she needed to be at her mother's side. When she arrived, Mary was able to say: 'Do you know, I think I may be finding it difficult to face the possibility that Dad might not get better'.

There is a complex, 'U-shaped' relationship between arousal/affect regulation and mentalising. When arousal is low, explicit mentalising is put to one side – we just get on with things without thinking too much about them. Equally, beyond a certain level of arousal, mentalising is impossible, and flight, fight or dissociation is activated. Mary's initial response to the possibility of losing her husband was a non-mentalising one: denial and projection. The problem was attributed to the doctors and their tablets. She continued to keep her feelings at bay – focusing on the doctors' views rather than her own emotions. Only when her daughter arrived was she able to begin to look at her own feelings in relation to John's likely demise, and how difficult she had been finding it to face the situation.

This example illustrates three key aspects of mentalising. First, the interpersonal aspect, and its link to secure attachment. Overcoming denial was made possible by Elizabeth's arrival, providing Mary with the secure base she needed to alleviate distress, lower her arousal and begin to explore her feelings. 'Awareness of awareness' enabled her to see how her perception of reality had been distorted by the need to ward off painful affect.

This example also shows how mentalising is a graded rather than an all-or-none phenomenon, depending on the attachment context. As the painful truth began to sink in, Mary moved from non-mentalising, through partial awareness of others' states of mind ('the doctors seem to think . . .') to fuller self-mentalising ('I think I may be finding it difficult . . .').

Third, it illustrates how mentalising can apply at five distinct levels, and how at any given point all, or some or none of these may be operating:

1   *self-mentalising* – being aware of one's own feelings
2   *other mentalising* – awareness of what the other might be feeling
3   *self-with-other mentalising* – what one might be feeling towards another
4   *other-with-self mentalising* – what the other's feelings towards oneself might be
5   *self-and-other mentalising* – being able to read the interactions between oneself and another from a neutral vantage point.

The following examples introduce the developmental aspect of mentalising, and again illustrate the importance of context, and relationship between self-mentalising and mentalising in relation to others.

Mentalising and motherhood

A six-month-old baby cries in the night, waking her parents. Her mother, still in bed, turns to her partner. She says: 'Oh, the little fiend, she *knows* I've got to get up really early tomorrow to go work. I'll be really washed out. She's just doing it to punish me'. She then goes to her child, saying to herself, or out loud to the baby: 'You poor little thing . . . I wonder what it can be this time . . . are you hungry, too hot, is your nappy wet . . . did you have a bad dream?' She picks the child up, soothes her, does what is necessary, and in a few minutes the whole family is asleep again.

Contrast this with a similar situation but where the care-giver might be alone and/or stressed or intoxicated. She will still, eventually, go to the crying baby, but now she might shout at her: 'You little devil . . . you're just doing this to annoy me . . . how *dare* you wake me up like that . . . now *get back to sleep!'*

In the first case the mother starts with a lapse of mentalising – in her sleep-deprived state she cannot differentiate between her feelings and those of the baby ('equivalence mode', see below). Her experience of her child's crying is seen only from the perspective of her own feelings of panic and paranoia. But the presence of her partner enables her to retrieve a mentalising stance and to reflect about her own state of mind, and that of her child. She can contain her irritation and resistance to being woken, to bracket them off, seeing them for what they are – her feelings, not those of the baby. This clears the way for her to offer a secure attachment response to the distressed child, based on responsiveness and the capacity to put herself into the child's shoes. This might be compared with a therapist, who, like any ordinary mortal, has good days and bad, life difficulties and problems, but who if these are not too pressing or overwhelming can put them to one side for the duration of the session.

In the second case the mother's capacity to mentalise is severely compromised. She is distressed and either highly aroused or drugged, both of which are inimical to mentalising (Bateman and Fonagy 2004). She is slow to respond, and when eventually she does, she sees the baby's distress only in terms of her own feelings rather than those of the child.

This type of self-referential response has been described by Lyons-Ruth (Lyons-Ruth and Jacobvitz 2008) as 'hostile/intrusive', typical of one group of parents whose children's attachment status is classified as 'disorganised'. The other main grouping is parents described as 'fearful'. A disorganised–fearful parent might, in this hypothetical example, simply lie in bed in a terrified and helpless state unable to respond to their child's distress.

These responses are reminiscent of the reactions of mental health professionals when confronted by disturbed behaviour in their patients (cf. Chapter 10). Like the first mother, an initial reaction is often dominated by overwhelming countertransference, high anxiety levels and compromised mentalising. The patient may be seen by the staff as deliberately 'winding us up', malevolent or dangerous. This in turn can drive non-mentalised responses such as instant discharge from hospital or, conversely, over-protective use of compulsory detainment. With the help of staff support and supervision these reactions, like those of the sleepy mother and her partner, can be defused, and a mentalising attitude regained.

Abigail: Sexual abuse and mentalisation

While her lone-parent mother was doing an evening shift at the local supermarket, 10-year-old Abigail was left with a seemingly helpful and friendly neighbour, who in fact was sexually abusing her. When Abigail refused to go to the babysitter any more her mother flew into a rage, threatening to put her into care. Abigail said that the man was 'not very nice', but this again provoked a furious response, and she was told that she had no right to say such things about such a kind man.

Linehan (1993) suggests that people suffering from borderline personality disorder have grown up in an 'invalidating' environment. Abigail is twice invalidated here, first by her abuser and second by her mother who failed to respond to her distress cues. The mentalising response is inherently validating. Had her mother been able to mentalise, she would have interpreted Abigail's refusal to go to the babysitter as meaningful and motivated by the need to protect herself. She would perhaps also have been stimulated to self-mentalise, and consider the feelings *she* had about his man – that there was something 'creepy' about him – feelings she had pushed to one side in order to survive economically. As with rhesus monkeys faced with variable foraging conditions (Suomi 2008), this hypothetical mother's care-giving skills are impaired by being subject to severe psychological and environmental stress. Stress is the enemy of mentalisation: when anxiety reaches a certain level the mentalising brain goes 'offline', and the mind moves into 'survival mode' (Allen 2006).

Partial mentalising: The case of Hamlet

An example of partial mentalising is to be found in Hamlet's famous lament about his depression:

> I have of late – but wherefore I know not – lost all my mirth, forgone all custom of exercises; and indeed it goes so heavily with my disposition that this goodly frame, the earth, seems to me a sterile promontory, this most excellent canopy, the air, look you, this brave o'er hanging firmament, this majestical roof fretted with golden fire, why, it appears no other thing to me than a foul and pestilent congregation of vapours. What a piece of work is a man! How noble in reason! How infinite in faculty! ... In apprehension how like a god! The paragon of animals! And yet, to me, what is this quintessence of dust? Man delights not me: no, nor woman neither, though by your smiling you seem to say so.
>
> (*Hamlet*, Act II, Scene 2)

Here Hamlet is mentalising his depression, able to contrast his perception of the world with its actuality, and to see how his 'Freudian' college friends Rosencrantz and Guildenstern wrongly think the problem must be to do with sex, while his libido is in fact depression-crushed. His mentalising is present but partial: he knows that he doesn't know – 'wherefore I know not'. The rest of the play is an exploration of this not knowing and the emotional paralysis that stems from it. The play's action finally forces him to face his oedipal ambivalence – his hatred of and reverence for the father-figure Laertes. Only in Act V is Hamlet able to risk ('explore'), with the reassuring presence of Horatio his secure base, the potentially lethal consequences of action. In a fully mentalising state, armed with an understanding of the meaning of one's psychological impediments, one is free to choose and to act.

To summarise the phenomenology of mentalising: it (a) starts from the capacity to empathise, to be able to put oneself in another's shoes; (b) encompasses the ability to see and evaluate oneself and one's feelings from the outside and those of others from the inside; (c) denotes a capacity to differentiate feelings *about* reality from reality itself; (d) is a graded rather than all-or-nothing phenomenon; (e) is related to arousal; (f) is enhanced by the presence of a secure soothing partner or other intimate.

Conceptual origins of mentalising

The notion of mentalising has four distinct intellectual roots (cf. Choi-Kain and Gunderson 2008): cognitive psychology; psychoanalytic object relations theory; francophone psychoanalysis; and attachment-influenced developmental psychopathology. Let us consider each in turn.

Cognitive psychology and ethology

Cognitive psychologists have adopted the philosophical notion of 'theory of mind' to explain some of the difficulties experienced by people suffering from autism, and the formal and developmental differences between autistic and 'normal' modes of thought (Baron-Cohen 1995; P. Hobson 2002). In order to operate in the intensely social world of human interaction it is necessary to understand that others have minds similar, but never identical, to one's own.

Children normally from a very early age are able to distinguish between animate and inanimate objects and, among the animate, between persons and non-human living creatures. It has been suggested that the social difficulties experienced by autistic individuals arise in part from their inability to conceptualise others as having minds, and therefore viewpoints, different from their own. People are not clearly differentiated from inanimate objects, and cannot be understood to have projects, desires and plans that may or may not intersect with those of the autistic subject. As a result the interpersonal world is experienced as inexplicable and unpredictable, triggering defensive withdrawal and self-preoccupation.

In normal children, 'theory of mind' has been elegantly demonstrated to develop in the first five years of life. In 'false belief' tasks children are asked to predict where someone who has gone out of the room might search for a missing object on their return. Unknown to them, but not to the observing child, it has been moved from one container to another. Until around the age of three children assume that others' view of the world is identical to their own and therefore that the 'deceived' subject will still know where to look for the missing object despite its having been moved. By the age of five, children can see that deception is possible and therefore one person's mind will view the world differently from another's, depending on information available – and that the searching adult will therefore be likely to look in the wrong place. It is only a small step from this to mentalising – i.e. the view that 'the world' is filtered through a perspectival mind, which may be more or less accurate in its appreciation of reality.

This classic experiment is usually seen as an illustration of the developmental aspect of cognition: how a child begins to understand that the world looks different from different points of view. But implicit in the study is also the idea of social relations. Armed with a theory of mind a child can begin to understand the part played by deception, possession, competition for resources (the 'object' is usually something desirable to eat) in social groups, and to know when these are playful and when 'for real'. Such skills are also present in the non-human world including some birds, but especially in our primate ancestors. Primatologists Cheney and Seyfarth (2007, pp. 270–272) suggest that *understanding social relations* is the foundation stone for the development of language:

> To survive, avoid stress, reproduce, and raise offspring who are themselves successful, individuals need both a system of communication that allows them to influence other animals' behaviour and a *system of mental representation* that allows them to recognise and understand other animals' relationships ... Because these mental representations concern animate creatures and are designed to predict behaviour, they include *information ... about other individuals' mental states*, and about the *causal relations between one social event and another* ... Long before our ancestors spoke in sentences they had a *language of thought* in which they represented the world ... in terms of actors, actions, and those who are acted upon.
>
> (emphasis added)

Freud's (1911) 'two principles of mental functioning' needs to be revised in the light of these ethological observations. Freud contrasts 'secondary process' (verbal, propositional thought) on one hand and 'primary process' (imagic, non-logical, non-verbal, atemporal thinking) on the other. But if Cheney and Seyfarth are right, even primary process thinking is fundamentally linguistic, because social relations are. 'Primary process thinking' is about what one person (a subject) does (a verb) to another (an object). Perhaps this is what Lacan (1977) refers to when he states that 'the unconscious is structured like a language', or Rycroft's (1995) view that psychoanalysis is a 'biological theory of meaning'.

The contrast is between the 'language of thought', largely unconscious and concerned with intimate social relations (sexuality, dominance, security, etc.), and 'language as we know it', or 'language proper'. While the latter can and is used in the service of the language of thought – for pleasure, seduction, dominance, obfuscation, etc. – it is not directly tied to the representation of social relationships. Thus in a clinical setting, patients' words may be used not just as informative, but also as performative communications whose function is to produce an effect in the analyst – excitement, diversion, holding-at-a-distance, etc. (cf. Busch 2009). Mentalising refers to the ability to 'read' the unconscious, decoding the language of thought from its manifestations in language proper.

A key difference between the two modes of thinking is that the 'language of thought' is largely asyntactical and therefore tends towards symmetrisation (Matte-Blanco 1975), while language proper is highly syntactical, allowing for infinite subtlety and complexity in expressing differences ('asymmetries') as well as similarities. In the language of thought, a father, a work-rival and a therapist might all be 'transferentially' represented in the mind in fairly similar ways, while in language proper, with the help of affect regulation and mentalising, the differences between these varying stimuli and the contexts in which they arise can be carefully appraised.

When psychoanalysis is successful it liberates what Henry Rey called 'the render unto Caesar' function (Rey 1975, personal communication) – rendering unto the father that which belongs to him, to the boss that which is relevant to her, etc. This applies to the subject's relation to their body as well – similarly rendering unto the mouth that which belongs to the mouth, to the genitals that which belongs to them, and so on.

In summary, the cognitive aspects of mentalising refer to the use of secondary processes to observe primary processes, language proper to describe the 'language of thought'.

Bion and object relations

Bion (1962, 1967) proposed a schematised theory of the origins of thinking. He was concerned with a general theory of origins of thought itself, rather than the specific mind-reading skills that the term 'mentalising' attempts to capture. Nevertheless his ideas help us look more deeply into what is involved in mentalising.

Bion starts from Freud's idea that, ultimately, thinking – the 'mind' itself – is a response to, and a bulwark against, absence and loss, and consequent frustration. Thinking maintains equilibrium in the inevitable gaps in attachment continuity – the five-year-old child goes happily to school because he carries with him a thought/memory/image of a loving parent in his mind to whom he can turn in times of stress or danger. For Bion, thinking – which might also be called 'image-ination' – arises in response to an absence: 'no breast, therefore imagine a breast'. Absence equates to loss and is, in Bion's Kleinian worldview, experienced by the infant as inherently 'bad' and frustrating, and therefore in need of expulsion/projection from the paradisical inner world of 'goodness'.

Bion differentiates between 'thoughts' and the 'apparatus' (his word) that thinks the thoughts. Thoughts must be 'contained' by a thinker who can think them. He calls the capacity to think thoughts 'alpha function'. Alpha function transforms 'beta elements' ('thoughts without a thinker') into 'alpha elements', which are then available for being thought about.

Bion postulates a conflict between the desire to rid oneself via projection of those 'bad' thoughts that, because they arise from loss, are inherently disturbing, and the capacity to modify them so that they can indeed be 'thought'. He sees the outcome of this conflict as depending in part on the possibly genetically determined capacity of the infant to 'tolerate frustration' (which in his model is needed for thinking as opposed to evacuation), and in part on the ability of the 'breast' to help the infant with his frustrations, to accept projections and gently to return them in a form in which they can now be 'thought'. This process is closely linked with the *naming* of feelings: e.g. 'mummy's going away for a minute, but don't worry because she will be back soon'. Explicit mentalising/alpha function involves words; words help us bridge the gaps in existence caused by separations, whether involuntary or 'caused' by expulsive hatred.

In Bion's view, in the absence of a containing mother, or where there is little ability to tolerate frustration, the outcome will be 'excessive projective identification', which sows the seeds of psychopathology in later life, including a deficit in the capacity for mentalising. In the example in the previous section, the stressed mother projectively identifies her infant as her persecutor, rather than being able to mentalise herself into a receptive state of mind. This in turn may interfere with the infant's developing capacity to mentalise, since his or her feelings will not have been recognised and 'real-ised' (Bion's word) by the mother, and, instead, the mother's feelings ('you just want to wake me up to wind me up') will have invaded the infant self as an 'alien' nidus, i.e. a malign 'nest' (cf. Fonagy et al. 2002).

Bion homes in on the 'recursive' aspect of thinking. As Cheney and Seyfarth (2007, p. 280) put it:

> mental states are recursive, because nested inside the mental state is its content ... An example is 'She thinks he doesn't know that she likes him'. We suggest that recursive thinking first appeared in the social and technological knowledge of hominids who could gain a reproductive advantage by representing the mental state of others (and themselves).

In Bion's account, successful transformation of 'beta' into 'alpha' elements leads to the establishment of a 'contact barrier', as originally proposed by Freud, between unconscious and conscious thinking. This means that an individual can differentiate between the somatic sensations, unnamed desires and proto-feelings that comprise 'preconceptions' on one hand (beta elements), and, on the other, thoughts or 'conceptions' (alpha elements) that form the stuff of rational thought. This enables an individual to distinguish reality from phantasy confidently, a key component of the ability to mentalise. Where the contact barrier is weak, phantasy can invade or flood rational thought, leading to a distorted perception of reality, and inability to 'factor in' one's own emotional states in any situation. This weakness may be genetic (as in autism), developmental (in abusive or neglectful environments) or situational (as in intoxication or high levels of arousal).

A further link between the ideas put forward here and Bion's schema is his notion of 'K' and 'minus K'. K represents knowing or knowledge, 'minus K' 'not-knowing', which Bion sees as arising from 'attacks on linking' (his version of the oedipal child's resentment of parental intercourse). Bion's K equates to the attachment-theory-derived notion of 'exploration' which forms the title of this book. Just as exploration is inhibited by anxiety, and replaced by attachment behaviour, so for Bion fear drives out K – the role of the analyst being to identify this fear, so that K becomes possible.

Containment and maternal alpha function play a similar role to that of the secure base as facilitators of exploration or self-knowledge. Where the two models differ is that for attachment theory, minus K or not-knowing is seen as an emptiness, a deficit, while for Bion it is an active state of hatred and destruction of the object felt to fail.

Francophone psychoanalysis

Francophone psychoanalysis can be differentiated from its Anglo-Saxon cousin in a number of ways, including greater adherence to Freud's early ideas, and to psychoanalysis as a self-sufficient philosophical *Weltanschauung*. In their approach to mentalising, Lecours and Bouchard (1997) take Freud's idea – contained in his unpublished 1895 'Project' (Freud 1895) – that thought represents the *binding* of otherwise untrammelled drive-energies (Bion sees this binding in interpersonal rather than intrapsychic terms – the mother 'binds' the child's projected affect). In the absence of such binding, psychic energy, as they see it, is either discharged through action or diverted into somatic processes – emerging clinically as 'acting-out', or somatisation.

Luquet (1981) and Marty (1991) start from the clinical phenomenon of somatisation disorders, conceived in terms of *pensée opératoire* – 'operational' or robot-like thinking, devoid of affect. *Pensée opératoire* is the French equivalent of the Anglo-Saxon notion of alexithymia – the inability to put feelings into words. Mentalising from this perspective is the antithesis of *pensée opératoire*, or, as Lecours and Bouchard (1997) put it, 'disruptive impulsion' (i.e. 'acting-out'). Mentalising encapsulates the capacity to transform drives into feelings, and to represent, symbolise, sublimate, abstract, reflect and make meaning out of them. Without mentalising, repeating (i.e. acting-out) is inevitable. As Freud famously put it, 'hysterics suffer from reminiscences'. If traumatic reminiscences are remembered – put into words, mentalised – they no longer need to be enacted. With the capacity for mentalising goes freedom. Santayana's equally well-known version of this idea (1905, p. 102) is that 'those who cannot remember the past are condemned to fulfil it' (often misquoted as 'repeat it').

While mentalising is in English neologistic, the term has been current in francophone psychoanalysis for a quarter of a century. Lecours and Bouchard (1997) put forward a sophisticated hierarchical classification of *degrees* of mentalisation. At one extreme lie 'unmentalised libidinal excitations' which emerge chaotically as 'somatisations, crude violent behaviour and self mutilation that force defantasised conflicts into the interpersonal arena' (Lecours and Bouchard 1997, p. 862); at the other an abstract reflexive stage, which, in a psychoanalytic context might enable a patient to say to his analyst: 'I know that whenever I feel this tired-exhausted feeling, I have left something aside, that I am angry but cannot somehow feel it' (Lecours and Bouchard 1997, p. 865).

This francophone account of mentalising is compatible with Stiles et al.'s (1990) 'assimilation model' arising from a quite different psychotherapy research tradition. Here 'problematic experiences' are seen as lying on a spectrum ranging from those indistinctly felt, if at all [corresponding perhaps with Bollas' (1987) 'unthought known'], at one end, to problems that can be clearly articulated and worked on at the other. Psychoanalytic approaches, helping clients to translate their inchoate feelings and actings-out into 'mentalised affectivity' (Fonagy et al. 2002), are more appropriate to the dimly sensed 'unconscious' end, while more cognitive therapies would be appropriate for the 'known knowns'.

To summarise so far: Bion implicitly, and the francophones explicitly, developed the concepts subsuming mentalising long before its arrival into the world of empirical, attachment-influenced psychoanalytic research.

Developmental psychopathology

Fonagy et al. (2002) see a deficit in mentalising as one of the key difficulties facing people suffering from borderline personality disorder. Their developmental approach proposes a staged model of affective/cognitive understanding of one's own and others' states of mind. Psychopathology is seen in terms of the persistence into adult life of earlier and more 'primitive' stages of psychological development – a model echoing the Hughlings-Jackson account of neurological deficit, adopted by Freud in his picture of psychosexual development, from oral through anal and phallic stages to genital maturity.

While influenced by francophone psychoanalysis, Fonagy and his colleagues bring a British empiricist and Winnicottian interpersonalist ambience to the discussion. In Winnicott's (1971) image of 'transitional space', Bion's conscious/unconscious contact barrier is expanded into a buffer *zone* – a 'two man's land' – in which reality and phantasy overlap. In this *spielraum* disbelief is suspended: thoughts and feelings can be played with as though they were real, while reality can be safely handled at a distance in the phantasy zone. Wright (1991), in the British Independent tradition and drawing on Winnicott, anticipates the idea of mentalisation in his discussion of 'vision', which – literally and metaphorically – he sees as bridging the inevitable separations of human existence. The child sees himself in the mother's face (see Chapter 3 below), and understanding is predicated on this 'seeing'.

The introduction of the Winnicottian model is seen most explicitly in Fonagy and Target's (1997) distinctions between teleological, 'pretend' and 'equivalence' modes of thinking, the last of these also owing a debt to Segal (1991). They see the developmental route to mentalising as passing through three preliminary stages.

The first stage, *teleological* or goal-focused thinking, sees others' behaviour not in terms of desires, plans and projects but in an 'if this then that' way. Pets are good at thinking teleologically. A leash taken up 'means' 'walk'. Thinking teleologically, which could also be described as associatively, is non-mentalising in that the dog is unlikely to fathom whether his master is skulking off after a row with his wife, drawn to the beauties of a spring day, or seeking solitude in order to work out how to order the chapters for his new book. Similarly preverbal, pre-mentalising children 'know' a huge amount about their world and the causes and consequences of actions, without being fully able to read other people's minds.

Peter and the nurse

Peter is an example of someone who, in an 'if this then that' way, would regularly harm himself when thwarted, but who was for the most part out of touch with his own feelings and those of others. He thus had great difficulty in understanding how the emotional states underlying his deliberate self-harm episodes came about. Rather than thinking 'I cut myself because I felt rejected and believe that no one really understands or cares about me', he would think (and say) '*Of course* I cut myself; they refused to give me the medication I asked for'.

Peter suffered from borderline personality disorder and was referred from the in-patient unit to our borderline clinical for assessment. Towards the end of a difficult interview I asked him if he felt anyone on the ward understood him. No one, he insisted.

'What about your "key-worker"?' (whom I knew to be an excellent nurse), I asked.

'Oh, she just thinks I'm a waste of space like everyone else', he replied.

'Do you really mean that?'

'Well, I don't suppose she really does, that's just the way I feel about it most of the time.'

Here, momentarily, is Peter mentalising, moving on from teleology – he sees that the nurse doesn't really reject him but that it is his *perception* of her attitude that is the problem. Getting him to that point entailed a mild challenge, while helping him to feel sufficiently 'held' that his arousal levels were sufficiently low for them not to negate his fragile mentalising capacities.

Second, in *equivalence* mode the world 'as it is' is mistaken for – seen as equivalent to – the world coloured by feelings (unlike Hamlet above, who clearly could differentiate the two). For example, a child unable to differentiate pretend from equivalence would be *un*able to ask: 'Mummy, are you really cross with me today, or just worried about that bill?'. In equivalence mode the external world is suffused with the feelings belonging to the inner world.

Naomi: Equivalence thinking vs. mentalisation

Naomi was a 30-year-old unmarried secondary school biology teacher. She found intimate relationships very difficult. Whenever she formed the beginnings of a relationship with a man, she felt used, taken over or misunderstood, and that she was losing her sense of self – at which point she would bring things to an abrupt halt.

She came into therapy after several episodes of suicidal depression. The child of a single parent, she had and continued to have a very close relationship with her mother, whom she felt she had to protect and look after.

In the course of therapy she was critical of her therapist in minor ways – complaining about his dusty room, the unartistic arrangement of his pictures and his insistence on commenting on her late arrival for sessions. On one occasion she informed me that I was clearly bored with her, since I kept yawning and, what was more, I obviously had to drink strong black coffee before her session in order to stay awake – and there was the proof (pointing to an empty cup on the desk).

Her conviction that the cup symbolised my boredom looked to me like an example of the pre-mentalising state of equivalence mode – her feelings about the cup represented primarily the state of her inner world. Admittedly the cup could symbolise in some way the mild feelings of disarray she evoked in me, and might have represented a minor acting-out of those feelings on my part.

The threat and anxiety associated with being in the intimacy of the therapeutic situation meant that for Naomi only one view was possible – that her therapist couldn't tolerate being with the 'boredom' of her depression. The lack of 'contact barrier' between the unconscious and conscious mind meant that she took what was a product of her depressive imaginings to be the real thing.

In an attempt to enhance mentalising, I said: 'Oh dear . . . while it is not impossible that I might be bored (although I really don't believe that I am), it is difficult for you to consider that I might be tired because I had a bad night, or simply like the taste of coffee. Although, knowing how easily you feel marginalised, it *was* careless of me to leave it there. The cup is important: I wonder if it has brought us to your feelings of disappointment towards those – me included – whom you feel don't really understand you?'

Unmitigated transference – the perception of the therapist as 'bored' with her in the same way that her abandoning father had been – is antithetical to mentalisation. Therapy can be seen as an attempt gradually to help patients *see* transferential feelings for what they are, i.e. to move from an 'equivalence' mode in which perception and reality cannot be separated to an 'as if' or 'partially pretend' mode, in which reality is always questionable and provisional upon accuracy of perception. The dilemma with a client like this is that of *interpreting* her state of mind. The therapist has to enter (and therefore validate) the client's worldview before challenging it.

The intervention tried to strengthen the boundary between fantasy and reality by proposing a difference between what is and what merely might be the case. Tentatively it tried to move the therapeutic discourse from the concrete to the metaphorical. Metaphor is inherently mentalising in that an image, while containing an important psychological truth, is by definition in the mind rather than 'out there' in reality. The idea of the cup as a metaphor for her bad feelings about herself had the potential to strengthen Naomi's mentalising capacities: metaphor-making enhances playfulness and the use of 'transitional' space as the participants add to and creatively modify each other's imagery. But for someone in equivalence mode metaphors can also be confusing, merely adding to the breakdown of reality testing rather than strengthening it.

Third, in '*pretend* mode' the external world is shut out, and the child inhabits an exclusively imaginary space, untempered by reality testing. Trapped in 'pretend' mode, an individual may withdraw into a realm of phantasy or become over-controlling, for example insisting that an 'imaginary friend' be fed or dressed in parallel with themselves ('controllingness' is a common developmental sequel to disorganised attachment in infancy; Lyons-Ruth and Jacobvitz 2008). In contrast to equivalence mode, where the 'contact barrier' between reality and phantasy is over-permeable, in 'pretend mode' reality is rigorously excluded, the boundary becoming rigid and impermeable.

Tom's 'pretend-iousness'

Therapy itself can sometimes reinforce 'pretend' modes of thinking – becoming a 'psychic retreat' (Steiner 2002), or 'the disease of which it purports to be the cure' (Reik 1922). The client may attempt to withdraw from the world into the therapy space and imagine a blissful all-excluding relationship with an idealised therapist. The realities of the client's life are not mentioned or, if they are, it is without real affective involvement.

Tom's life was a mess. He drifted from one superficial relationship to another, feeling depressed and cut off from his children who lived with his divorced wife. None of this was discussed in therapy. Prior to each session he would consult his dream diary, memorise it and then regale the therapist with endless and complex dreams, full of portentous themes. Eventually the therapist, normally rather adept at dream interpretation, said 'I really can't make head or tail of these dreams – they seem to me as confused as your life is at the moment . . . perhaps that is what we should be focusing on'. Only then was Tom able to acknowledge his helplessness and vulnerability and fear that the therapist would think him and his life stupid and inadequate.

In pre-mentalising modes – which as temporary states are normal in both children and adults, but if persistent may be associated with psychopathology – the child cannot see that the way the world as *perceived* has to be taken into account when considering what is or is not the case. Mentalising implies the capacity to differentiate between pretend and equivalence modes, to keep them separate and to allow traffic between them, along the lines of Bion's semi-permeable 'contact barrier' between conscious and unconscious thought.

Mentalising is both an acquired skill and a process that characterises particular states of mind. Adults perfectly capable of mentalising under propitious circumstances may lose that capacity when subject to stress, high arousal, danger, intoxication, etc. Indeed, in a flight/fight situation mentalising can be disadvantageous. If one is about to be eaten by a lion one doesn't want to spend too much time imagining what's going on in the lion's mind. Although children brought up in secure families can succeed in theory of mind tasks sooner than those from less favourable backgrounds, the latter also achieve a degree of mentalising capacity by the age of six (Gergely 2007). Affect regulation is intimately connected to mentalising – only when feelings are held within manageable limits can one begin to think about them. A dynamic model is therefore needed that takes account of both developmental and contextual factors in gauging the degree and relevance of mentalising in any given situation.

What are the developmental and contextual processes that facilitate the achievement of mentalising in children and adults? Fonagy emphasises the intense interactive processes between care-giver and child in the early years of life (Fonagy et al. 2002). In normal development 'transitional phenomena', especially *mirroring* interactions between care-giver and child, provide the basis for a sense of self. The child learns who he is and what his feelings are through the capacity of the care-giver to reflect back his gestures via playful mirroring responses. As development proceeds, playing alone or with others, his imaginative development *and* sense of what the world is 'really' like develop *pari passu*. He begins to build up a picture of where internal and external reality begin and end. This enables him to be aware of the contribution of his own feelings to his appreciation of the world. In parallel with this emergence of self-mentalising abilities, or possibly prior to them, he begins to take into account others' mentalising as an explanation for their actions and reactions. The role of the care-giver moves from mirroring to 'triangulation' (see Cavell 2006 and Chapter 6 below) in which there is a continuous dynamic interplay between the child's perceptions and those of the referenced care-giver, reinforced by language as the 'fixer' of perceptual flux.

The family game 'Pictionary' graphically illustrates and plays with this triangulation process. Players are divided into two teams. A neutral adjudicator has a list of words or phrases. A member of each team, armed with pencil and paper, is given the first item on the list by the adjudicator and, without using words, draws a picture illustrating the word or phrase, which then has to be guessed by the other members of the team. As soon as it successfully identified, the next member of the team applies to the adjudicator for the next word on the list, and so on. The first team to identify all the words correctly is the winner. The game plays with mentalising in that the task is to guess what word is 'in' the mind of the person drawing the picture. Triangulation is necessary in that the players check whether they have got it right or wrong against the drawer's negative or affirmative non-verbal response, and with each other. The word is the common currency that links one mind with another, which has to be translated into, and from, the language of thought.

Another analogy drawn from the world of games comes from Dennett's (2006) exploration of the psychology of religion. He describes how card-games are taught initially by placing cards, normally hidden, 'face-up' until the novice has grasped the rules and can begin to learn from the experience of playing itself. Dennett argues that the notion of an all-seeing 'God', and the omniscient narrator in a novel, are two examples in which similarly all the 'cards' in the human game are 'visible', thereby helping us to understand motives and feelings which in real life are never fully transparent. Psycho-analytic psychotherapy as a mentalising discipline can be seen as a third example of 'facing-up', in the sense that the patient's transferential feelings and the countertransferential responses of the analyst *qua* analyst (i.e. putting her own non-analytic responses to one side for the duration of the session) are potentially fully available for examination and discussion.

'Earned security' and mentalising

In normal development the constant circulation of thoughts, feelings, images and words from the care-giver's to the child's mind helps build up mentalising capacities. A key notion underlying the concept of mentalising was the empirical finding that when parents' attachment status was assessed before the birth of a child, high reflective function (RF) in the parent pre-dicted secure attachment in the child, even when mothers reported that they themselves had been deprived or harmed in childhood (Fonagy et al. 1997). This suggests that RF – i.e. the capacity for mentalising – is protective against the psychologically damaging impact of childhood deprivation or harm. Potential borderline personality disorder sufferers may have had develop-mental experiences that compromise RF; conversely, those who are resilient have the mitigating mentalising capacity that counteracts the psychological harm done by trauma. 'Earned security' (Hesse 2008, p. 568) is a term used to describe this latter group, who despite unpropitious developmental cir-cumstances develop secure attachments and mentalising capacities.

A contemporary example might be that of the US President Barack Obama. Coming from a difficult background, with an absent father, switches of continent and care-giving from mother and problematic step-father to his grandparents, he showed preternatural mentalising capacities. These are manifest in his autobiography (Obama 2008). Here he is describing a train journey across Kenya as he searches for his missing father and family:

I tried to imagine the sensations some nameless British officer might have felt on the train's maiden voyage as he sat in his gas-lit compartment and looked out over miles of receding bush. Would he have felt a sense of triumph, a confidence that the guiding light of Western civilisation had finally penetrated the African darkness? Or did he feel a sense of foreboding, a sudden realisation that the entire enterprise was an act of folly, that this land and its people would outlast imperial dreams? I tried to imagine the African on the other side of the glass window, watching this snake of steel and black smoke passing his village for the first time. Would he have looked on the train with envy, imagining himself one day sitting in the car where the Englishman sat, the load of his days somehow eased? Or would he have shuddered with visions of ruin and war?

(Obama 2008, p. 368)

This is high-level mentalising. The author imaginatively puts himself in opposing shoes, speculating about what each might be feeling, and qualifying his speculations with provisionality; guessing how someone else might be feeling needs always to be 'checked out' – triangulated. The mentaliser is always aware that he is mentalising – thinking about his own thinking. With his manifold gifts of intelligence, sporting prowess, good looks and a strong marriage, Obama illustrates many of the established features of resilience and earned security. (In the spirit of mentalising, the dangers of 'psychoanalysing' public figures should here be acknowledged – a fault to which Freud was not immune in his psychobiography of another US President, Woodrow Wilson.)

The general premise underlying the developmental approach is that secure attachment leads to the emergence of mentalising, and, reciprocally, that the capacity for mentalising is a marker of secure attachment. There is an impressive array of evidence (e.g. Slade 2005; Meins 1999) that mothers' capacity to be 'mind-minded' in relation to their offspring, and to be playful with them, is robustly associated with secure attachment measures in those children. Conversely, accumulating studies suggest that extreme forms of insecure attachment, especially disorganised attachment, compromise mentalising abilities in later life. As we shall see in Chapter 10, this in turn may act as a vulnerability factor for the emergence of borderline personality disorder.

Possible psychoanalytic objections to mentalisation

To return to our theoretical discussion, mentalising as a concept has three distinct intellectual roots. Bion and the cognitive psychologists draw on a philosophical tradition going back to Kant's distinction between the thing-in-itself (known only to God) and our appreciation of it. The francophone psychoanalysts remain true to Freud, linking present-day clinical experience with his unpublished 'Project' (1895) and early drive-based formulations. In the tradition of Anglo-Saxon empiricism, Fonagy and his colleagues link clinical experience with the findings of developmental psychopathology. What makes the latter's use of the term distinctive is its precision and restrictedness. The francophones and Bion aim for a global explanation of the process of thought itself, whereas Fonagy et al. concentrate on a specific aspect of thinking – the ability to understand others and oneself as intentional agents. Paradoxically, this more modest aim may provide more potency than attempts to use psychoanalytic ideas to explain the entire workings of the human mind.

When we compare the Fonagy notion of mentalising with Bion's formulations, there are striking similarities and significant differences. Bion sees the capacity for 'thinking' as dependent on the mother's (and by implication the analyst's) capacity for 'reverie', i.e. to love her infant in a way that enables her to tolerate his projections, to contain them, metabolise them and return them for re-introjection when the moment is right.

This can be compared with the Fonagy model in which the infant's sense of self, his security and ultimately his capacity for reflexive function depend on the mother's capacity to put her own feelings to one side, to mirror accurately his states of mind, within the context of a secure base. This helps the child acquire an internal image of himself, introjected from his mother's responsive and accurate reflections of his moods, feelings and desires.

A key feature of both models is the notion of affect regulation. In Bion's terminology this is 'frustration tolerance'. In the Fonagy model secure attachment means modulation and down-regulation of painful affect, aided by a care-giver who is not unduly upset by infant's distress, and knows not to 'take it personally'. This relative calmness in the face of distress fosters mentalising, since clinical, developmental and neurophysiological studies all show that excessive arousal and mentalising are mutually incompatible (Bateman and Fonagy 2004).

Similarly, mentalising can be related to the contrast between paranoid-schizoid and depressive position thinking so central to the Kleinian approach. To be in the depressive position implies a capacity to accept that both love and hate are partial, split-off feelings and are inevitably at times directed towards the same object. A mentalising perspective is consistent with this in that it visualises a thinker able to say to himself or herself: 'I know I feel hateful towards you right now, but I realise that I am just in the grip of an emotion, and that you are in reality a loving parent as well as a depriving one'.

There are also important differences between Bion's alpha function/containment theory and mentalising. Bion attempted to devise a theory that would encompass psychotic thought disorders. But it seems unhelpful to view everything that is not mentalised as 'beta elements', since people with compromised mentalising skills can still get along fairly well in many aspects of their lives. Not all of them are in any meaningful sense 'psychotic', even though it might be argued that there are 'psychotic islands' within otherwise normally functioning personalities, which can emerge under conditions of extreme stress, not excluding the analytic couch.

Second, there is a contrast in the emphasis each places on where the responsibility for health or pathology lies. In the Bion model the mother's role is relatively passive, as the term 'reverie' implies, albeit as a form of 'active listening'. Her job is to 'dream' her infant. The child by contrast is the instigator: his inability to tolerate frustration and to evacuate unwanted feelings is what underlies the ability or inability to think productively and to know what is real and what is not. In the Fonagy model the secure-base-providing mother moves fluidly into her infant's mental space, providing the 'marking' and 'contingent' responses that the child requires (see Chapter 3). While Bion's model is less purely intrapsychic than classical drive theory as drawn on by the francophone analysts – more 'object relational' – it is not fully interpersonal in the way that the Winnicott–Fonagy approach is. For the latter there are two interacting subjectivities in interplay with one another, while for Bion the '(m)other' is mainly a receptacle for the infant's projections, and there is no clear interpersonal mutually mentalising space between.

Third, for all its quasi-mathematical formulation, the Bion model is essentially a metaphor, explicitly derived from alimentation. Bion writes almost exclusively in terms of 'breast/nipple' and mouth. Much of the research underlying the Fonagy model focuses on observable facial and eye contact between mother and child and, more recently, on the findings of neuroimaging (Zeki 2008). A model, as opposed to a metaphor, can be operationalised and subject to experimental confirmation or disconfirmation; a metaphor is more akin to a poetic image that can be felt intuitively to be more or less 'true'. The two approaches come from different worlds of discourse.

A number of other possible objections to the concept of mentalising flow from this discussion. The Fonagy view is essentially an environmental/deficit model – i.e. the child is deprived of the capacity for mentalising by deficient or malevolent parenting. Psychoanalysts such as Caper (1999) have argued strongly against this, both theoretically and technically, seeing it as essentially anti-analytic and leading to collusive and ultimately unhelpful 'support', rather than radical psychic change. This approach might also be criticised from a sociological perspective as an implicitly mother-blaming manoeuvre in which the role of absent and abusive fathers is downplayed, and failing to take account of social pressures leading to family breakdown.

By contrast, Bateman and Fonagy (2004) argue that the inability to mentalise is a structural deficit, and that until mentalisation is instated, 'normal' psychoanalytic interpretations and reconstructions are unlikely to be effective. Their therapeutic rubric for people suffering from borderline personality disorder is specifically designed to foster mentalising – for example through the use of groups as well as individual therapy so that patients can regularly see themselves and their actions reflected through the eyes of their fellow sufferers. Therapy is necessarily supportive as well as interpretive, in the sense of providing and constantly aiming to repair a 'secure base', because psychological and physiological security are preconditions for mentalising.

A further objection comes from the view that mentalising is just another word for the familiar psychoanalytic concept of insight (Choi-Kain and Gunderson 2008). Bateman and Fonagy (2004, p. xi) explicitly characterise mentalising as a 'new word for old concepts'. However, insight usually refers to specific nuggets of self-understanding – e.g. that someone tends to become aggressive when confronted by older men, or compulsively seductive with married women, and to understand these tendencies in oedipal terms – while mentalising refers to a *process*, or function. Fonagy postulates a specific defect in the *apparatus* of thought (to use Bion's word), and therapy is designed to help establish reflective capacity, before the traditional aim of insight-promotion can be pursued.

Mentalisation might be accused (if abstract nouns can stand accused, cf. President Bush's 'war on terror'!) of being too 'cognitive' for psychoanalytic taste. What, it might be asked, is the difference between psychoanalytic-fostered mentalising and cognitive behavioural therapy (CBT) where the patient is encouraged to examine his erroneous thoughts and how they might be modified? One answer to this might be to argue that there are indeed overlaps between psychoanalytic mentalisation-based therapy and cogni-tively influenced treatment such as CBT and dialectical behaviour therapy (Linehan 1993), and that integrative approaches represent the future of psy-chotherapies generally (Holmes and Bateman 2002; Gabbard et al. 2005). However, CBT approaches to borderline personality disorder are likely to be as relatively ineffective as traditional psychoanalytic ones if they fail to address first the need to establish the *capacity* for mentalising, before moving on to examining specific instances where it succeeds or fails.

Finally, the mentalising approach espoused here is very different from CBT, which suggests that, since 'there's nothing good or bad but thinking makes it so', all we need to do to change our 'reality' is to change our minds. Mentalising (life couching as opposed to life coaching!) argues that the route to reality is acknowledgement that perceptions will always be mind-forged. Change comes about (a) interpersonally through collaborative reality-testing ('triangulation'; see Chapter 6 below) with a trusted other and (b) intrapsy-chically by observing and accepting the unconscious mind at work, and the anachronistic distortions that brings.

Conclusion

In the end psychoanalytic ideas stand or fall by their capacity to improve clinical outcomes. This chapter has, I hope, offered a balanced account of mentalising, albeit one mildly biased in its favour. I believe that awareness of mentalising can help clinicians to see more clearly what they are intuitively doing and saying in the consulting room. Mentalising is not so much an explanatory concept as a description of one aspect of intimate relationships, especially when they are in need of repair.

Thinking about mentalising has arisen out of the need to understand and work effectively with different groups of difficult patients. Each of the four theoretical traditions discussed takes as its starting point a particular clinical/ diagnostic phenomenon. Cognitive psychologists want to understand the social and interpersonal deficits associated with autism. Bion was preoccupied with thought disorder as seen in 'psychosis' (using the term psychoanalytic- ally rather than psychiatrically) in the consulting room, when faced with patients who suffer from deficits in 'linking' and are thus unable to make connections between their own thoughts and/or their analyst's interpret- ations. The francophone psychoanalysts started from somatisation disorders: people, in their view, who tend to manifest emotion somatically rather than verbally. Fonagy and his colleagues focus on the painful relationships with self and others characteristic of borderline personality disorder.

Mentalisation encourages therapists as well as patients to subject their ideas and feelings to constant scrutiny, in order to arrive at a greater approximation to the truth. 'Countertransference' in its modern interpretation is a specific example of mentalising – the therapist must always be asking herself 'what am I thinking and feeling at this specific moment with this particular per- son?'. That stricture applies to theoretical predilections as much as it does to responses to our patients. If taken seriously, mentalisation-informed use of countertransference is decentring and postmodernistic. There are no fixed theoretical reference points for the fully mentalising therapist, no certainty other than that the conviction that there can be no certainty – no fixed point in a turning world, no 'O' (cf. Bion 1987), no ultimate reality. Every theor- etical viewpoint, including the attachment-informed mentalising-based one, must be subject to question – how does it come about that I adopt this or that position? What and whose conscious and unconscious interests does it serve? Where does it come from? What is its justification and how do I know that that is not merely a rationalisation? Living daily with that challenge is a pedagogic, practical and moral task for therapists.

Chapter 3

Attaching

People in search of therapy are in varying states of unhappiness, conflict, trouble, mental pain and psychological illness. Psychoanalytic therapy's unique contribution is that it offers a locus where distress is both re-experienced and examined. Clients' descriptions of their difficulties 'entail' the experience being described. Encountering a therapist is in itself anxiety-arousing: how that anxiety is managed, defended against, succumbed to or circumvented tells the patient's story for him. The problematic lineaments of the therapeutic relationship make manifest the very difficulties with which the client needs help. The skill of the therapist lies in being able to engage in such a relationship, while simultaneously observing and helping the client learn from those observations. In this chapter I enumerate the component parts of the therapeutic relationship.

From an attachment perspective, understanding the therapeutic relationship arises out of a theoretical and practical conceptualisation of intimate relationships in general. These encompass the parent–child bond, spousal and romantic relationships and sometimes relationships between siblings and close friends or 'buddies'. In each there is a balance between the wish for intimacy and characteristic defences against closeness, often based on previous, often adverse, developmental experience.

Attachment styles

Attachment theory offers a model of the therapist–client relationship as the medium within which this unique interchange occurs. Distress triggers attachment behaviours. Once activated, attachment overrides all other motivations – exploratory, playful, sexual, gustatory, etc. Attachment behaviour involves seeking proximity to a figure able to assuage distress; in the case of children, one who is older and wiser. Once soothed and safe, and only then, the sufferer is able to explore his or her world, inner or outer, in the context of 'companionable interaction' (Heard and Lake 1997) with a co-participant.

The mutual incompatibility between threat-triggered attachment behaviour and exploration is the leitmotiv to which attachment in its clinical guises continually returns. In infants and young children this is manifest in observable behaviours – pulling 'in' to the secure base figure when threatened, turning 'out' into the world of play and exploration when secure. Inhibitions and compromises of this pattern are the mark of insecurely attached children. In adults these shifts are usually more subtle, although most will have had the experience of 'holding on to'/'holding in' pain – whether physical or emotional – while in the public arena, until the secure presence of a loved one makes 'letting go' possible, usually with physical accompaniments such as holding, hugging and tearfulness.

The architecture of the therapeutic relationship is (a) a person in distress, seeking a safe haven, in search of a secure base; (b) a care-giver with the capacity to offer security, soothing and exploratory companionship; and (c) the resulting relationship with its own unique quality, not directly derivable from either of the contributors. This process applies both to the initiation of therapy and to the start of each session, as well as to moments of emotional arousal as they occur within the session. One of the key aims of therapy is to elicit and identify buried feelings. In the course of a session there will be an iteration between affect arousal, activation of attachment behaviours, and their assuagement; followed by companionable exploration of the triggering feelings; leading to further affective arousal, and so on.

This process is inevitably coloured by past experience, especially expectations about how a care-giver will respond to expressed distress. This can be construed as transference in that the client brings to the relationship largely unconscious schemata, or internal working models, based on, but not identical with, previous experiences of care-seeking.

Most therapy-seekers will have had sub-optimal or adverse attachment experiences in the past. Their attachment styles are therefore likely to be insecure. Insecure attachments can be subdivided into (a) organised and (b) disorganised. As mentioned in Chapter 1, organised attachment was originally classified, on the basis of a child's response to separation in the Strange Situation (Ainsworth et al. 1978) into two typical patterns: avoidant, in which attachment needs are minimised in the face of brusque care-giving; and ambivalent, in which they are exaggerated as a way of remaining close to an inconsistent care-giver. Both are effective in providing security, but at a price: inhibition of exploration for the sake of security.

Disorganised attachment is a relatively uncommon pattern in general population samples, but seen in as many as 70% of families with overt psychological or social difficulties (Van Ijzendoorn and Sagi-Schwartz 2008). The essence of disorganisation is that *no* clear structure of care-giver–child interaction is seen, the child resorting to bizarre behaviours such as rocking, head-banging or dissociative states in which he or she appears emotionally inaccessible.

Organised insecure attachment patterns can be seen as necessary psychological defences, both in infants and in adults, in the sense that anxiety is held within manageable bounds while achieving a modicum of security. The concept of 'attachment styles' characterises typical ways of handling intimate relationships. In organised insecurity, defences are essentially interpersonal: compromises or trade-offs in which a child's conflicting psychological needs – for security on one hand and for full emotional expression and exploration on the other – are negotiated between care-giver and care-seeker. Disorganised attachment is a more autistic defence in which the child resorts to dissociation and self-soothing as a way of hanging onto a semblance of psychological integrity in the face of overwhelming attachment anxiety. Later, there may be an attempt to manage anxieties by control or coercion of others.

Classifying attachment styles in adults, Shaver and Mikulincer (2008) see insecure attachment as a spectrum ranging from deactivation (corresponding to avoidance in children) of attachment needs at one pole to hyperactivation (corresponding to ambivalent attachment) at the other. This hyperactivation/ deactivation dichotomy captures the relational expectations clients typically bring into the consulting room. Some seem 'switched-off', cool, intellectual, describing their difficulties in clichéd, minimalist ways, resistant to therapists' probes for feelings. Others overwhelm the therapist and themselves with emotion, seemingly confusing present and past, leaving little space for the therapist to stem the tide of emotion or assuage distress so that difficulties can be reflectively considered. The difficulties associated with disorganised attachment styles will be considered in detail in Chapter 10.

However, real-life therapists are far from passive observers, neutral elicitors of 'material' or objective commentators on their clients' difficulties. They themselves may well have insecure attachment styles, usually towards the hyperactivating pole (Diamond et al. 2003). Therapist and patient actively engage in an attachment/exploration cycle, in which the actuality of what the therapist offers and the client wants is counterpoised with long-established expectations and characterological attitudes, threatening that very process of productive engagement.

Mallinckrodt et al. (2005) illustrate how skilful therapists accommodate to and gradually modify the presenting stance of the client *vis-à-vis* attachment. They suggest that successful therapy requires initial 'concordance' (cf. Racker 1968) on the part of the therapist. This means partial acceptance by the therapist of the role allocated by the patient's unconscious expectations and procedures. This might mean allowing for a degree of intellectualising with deactivating clients, waiting patiently for the client to begin to allow feelings to surface, for example in relation to breaks – 'I used to take gaps in my stride, just telling myself that you were a hard-working professional and were entitled to holidays; now I really resent your going away, and wonder who you are going away with'. Conversely, with hyperactivating clients, a degree of boundary flexibility and gratification might be allowable, accepting inter-session letters and text-messages, and occasionally offering extra sessions. Later the therapist will move to a 'complementary' (as opposed to 'concordant'), more challenging role, thereby disconfirming maladaptive client expectations and opening the way for psychological reorganisation. Secure therapists redress their client's attachment insecurities, while insecure ones more likely reinforce them.

From an attachment perspective, the therapeutic relationship can be seen as the resultant of two opposing sets of forces. On one hand the analyst attempts within the limited framework of therapy to provide a secure attachment experience – to identify and assuage attachment needs and to facilitate exploration; on the other, the patient approaches the relationship with prior expectations of sub-optimal care-giving, and, unconsciously assuming an unloving and/or untrustworthy care-giver, aims mainly for a measure of security. The attachment viewpoint suggests that the therapeutic relationship is shaped both by the dynamic of its actuality and the distorting effects of transference. As therapy proceeds, the soothing presence of the analyst enables the client to expose himself to, tolerate and learn from increasing levels of anxiety.

Emotional connectedness

What makes a potential secure base 'secure'? How does an infant 'know' to whom to turn when attachment behaviours are activated? How does an attachment hierarchy, normally with mother at the apex, followed by other kin such as aunts, older siblings, father, grandparents, and non-kin 'alloparents' (Hrdy 1999) such as child-minders, become established? For adults, at what point does friendship and companionship become 'love', and what is the relationship between this and the establishment of a secure base? (Attempting to tap into this vector, I routinely ask clients at assessment 'who would you contact first if there were an emergency or crisis in your life?', and also ask for an account of what 'love' means to them, and their loves, requited and otherwise.) Relatedly, when does a therapist move from being a helpful professional into the role of an indispensable attachment figure, and how does this connect with the establishment of an 'analytic process'? Attachment research suggests at least partial answers to some of these questions.

Konrad Lorenz (1959), Bowlby's mentor and colleague, became famous for his imprinting experiments in which he showed that goslings would follow and take as their mother any largish moving object to which they were exposed in the first few hours of life – whether this be the actual mother, Lorenz himself, or even a cardboard box. Imprinting temporal 'windows' do not seem to apply to the much more fluid relational system of primates, and especially humans. Ongoing intimate proximity, availability, together with the 'knowing' – the holding in mind through absence and interruption that is integral to parental (and spousal) love – are some of the essential ingredients. The mother–infant literature suggests that, among other characteristics, a secure base parent also offers responsiveness 'mastery' (Slade 2005);

healing will be about our awareness of and responses to / ability to tolerate anxiety

reliability and consistency; 'mind-mindedness' (Meins 1999); and the ability to repair disruptions of parent–infant emotional connectedness (Tronic 1998). As we shall see, each of these forms threads that also run through the fabric of successful therapeutic relationships.

Overall, *care-seeker–care-giver emotional connectedness* is the key feature of secure base (Farber and Metzger 2008). The restriction, exaggeration, or uncoupling of such connectedness is what leads to the three varieties of insecure attachment. No less than in secure relationships, in insecure attachments the attachment figure is present in the mind of the care-seeker as a sought target for attachment behaviours, but there is a discrepancy between what is desired and what is available. Transference analysis in therapy attempts to place the minutiae of this disjunction under the therapeutic microscope.

Contingency and marking   *Interactive sequences*

Are there analogues of therapeutic intimacy in developmental studies of parent–child interaction? Gergely and Watson's (1996) landmark paper focuses on affective sequencing between parents and infants. They identify 'contingency' and 'marking', in the context of intense mutual gaze, as the basis of mirroring sequences in which, to use Winnicott's (1971, p. 51) phrase, the 'mother's face is the mirror in which the child first begins to find himself'.

'Contingency' describes the way in which the care-giver waits (her response is 'contingent upon') for the infant to initiate affective expression. Her response is then 'marked' by an exaggerated simulacrum of the infant's facial and verbal affective expression. For example, the child might be slightly down-at-mouth; the mother might then, while maintaining intense eye contact with her child, twist her face into a caricature of abject misery, saying, in high-pitched 'motherese', 'Oh, we *are* feeling miserable today, aren't we . . .'. She thereby offers the child a visual/auditory representation of his own internal affective state. This sets in motion the child's capacity to 'see' and 'own' his feelings.

Contingency gives the child the message that he/she is an actor, a person who can initiate and make a difference to the interpersonal world in which he/she finds herself or himself, and introduces him/her to the dialogic nature of human meanings. Marking links representation (initially in the mother's face, then re-represented in his own mind) to the child's own actions and internal feelings, while 'tagging' that these are his/her, not the mother's, feelings. This proto-linguistic envelope has a soothing, affect-regulating, quality.

These interactive sequences thus involve (a) *affect expression* by the child; (b) *empathic resonance* on the part of the mother, able to put herself into the shoes of the child; (c) *affect regulation* in that the parent tends to up-regulate or down-regulate depending on what emotion is communicated (stimulating a bored child, soothing a distressed one). The result is (d) mutual pleasure

When offered this contingent / mirroring - feels awful?

and playfulness, or, to use Stern's (1985) phrase, the evocation of 'vitality affects', or *enlivenment*, leading to (e) *exploratory play*/companionable interaction (Heard and Lake 1997) – 'exploring in security'.

Goal-corrected empathic attunement

Similar sequences are arguably to be found in therapist–client interactions. McCluskey (2005) describes a series of empirical studies in which she films and rates student therapists and simulated clients. She shows that initial attunement, a mirroring *affect-identifying* response on the part of the therapist, in itself is insufficient to make up a satisfactory therapeutic interaction. Further steps are needed in order to release exploration and companionable interaction. The next is affect-regulating as the therapist takes the communicated feeling and, through facial expression, tone of voice and emphasis, modifies or 'regulates' it: softly expressed sad feelings are amplified, perhaps with a more aggressive edge added; manic excitement soothed; vagueness of tone sharpened. Mirroring here becomes dialogic.

These moves are comparable to the 'marking' of the Gergely and Watson (1996) schema. The therapist might say: 'you did *what*?!'; 'that sounds *painful*'; '*ouch!*' 'it sounds as though you might be feeling pretty sad *right now*'; 'I wonder if there isn't a lot of *rage* underneath all this'. A historic example comes from Freud's Dora case, in which he writes in a footnote that he took note of the 'exact words' that Dora used 'because they *took me aback*' (emphasis added; cf. Bollas 2007, p. 31).

It is interesting to compare this empirical account with Grotstein's (2007, p. 29) account of his analysis with Bion:

> virtually every one of the words in my associations was taken up, used, and rephrased so that I was receiving from him in a somewhat altered and deepened version what I had uttered. It was like hearing myself in an echo chamber or sound mirror in which I was being amplified while being edited . . . what the classical analyst would point to as a resistance he would point to as a focus of great anxiety.

The therapist is a 'sound mirror', representing the analysand's self to himself. Further, 'resistance' is reframed as anxiety that has to be soothed if the analysis is to progress. Thus two very different theoretical and evidential standpoints arrive at similar technical conclusions: Bion's quasi-mathematical consulting-room account of transforming beta elements through the analyst's containing alpha function, and Gergely's use of Mead's theory of gesture and self-representation based on empirical studies in developmental psychology. The common theme is affect regulation and mirroring as the pathway to self-understanding.

Translating this into consulting-room practice, the therapist communicates to the patient that he has heard and felt her feelings, regulates their intensity and implicitly or explicitly adds something, e.g. the sadness that underlies mania, the anger that can be an unacknowledged feature of depression. The security associated with being understood leads to enlivenment on the part of the patient. This in turn opens the way for companionable exploration of the content or meaning of the topic under discussion. McCluskey (2005) dubs this sequence *goal-corrected empathic attunement* (GCEA), in which there is a continuous process of mutual adjustment or 'goal-correction' between client and therapist as they attempt, emotionally and thematically, to entrain the client's affective states and imagine the contexts that engender them. Mentalising is an umbrella term covering all aspects of this process.

Rupture and repair

Such sequencing is of course a council of perfection. Like parents and spouses, and indeed anyone whose goal is intimate understanding of another person, therapists regularly 'get it wrong'. Tuckett et al.'s category (2008) of therapist actions which they define as 'sudden and glaring reactions not easy to relate to the analyst's normal method', can be seen as ruptures, comparable to the normal and expectable ruptures in parent–infant connectedness, which in well-functioning parent–infant couples are 'repaired' as the parent responds to the child's signals of distress.

The GCEA framework tells us that being understood reduces anxiety, liberates vitality affects and initiates exploration. Conversely, being *mis*understood is anxiety-augmenting and aversive, triggering withdrawal and avoidance and/or defensiveness and anger. But just as security-providing mothers are able to repair lapses in attunement with their infants, so the capacity to repair therapeutic 'ruptures', a concept developed by Safran and Muran (2000) and to be developed further in Chapter 7, is associated with good outcomes in therapy.

Using the 'still face' paradigm, attachment researchers have looked at attachment styles in relation to the capacity of mother–infant dyads to resume affective contact following a brief one-minute affective withdrawal on the part of the mother in which she is asked to 'freeze' her expression (Crandell et al. 2003). Securely attached mothers' children are least disrupted by this procedure. Children with insecure mothers resort to self-soothing via looking at their own faces in the mirror when the link with mother is broken, but can generally resume contact once the break is terminated. Disorganised children are least likely to get back on track with their mothers on resumption, and most likely to resort to self-soothing, and fail to link up again with the security of the mother's gaze even when it becomes once more available.

Extrapolating from these findings to adult psychotherapy, therapists need to be highly sensitive to client reactions to discontinuities of contact both within sessions and in relation to the normal interruptions of holidays and

being understood reduces anxiety liberates vitality affects + initiates exploration

illness. Even though psychoanalytic psychotherapists are trained to focus on manifestations of 'negative transference', the evidence suggests that clients hold back negative feelings from their analysts no less than in other modalities of therapy (Safran and Muran 2000). An attachment perspective suggests that (a) in any intimate relationship daily misunderstandings are the norm; (b) the implications of these depend in part on prior expectations and attachment styles of both participants; and (c) the therapeutic issue is not so much to eliminate misunderstandings as to focus on them and find ways to put them to rights.

'Transferential' expectations are brought into play in relation to the regular mistakes, weaknesses and idiosyncrasies applicable to therapies and therapists. Therapist 'enactments' (e.g. starting a session late, drowsiness, inattention or intrusiveness) need to be non-defensively acknowledged. Such ruptures are understood as 'induced', often outside the awareness of both therapist and client (Wallin 2007) in the unconscious matrix inherent in an attachment relationship. Reflexively thinking about them by therapist and client together strengthens the therapeutic bond, and is itself a change-promoting manoeuvre, enhancing clients' capacity for self-awareness and negotiating skills in intimate relationships. This is illustrated in the following example.

Miriam: On not being 'helpful'

Miriam, single, in her mid-thirties, a computer programmer, presented with depression, and a wish to understand why she had found it so difficult to find the partner she so longed to share her life with. Her childhood broke apart when her parents divorced. She saw little thereafter of her controlling skin-flint obsessional father, except when she had to testify in a bitter parental court battle over child support. She had dealt with this by emotional withdrawal and concentrating on her career.

At assessment the therapist felt powerful compassion and a wish to be a 'good father' to this courageous woman – to foster her ability to find herself a loving partner, validate her attractiveness as a woman and take pride in her achievements. The strength of these countertransferential feelings suggested a split-off neediness, which, for survival's sake, Miriam had had to repress. They also represented a valid 'non-transferential' task for any therapist working with her. She really did need a safe person with whom she could explore both her longing for love and her rage at its absence. However, when invited to explore her feelings she felt 'put on the spot' and became very agitated. What she most wanted was also what she most feared. The first task was to acknowledge and soothe her anxiety (mainly through tone of voice and a receptive, expectant, non-demanding stance) before exploration could be embarked upon.

Ideally she would have begun to look at how untrusting she was of people in general (therapists included), and how the template for this might have been her father and distracted mother. Understanding how she unconsciously 'chose' untrustworthy men who confirmed her negative expectations would perhaps have been possible once her attachment anxiety reached more manageable limits. Instead, the therapist became caught up in an egregious instance of acting-out, albeit apparently for the best of motives. He wanted to 'be' the good father she hadn't had. He found himself recommending that she might prefer to see a female therapist, working nearer her home, who would be able to offer more frequent sessions. Not surprisingly, rather than being enthusiastically responded to, this resulted in a period of confusion and missed sessions.

When eventually a more secure attachment relationship was re-established, therapist and patient were able to see how this episode represented a replay of her parents' divorce, where she was abandoned by her father to her mother, reinforcing her feelings of unwantedness and sexual insecurity, and triggering further emotional withdrawal. Not only had the therapist failed to provide a secure base, he had actively fostered insecurity through an unconsciously driven enactment of both his own threateningly strong countertransferential feelings and the client's negative expectations of herself and her ability to elicit love in those whose business it was to care for her.

In this example Miriam's initial unbearable attachment anxiety meant that exploration was powerfully inhibited: 'I can't really talk, I feel so put on the spot'. As she was unable to think about her feelings, they were transmitted via projective identification or the 'language of thought' to the therapist. Miriam unconsciously communicated the longing she felt for a good father, too painful to be directly experienced (since that would mean being in touch with the misery that his actual absence entailed), manifesting in the therapist as his 'positive' countertransference. The levels of attachment anxiety were so great that neither she nor her therapist was able to think clearly (mentalise) – he could not 'be a secure base'; she could not turn to one. This opened the door to an 'enactment' in which the therapist replayed her father's abandonment via his suggesting transfer to a more 'convenient' (? less anxiety-arousing) female therapist. Turning passive into active, Miriam's response was then to communicate her feelings of abandonment indirectly via her missed sessions.

'Paternal' aspects of the attachment/therapeutic relationship

A key early finding in attachment research (Ainsworth et al. 1978) was that attachment classification in the Strange Situation was a relational and not a temperamental feature, since at one year children could be secure with mother and insecure with father or vice versa (by 30 months the maternal pattern tends to dominate; Ainsworth et al. 1978). Nevertheless the role of fathers in attachment has been relatively neglected, in the case of disorganised attachment because, sadly, most of the children studied come from mother-only families (Lyons-Ruth and Jacobvitz 2008). The Grossmanns' longitudinal studies (Grossmann et al. 2005) are an exception, showing that paternal contribution in childhood to eventual security in early adulthood is as important as that of the mother, and that combined parental impact is greater than the sum of each alone.

The Grossmanns delineate the 'paternal' role as somewhat different from the 'maternal'. (The sexist implications of this dichotomy are acknowledged, and should perhaps be reframed as 'security-providing' and 'empowering' parental functions.) When asked to perform a brick-building or sporting task (e.g. teaching a child to swim), successful security-providing fathers offer their offspring a 'you can do it' message, creating a zone of protection, within which sensory-motor development can proceed. In the Strange Situation, as compared with mothers, fathers tend to use short bursts of intense distraction and activity as comforting manoeuvres, in contrast to the more gentle crescendo and diminuendo of hugging and soothing characterising female care-givers.

In child development studies measures of maternal sensitivity are insufficient to capture security-providing functions, and a dimension of 'mastery' also contributes to the variance, communicating not just intimate protectiveness but also the presence of a competent adult in charge of the play-space. This links with the Vygotskian notion of the 'zone of proximal development' where the child is directed to tasks that are neither too easy nor too hard (Leiman 1995), and also the physical 'defensible space' surrounding the child whose security it is the parent's responsibility to guarantee. Similarly, therapists provide therapeutic space (which is also a 'space of time', cf. Lakoff and Johnson 1980), and are mindful of Freud's (1914/1958) injunction that interpretations should be aimed at patients' emergent thoughts, being neither too 'deep' nor too superficial.

Effective psychotherapy has *both* a soothing and an empowering function. McCluskey (2005, p. 87), drawing on Heard and Lake (1997), captures this in her emphasis on the *goal*-oriented aspect of exploration. She sees the outcome of secure attachment through effective assuagement of attachment behaviours as being the

> effective capacity to influence one's environment . . . What is sought by the care-seeker . . . is a relationship with someone which puts them in touch with how they might, with or without help, reach their goals for themselves; or if their goals are unrealisable . . . the interaction promotes that sense of well-being [*cf. 'vitality affects'*] that comes from being in touch with another person who can stay with and *name* what one is experiencing rather than denying it, changing it, or fleeing from it.
>
> (emphasis added)

In the Western world, 'naming' is construed as a 'paternal'/masculine function. In Henry Reed's (Gardner 1972) classic Second World War poem,

Naming of Parts, a dreamy military recruit is being instructed by his company sergeant in the dismantling, cleaning and reassembly of a firearm, while his thoughts keep drifting into a (? maternal) reverie towards the scents and sights of the surrounding flowers:

> Today we have naming of parts. Yesterday
> We had daily cleaning. And tomorrow firing. But today,
> Today we have naming of parts. Japonica
> Glistens like coral in all of the neighbouring gardens,
> And today we have naming of parts.

Lacan's punning '*le non[nom] du père*' (the name of the father; the *no* of the father) encapsulates the 'negative' paternal oedipal prohibition that severs the infant's phantasy of merging with the mother, but also the 'positive' liberating, linguistic function that enables one to stand outside, think about and manipulate experience and ultimately to understand one's self (which in Western culture includes the patronymic). In order to alleviate client anxiety, the therapist needs not just to be empathic, but also to communicate 'mastery' (with its 'paternal' resonance) – a sense that she knows what she is doing, is in control of the therapy and its boundaries (without being controlling) and is relaxed enough to mentalise her own feelings. Mastery and empathy are not mutually exclusive (as they are implicitly in the Reed poem), but denote a good 'primal marriage' of sensitivity and power that forms a basis from which the client can begin to tackle his life-problems.

The 'fundamental rule'

A feature of secure relationships, whether parent–infant or spousal, is the presence of open communication (e.g. 'I can say anything to my mum/husband and know she/he will listen without judging me'). This is the novelist Joseph Conrad's (1904/1963, p. 205) formulation of intimacy between two people:

> The frank unreserve, as before another human being, of thoughts and sensations; all the objectless and necessary sincerity of one's innermost life trying to react upon the profound sympathies of another existence.

Freud's 'fundamental rule' (i.e. an invitation to the patient to say anything that comes into her/his mind, however irrelevant or embarrassing it might seem), could be seen as an attempt to establish a similar culture within the consulting room. Much of the work of psychoanalytic psychotherapy revolves around identifying and removing barriers to such free communication. 'Free association' typically requires a contingent interactive culture in which the therapist awaits and follows the client's lead. Unfettered communication becomes possible once an atmosphere of security is established, often following the identification of, and challenge to, the myriad ways in which clients habitually avoid emotional intimacy in the service of security.

Bollas (2008) bemoans the attrition of free association in current psycho-analytic practice, which he sees as having been driven out by an excessive preoccupation with transference interpretation. For him a mark of 'good' analysis is that it liberates the flow of free association. While excessive emphasis on 'you mean me' interpretations (Budd 2008) may bedevil certain rigid analytic approaches, there is no intrinsic opposition between transfer-ence interpretation and free association. Indeed Freud viewed transference interpretations as necessary only when the flow of free associations was inter-rupted. Interpretations can be seen as means of identifying ways in which the patient feels insecure in the presence of the analyst. An interpretation that acknowledges and helps understand a painful affect – if transferential in relation to the therapist – facilitates exploration, once greater security/ intimacy is re-established.

Thus far I have concentrated on anatomising the therapeutic relationship, as opposed to the meaning-making and change-promoting aspects of what makes therapy therapeutic. The tripartite division is of course artificial in that a good therapeutic alliance in itself promotes – and, indeed, some argue is a proxy for – change (Stiles et al. 1990). Likewise, a feeling of positive change strengthens the therapeutic bond, and the exploration of meaning can strengthen the therapeutic alliance, while thinking about that alliance is a central part of the meaning-making process. Nevertheless, without secure attachment it is unlikely that mutative work will be done. However accurate the interpretation, if the analyst is not experienced as a secure base, it will fall on deaf ears. Our next task then is to look at how attachment can inform meaning-making, which for most analytic therapists is what their work is most obviously about.

Chapter 4

Meaning

Meaning-making is intrinsic to all therapy, from folk remedies and Shamanic rituals to psychoanalysis itself. All rely on an explanatory framework bringing order to the intrinsically inchoate experience of illness, whether physical or mental (Holmes and Bateman 2002). An explanatory framework, or 'formulation', both is anxiety-reducing in itself and provides the scaffolding for the mutual exploration that follows once attachment anxiety has been assuaged. A symptom or troublesome experience is 'reframed' (a term originating in systemic therapy) into a new explanatory system or model, which helps make sense of the sufferer's mental (or physical) pain. The use of the word 'sense' here acknowledges that meaning transcends mere cognition and ultimately derives from bodily experiences.

Psychoanalysis' search for meaning does not in itself make it different from other therapies. Its distinctive contribution is (a) the idiographic search for specific and personal meaning, rather than assignation to pre-determined diagnostic categories (although these are not entirely eschewed – 'oedipal', pre-oedipal', etc.) and (b) providing a technique and conceptual framework for exploring unconscious, relational and developmental meanings. We shall now consider each of these in turn.

Unconscious meanings

At least four distinct connotations are associated with the idea of the unconscious in contemporary psychoanalytic debate. Classically, a primal trauma is postulated in which the infant encounters his/her utter vulnerability in relation to the nurturing body of the mother. Awareness of that helplessness, together with dimly perceived, but equally traumatic, intrusion of her sexuality (cf. Chapter 9), results in 'primary repression' – radically banishing to unawareness thoughts and feelings of fear and desire that would otherwise overwhelm the fragile infantile mind. The abolition of these unthinkable thoughts constitutes the origins of the unconscious, a psychic zone that cannot manifest itself directly, but that nevertheless reaches consciousness via dreams, psychosis and creativity. From an attachment perspective this could be seen as a primitive apprehension by the infant of his or her overwhelming dependency on the mother for survival.

The neo-Kleinian approach (Hinshelwood 1994) similarly assumes a trauma intolerable to the infantile mind. Here, however, it is the infant's feelings of rage and envy directed towards the indispensable – but autonomous and uncontrollable – breast, rather than its sexual or security-providing properties, that have to be kept out of the mind. Repression is one means of achieving this. More important are splitting and projection, in which unwanted feelings are relocated into an intimate other. This may be the loving mother/breast herself, who in turn helps with the process of re-introjection. When that fails, others may be unwittingly pressed into service for the sake of psychic survival. The latter, described in terms of 'excessive projective identification', is associated especially with complex and disturbed states of mind (see Chapter 10), but can hold sway temporarily when anxiety reaches unmanageable levels, as in the example of Miriam above.

A third tack, typically that of neo-Jungian and Winnicottian variants of object relations, views the unconscious as not so much the repository of the unbearable as the wellspring of creativity and power. Working joyfully in tandem with, rather than ruefully acknowledging the power of, the unconscious is the task of the conscious mind and is the basis for healthy/ creative living.

Fourthly, in a radical divergence from Freud's original concept, the relational and attachment-influenced approach advocated in this book suggests that the consciousness–unconscious divide is not fully captured in terms of repression and splitting/projection. Both are indeed necessary as a way of avoiding painful feelings, especially those associated with adverse developmental pathways when faced with environmental trauma or neglect. But the 'Freudian unconscious' here is merely one facet of the *pervasive* unconsciousness of mental processes, whether due to intrinsic automatism (such as digestive processes), repression or absence of mentalising skills. Cheney and Seyfarth's (2007) 'language of thought' baboons are unconscious in the sense of being unaware of their awareness, yet they need to be continuously thinking about social relations throughout their waking day (perhaps even processing those 'unconscious thoughts' in their sleep, since we know that animals dream). These thoughts are not so much repressed as unexpressed.

In this secular version of psychoanalysis, what is at stake is not so much 'the unconscious' as consciousness itself. Current interest in mindfulness (Mace 2008) and mentalising-fostering therapies as therapeutic tools reflects this changed perspective. Here, enhancing awareness in its widest sense is a goal of therapy, seen as the acquisition of a necessary social skill, rather than the consequences of undoing repression. Just as having a 'language of thought' helps baboons negotiate their limited but intense social field, so consciousness of consciousness makes humans happier/more successful/fitter

(in the evolutionary sense) than those who lack such skills. Those with felici-
tous developmental experiences acquire and pass on such skills in the bosom
of their families; those less fortunate may need psychotherapy if they are to
achieve or regain a positive developmental track.

Relational meaning

The meanings or patterns that form the basis of psychoanalytic work
are essentially interpersonal or relational, i.e. they are concerned with what
one person feels *vis-à-vis* another – love, envy, desire, hatred, inadequacy,
rejection, excitement, fear, etc. Even when the symptom to be elucidated is
apparently intrapsychic, e.g. depression, it can be translated psychoanalytically into a relational context. As conceptualised by Freud (1917), the
self-hatred of depression might denote hostility towards another turned
inwards; from an attachment viewpoint depression relates to loss and might
indicate despair and disconnectedness following a sense of abandonment by a
care-giver. From this follows the significance of transference, since it is the
relationship to the analyst that often provides the clue to the recurring (and
therefore characterological) relational/contextual pattern that underlies the
patient's problem.

Whether *every* aspect of what the patient brings to the therapeutic table is
grist for transferential interpretations is open to debate (Budd 2008). It may
be that transference interpretations achieve their positive effects because,
conveying a sense of mastery, they provide a consistent and coherent rubric
of meaning for the therapist, which in turn is reassuring for the patient; this,
as we saw before, is in itself security-promoting. Meaning – based on any
explanatory model – is the therapist's secure base, and a secure therapist is
likely to be an effective one.

There is a balancing act between the tolerance of unknowing, or Keats'
'negative capability', implicit in Bion's 'beyond memory and desire' impera-
tive, and the therapist's need to co-construct meaning with the client. In
any session, or indeed at any given moment in a session, the therapist will
be working to a formulation (a mini-theory or hypothesis) with which to
make sense of what is going on between them, and in the client's life. The
recursive aspect of mentalising means that that formulation is always provisional, open to 'visions and revisions' (Eliot 1986), itself to be subject to
further formulation.

More about Miriam

Miriam, in the previous chapter, felt inhibited and 'put on the spot' in therapy. She described in one session how difficult it was for her to do what
she wanted when she was with someone else, even though while by herself she
was perfectly capable of knowing her own mind. She gave the example of

choosing fabrics for her new house while shopping with a friend and being swayed in directions that she then regretted when making her choice. The therapist's formulations were guided by 'Malan's triangles' (Malan and Della Selva 2006). Making a present–past link in his mind, he wondered if the prototype for this kind of difficulty was her relationship with her father, whom she experienced as controlling and abusive, the anxiety associated with which drove out her capacity to think clearly. Attempting to complete the 'triangle', his formulation then moved to the present-therapist vector and wondered if a similar process was inhibiting therapy. He said: 'I wonder if this is affecting us right now. Perhaps if I weren't here behind you on the couch you would have no difficulty in thinking your thoughts'. She laughed confirmingly, leading to a new formulation arising from the observation that in disorganised attachment, intimacy arouses rather than assuages attachment anxiety. He then probed for more detail about the chaotic childhood she had endured.

Developmental meaning

Psychoanalytic meanings are typically developmental in that feelings that appear incomprehensible (i.e. meaning-less) in an adult make sense when translated (a linguistic metaphor whose origin implies the movement of an object in space, but also time) into a childhood context. This provides the rationale for infant observation as part of psychoanalytic training, in that the student learns how to make sense of the pre-verbal gestures and interactions of 'one without speech'.

The role of infant and childhood trauma (neglect; physical, emotional or sexual abuse; loss and bereavement) as precursor of later psychological difficulty is understood in terms of both (a) deficits in the ability of the child's cognitive and affective apparatus to comprehend the trauma fully and to 'defend against' it, and (b) deficits of the 'environment' (i.e. care-givers) to help cope with the trauma, especially if they themselves are the perpetrators. Therapy involves reawakening of painful affect, often via minor echoes of the traumatic situation in the transference (cf. Casement 1985), which can now be thought about in the context of a benign therapeutic relationship. As anxiety is brought within manageable limits, the overwhelming helplessness of trauma is replaced by the possibility of mastery via mentalising.

Unconscious meanings are by definition implicit. A distinctive aspect of the psychoanalytic approach is the view that no explanatory framework can be fully accessible to the conscious mind. As Freud pointed out, using the 'blind spot' analogy from the visual field, a fully reflexive self has to acknowledge that there will always be lacunae in its self-awareness. Psychoanalysts know that, however 'well-analysed', there is much that we do not know and can never fully know. Psychoanalysis is a recursive hall of mirrors (cf. Chapter 9), but also a 'beam of intense darkness' (Grotstein 2007).

Language

How do new meanings emerge in the cut and thrust of psychoanalytic work?

First, via close attention to language. From the outset, Freud saw the inherent ambiguity of language as an entrée to the unconscious, viewing words as 'switches' or junction points between conscious and unconscious thoughts or, to use a contemporary metaphor, nodal points in neural networks (Gabbard 2005). Analysis of linguistic ambiguity has been particularly emphasised in the British Independent tradition by authors such as Sharpe (1940) and Rycroft (1985), and in Lacanian psychoanalysis (Zeal 2008). To take a non-clinical example, a radio interviewer's comment to an interviewee was 'I'm delighted to see you share my passion for Chopin'. Were this to arise in a clinical setting, this might be noted as suggesting a degree of narcissism, since a less self-centred person would more likely have said 'I see we share a passion for Chopin', or 'we have in common an enthusiasm for Chopin'.

Tuckett et al. (2008) categorise some interventions as 'unsaturated' and 'polysemic' comments on the part of the analyst. 'Unsaturation' is Bion's (1988) chemical metaphor: an unsaturated solution is one that can always accept more without precipitation; an unsaturated compound is one capable of further reactions due to the availability of unfilled 'shells' or bonding possibilities. Polysemy means 'many meanings', so it and unsaturation refer to the possibility of multiple (or arguably infinite) meanings. As the literary critic Eagleton (2007, p. 22) puts it: 'language is always what there is more of'. Therapist and patient co-create a space from which to look at feelings, behaviours and speech-acts from all possible perspectives and angles – concrete, metaphorical, sexual, adult, child-like, coercive, intimidated, anxiety-influenced, and so on. The analyst is ever-alert to the puns, polyphony of the words and phrases used by the patient, and ready to explore the many meanings thereby revealed and concealed.

Tom and the unreliable driver

Tom, a keen runner, was negotiating an icy road on a dark winter's evening. The sides of the road were particularly slippery. The phrase 'be careful of the sides of the road' came suddenly into his mind. Then he remembered that this was precisely the instruction his father, a Second World War officer, had told him he had given to the jeep-driver when they were negotiating a minefield after D-day, minutes before they were blown up with near-fatal consequences. This free-associative anecdote emerged in a session in which the patient was resisting his therapist's push to talk about the many losses and traumata of his life. The transferential situation with the therapist – who was, in effect, saying 'come on, stop blocking the pathway to talking about your trauma' – evoked the metaphor of 'the road' (? 'less travelled') in this complex set of polysemic associations.

In the consulting room, sensitivity to the ebb and flow of attachment and exploration is the hallmark of the skilful therapist. As discussed in the previous chapter, GCEA entails 'secure base' responses to client distress. This is in part a matter of timing and tone of voice, but accurate verbal identification of feelings – i.e. the emergence of shared meanings – is in itself soothing, and the exploration that ensues once anxiety is assuaged is a 'conversation about a conversation'.

As in any intimate relationship – spousal, parent–child, sibling, close friendship – highly specific meanings derived from the minutiae of a person's life are co-created by therapist and client. Elaborating this personal vernacular or 'idiolect' (Lear 1993) is a crucial aspect of psychotherapeutic work. In Bollas' (2007) terminology, the 'receptive unconscious' of the analyst is tuned into the 'expressive unconscious' of the client; the task of the analyst's conscious ego, like that of the good-enough mother in Winnicott's (1971) model of the child playing 'alone in the presence of the mother', is to guard the therapeutic space in a non-intrusive way.

The meaning-making function of therapy picks out significance from this unending flux of the free play of the imagination, or stream of consciousness. 'Whole trains of thought sometimes pass through our brains instantaneously, as though they were sensations, without being translated into human speech' (Dostoevsky); 'these words represented in brief the thousand and one thoughts which floated through his mind' (Balzac). Language marks out meanings and preserves them from the erasing process of the unconscious' unending dynamic, Buddhism's 'monkey mind', ever moving from branch to branch in the brain's dendritic forest. Once verbally 'fixed', meanings can be considered, by therapist and patient together from all possible angles: tested, refined, held onto, modified or discarded as appropriate.

Main is credited with attachment theory's decisive 'move to the level of representation' (Main et al. 1985) – i.e. the instantiation in a mind of attachment relationships. Clearly 'representation' is not exclusively or necessarily verbal. 'Teleological' thinking, characteristic of pre-verbal, 'pre-mentalising' toddlers (Fonagy 2006b) (see Chapter 2 above) is both representational and meaningful in the sense that the infant begins to develop a mental map of the interpersonal world based on 'if this, then that' logic. However, the capacity to represent the Self and Others and their relationship *verbally* is a vital developmental step, enabling children to negotiate the interpersonal world that will be matrix of all future existence once the physical 'matrix' (i.e. mother) is relinquished. Language underpins a Self that becomes both a centre of experience and an object in the world which can be described and discussed and 'worked on' through the vicissitudes of everyday life, and, when necessary, in psychotherapy.

An analogy might be with the invention of musical notation around the start of the second millennium AD. Through oral tradition, music has been integral to culture throughout human history. But once notation was developed, far more complex musical structures became possible, starting with polyphony, and moving to its full symphonic expression in the nineteenth and twentieth centuries. Psychological theories, including psychoanalysis, can similarly be thought of as 'notations' with which to reflect and to elaborate the complexities of the inner life of the mind (cf. Bollas 2007).

Narrative styles and the meaning of meaning

The Adult Attachment Interview suggests that *how* we talk about ourselves and our lives, as much as *what* we talk about, probes the architecture of the inner world. Like the 'fluid attentional gaze' (Main 1995) of the secure infant who seamlessly negotiates transitions between secure base-seeking, social referencing and exploratory play, Main characterises secure narratives as 'fluid autonomous' – neither over- nor under-elaborated, able to balance affect and cognition in ways appropriate to the topic discussed.

In the context of therapy, secure narrative styles are 'meaningful' in the sense that they facilitate an open-ended 'language game' (Wittgenstein 1958) between therapist and client. In contrast, insecure styles lead to therapeutic conversations that are under- or over-saturated with meaning (dismissive or enmeshed respectively), or lack apparent meaning (incoherent), depending on whether they represent deactivating, hyperactivating or unresolved attachments. 'Meaning' is inherent in the interactive mutuality of a language game. Clearly it is possible to have a private language, as for example in psychosis, but it is only when it can be shared that it becomes meaningful in the sense used here. Therapy can be seen as continuously helping the client to move from private to shared meanings.

A key part of therapeutic work, then, far removed from an exclusive preoccupation with making 'correct interpretations', consists in moving the client towards the exploration of mutual meanings, based on a more secure narrative style – 'can you elaborate on that?', 'what exactly did you mean by that?', 'I can't quite visualise what you are talking about here; can you help?', 'what did that feel like to you?', 'I'm getting a bit confused here, can you slow down a bit?', 'there seems to be something missing in what you're saying; I wonder if there is some part of the story we haven't quite heard about?'. The therapist is probing in this kind of dialogue for specificity, visual imagery and metaphor that enable her to conjure up, in her mind's eye and ear, aspects of the patient's experience. This then becomes a shared object or 'third' (Ogden 1989; Benjamin 2004), which can be 'companionably explored' (Heard and Lake 1997) and, in the case of metaphors, played with and extended.

There is evidence to support the idea that successful therapy is associated with the replacement of insecure by more secure narrative styles (Avdi and Georgaca 2007), a move that I have called 'autobiographical competence'

(Holmes 2001). However, Eagle and Wolitzky (2008) question whether the notion of 'autobiographical competence' is necessarily a valid marker of progress in therapy. It could be a manifestation of compliance and/or intellectualisation, or emerge in the consulting room without necessarily denoting generalisation into the client's 'real life', or true structural change in the personality.

Main's schema contrasts the fluidity of secure styles with the fixity, prolixity or incoherence of the insecure. Psychic health is characterised by some psychoanalytic writers in terms of a harmonious and creative collaboration between unconscious and conscious parts of the mind (e.g. Loewald 1980; Rycroft 1985). Secure narrative styles are open-ended, 'polysemic' systems, 'infinite' [in Matte-Blanco's (1975) sense of the unconscious as an 'infinite set'], in contrast to the fixed, overwhelming or inchoate narratives of insecure attachment.

Finding the right meaning

As therapists we are continuously struggling to select the 'right' or true meaning out of the infinite range of possibilities. The client needs to know whether a particular comment on the part of the analyst, or idea they have generated themselves, 'feels right'. Damasio (1994) suggests that we use the body to let us know when our cognitive and intellectual faculties are on track. Implicit in Cavell's (2006) notion of 'triangulation' (to be elaborated in Chapter 6) is the idea that a child cross-checks the veracity and validity of their perceptions of the outside world with those of the care-giver and so begins to build up a picture of the real world distinct from his or her perception of it. While internal experience cannot be directly 'double-checked', the notions of mirroring and empathic attunement suggest that we learn about our inner world in a comparable way, using the care-giver's understanding to develop our own self-knowledge. In psychotherapy sessions the analyst makes guesses or suggestions about clients' states of mind, clients then compare this proffered empathic understanding with what their introspection tells them they are feeling. Exploring whether there is a near-match or a misalignment (empathy is never an exact match, more a 'rhyme' leading to further informed guesses), therapy helps the client gradually to know himself or herself better.

Mace (2008) reviews findings suggesting that the capacity for *attention* or 'mindfulness' is a psychological skill for therapists and clients alike. CBT therapists have found that adding mindfulness training to conventional therapeutic strategies reduces relapse rates in chronic depression (J. Williams et al. 2000) and borderline personality disorder (Linehan et al. 2006). Mace links mindfulness with the 'evenly suspended attention' advocated for therapists by Freud (1912), and Bion's (1970) admonition that analysts should abandon 'memory and desire' if they are to achieve receptiveness and spontaneity.

Attachment and empathy, apparently abstract concepts, are ultimately psychophysical phenomena. Proximity is sought – tactile (hugging, sitting on a lap), auditory (via a telephone) or visual (a picture, which may be in the 'mind's eye'). This lowers arousal – lowered heart rate, less sweating, releases oxytocin (Zeki 2008). A mentalising conversation (e.g. a therapy session) may also be seen in those terms. The physical posture and tone of voice of the client reveal his or her emotional state. The therapist imaginatively or even actually (via contingently marking and so altering their own physical posture) mirrors this state, which in turn, via 'mirror neurones' (P. Hobson 2002), triggers a version of the client's emotional state in the therapist's receptive apparatus. This can then be introspected, identified, verbalised. Change is thus set in train. When I feel out of touch with a client's affective state I concentrate my attention on a spot just above their sternum and try to resonate with their somatic feelings (a procedure I dub 'open heart therapy') until I get sensations that I can then put into words about how they might be feeling.

Finding the 'right' meaning emerges from a three-stage process. First, in a state of 'reverie' (Ogden 1989), the therapist 'tunes into' her own affective and corporeal sensory–affective world, i.e. her 'countertransference'. Describing such sensations in words constitutes stage two, an attempt at verbal description, transforming 'preconceptions' into 'conceptions' (Bion 1970). Stage three, the full expression of meaning-making, is the therapist's attempt to weave (a) her own affective reactions, (b) knowledge about the client's history and (c) relevant understanding of developmental/psychoanalytic theory into a pattern that captures the internal world of the client in the context of the interpersonal situation generated in the *in vitro* atmosphere of the session (cf. Canestri 2006).

Herein lies the argument for psychoanalytic pluralism. The therapist's affective response to the client is involuntary and, if the therapist is working well, ineluctable. Her task then is to find an appropriate theoretical metaphor or 'fit' with this countertransferential feeling. She might want to work with defences, with loss, with splitting, with the simultaneous need for and fear of attachment, with the fragile narcissistic self, with rage. The amalgam of countertransferential response and theoretical formulation forms the prevailing 'focus' (Balint 1968) of the session. The more theoretical perspectives are available to the therapist, the more sophisticated this response is likely to be.

Sandra's dreams – no escape from the wolves

Sandra started a session by recounting a long, complicated and terrifying dream. Towards the end of this nightmare she found herself *being pursued by a 'doctor' who was offering her a curative injection, but the syringe was full of strychnine.*

I immediately thought that this must be a comment on the 'treatment' that I was offering her, purporting to be helpful but experienced by her as potentially fatal. It seemed to say something about her attitude towards men, whose 'syringes' were at best ambiguous in her eyes.

For some reason – bringing oneself as therapist into the discussion prematurely can often appear heavy-handed and self-centred – I decided to hold my fire on this. Instead I said 'the end of the dream sounds very scary and persecutory . . .'.

She immediately responded by recalling a recurrent dream she had had as a child (a common occurrence – one dream leads onto another):

> I am in a wood with my younger brother at the back of our house. There are wolves there trying to 'get' us. I want us to climb up the trees to safety, but they are all pine trees with no lower branches. Eventually I find a makeshift platform that I had built and we huddle up there.

My immediate response was to think of the branchless trees as being like people without arms. The scenario of the dream typifies attachment behaviour when there is no 'secure base'. There is a threat, the child turns to the caregiver, but there are no comforting arms to nestle in. The base is insecure and the attachment seeker has to provide her own secure base – the ramshackle platform – as best she can. This seemed to encapsulate Sandra's attitude to the world. She daren't trust people too much and has to be excessively self-reliant (in the dream she inhabits a 'brotherly', masculine, alter-ego – every character in a dream, in a sense, being a manifestation of some part of the dreamer's psychological makeup), at a price of loneliness and depression. She 'pines' for closeness but there are no arms there to hold her.

She accepts my interpretation sceptically. To do so with open arms would mean coming down from her platform of self-reliance, admitting her dependency on me and running the risk of being thrown to the wolves of my therapy.

We are exploring unconscious meanings in three ways. First, in taking the dream seriously as representing a story about herself that needs to be decoded; second through the language and its reverberations implicit in the dream and its discussion – 'pine-ing', 'open arms', wolf metaphors; third through its reference to the relationship with the therapist. But the language we use to talk about the unconscious, the theoretical framework we bring to bear, depends on who 'we' as therapists are – characterologically, developmentally, sociologically, pedagocially, philosophically.

As an attachment theorist, I 'automatically' saw the dream in terms of an insecure base. Equally automatically, a Jungian might well have seen the dream in archetypal terms, the wood representing Julie's unconscious into which she fears descending, yet containing her predatory, beautiful persona (a woman who could, if only she would, 'run with wolves') and her creativity (the platform which she had built).

A neo-Freudian take on the dream might focus on the sexual connotations of the syringe and the upright trees, representing a masculine principle threatening to separate her from her mother and leave her defenceless (she lived with her single-parent mother until she was 10 years old, when the mother re-married).

A Kleinian analyst might have jumped to the conclusion that the dream was a perfect expression of the 'paranoid-schizoid position'. The image of the syringe can be understood in terms of projected 'envy of the breast' – i.e. the feeling that anyone who is able to give her something good (a healing injection) has something to be coveted, and is thus envy-provoking and not to be trusted. So the good medicine turns to poison. This theme is then repeated as the predatory wolves, representing her own voraciousness, rage and (again) envy, threaten to destroy the good reparative protectiveness she feels towards her younger brother.

It would be reassuring to be able to say that one interpretation was correct and the others wrong. In my view, to do so would also violate one of the essential pillars of psychotherapy – the capacity to tolerate ambiguity and uncertainty, to offer the patient one's views in a tentative manner so that they can be picked up or rejected at will, and in which the patient is the ultimate arbiter of what feels right.

To summarise, attachment theory's contribution to meaning-making underpins a meta-theoretical perspective in which it is not so much specific interpretations that count as the restoration or elaboration of the *capacity to find/make shared meanings*, irrespective of their content. The Boston psychic change group (Lyons-Ruth and the Boston Change Process Study Group 2001) have similarly focused on the mutative aspects of 'non-interpretive mechanisms' in psychoanalytic work. Therapist and client come together in a meaningful shared 'present moment' (Stern 2004). Meaning in itself is not mutative; it is the *mutuality* of meaning-*making* that matters. This brings us to the third leg of the psychotherapy tripod – promoting change.

Chapter 5

Changing

The purpose of psychoanalysis is to improve the lives of its clients. But, in contrast to 'suggestion-based' therapies (ranging from Freud's characterisation of therapeutic charisma and the placebo effect to the homework 'suggestions' of CBT therapists), psychoanalytic psychotherapy avoids explicit efforts to produce change, even if its implicit aims are no less 'mutative'. This paradox follows logically from psychoanalysis' theoretical base. People get into psychological trouble because of conflict between the conscious and unconscious mind. Direct appeals on the part of therapy to the sufferer's consciousness will therefore merely activate resistance of the unconscious to change in the status quo and be counterproductive. The unconscious must be approached by stealth, and taken unawares. Difficulties based on paradox require paradoxical means if they are to be overcome.

But what sorts of change does psychoanalysis aim to achieve? Alleviating specific symptoms is generally seen as flowing from the attainment of greater global psychic health. Contemporary psychoanalytic psychotherapy concerns itself primarily with problematic character traits rather than specific symptoms, the latter being seen as best treated, at least initially, pharmacologically or with CBT.

Different schools of psychoanalysis emphasise varying objectives and associated techniques. For classical psychoanalysis the aim was to help clients identify and express repressed emotions, especially oedipal desire, fear and rage, which, it was presumed, no longer manifest themselves symptomatically once brought into consciousness. A contemporary version of this is to be found in intensive short-term dynamic psychotherapy (ISTDP; Malan and Della Selva 2006). This approach sees the liberation of repressed emotion as (a) enlivening the restricted personality and (b) enabling repressed traumata and losses to be reworked, mourned and laid to rest. ISTDP posits an active, challenging, somewhat unstealthy therapist confronting defences, homing directly in on the affects that lie behind them.

Object relations psychoanalysis, especially in its neo-Kleinian version (Steiner 1996), emphasises integration of the personality as its therapeutic goal (Hinshelwood 1994). As the client re-assimilates projected parts of the personality, no longer extruding, via 'projective identification', intolerable affects into those around him, this leads to more harmonious interpersonal relationships and a strengthened sense of self and autonomy. The analyst focuses on the ways in which the patient's perceptions of, and dealings with, the external world – especially the analyst herself – are shaped by projective processes. These formulations are continuously fed back to the client as interpretations. The 'insight' that this facilitates is not just an intellectual event. The juxtaposition of the client's self-experience and an 'external' neutral account of its impact on the other (the analyst) creates an inner tension catalytic to personality restructuring.

The Winnicottian version of object relations views playfulness and creativity as a mark of psychic health. The therapist is a 'transformational object' (Bollas 1987), both 'real' and 'unreal' (and therefore available for projection), in which – in the play-space of the consulting room – the client begins to differentiate what belongs to the inner world and what to reality. A major job of the analyst is 'containment' (Bion 1970), 'holding' (Winnicott 1971), both of which precede interpretation, and without which interpretation is likely to fall on deaf ears.

Containment and holding both loop back to the therapeutic relationship and, in attachment terms, reflect the secure base that the therapist must provide if exploration is to be possible. To reiterate our leitmotiv, a sense of security is a precondition for the exploration of other affective states such as sexuality and aggression. In a series of brilliant experiments, Mikulincer and Shaver (2008) show how the experience of security, even if subliminal, enables insecurely attached people to confront rather than defensively deactivate or hyperactivate mental pain. In one study (Mikulincer and Shaver 2008, p. 317), participants who had completed a questionnaire tapping into attachment styles were asked to write a description of an incident in which a close partner had hurt their feelings. They were then exposed to security-enhancing subliminal 'primes' (words like 'love', 'secure', 'affection') or neutral ones ('lamp', 'building', etc.). Next they were asked to reconsider the hurtful event and to describe how they would feel if it were to occur again. In the neutral priming condition deactivators reported less, and hyperactivators more, pain than in the initial task. This would be expected if, with the passage of time, pre-existing defences were reinforced. However, in those exposed to the positive prime, both anxiety and avoidance were greatly reduced and the insecurely attached subjects' responses were indistinguishable from those of the securely attached. As Mikulincer and Shaver (2008, p. 318) put it:

> protective armour can at least temporarily [be] softened by an infusion of felt security . . . even a small security boost can allow an avoidant person to be more open to inner pain . . . which can then be addressed clinically.

Transposing this finding into the consulting room, the benign presence of the therapist offers a mutatively validating, encouraging environment, helping clients to face, bear, process, live with, master, transcend and incorporate pain and trauma. It is unimportant whether the latter is externally inflicted or arises from within, from the intrinsically rage- and envy-wracked psyche. Kleinian psychoanalysis is sometimes caricatured as focusing almost exclusively on negative emotions such as aggression, in contrast to more attachment-influenced approaches. In skilful hands there is, however, no real incompatibility. Positive priming, via the implicit validating presence of the analyst, is a precondition for meaningful exposure to negative emotions. Conversely, support without challenge can be collusive rather than mutative.

The paradox of commitment to change without its overt promotion reflects itself in differing analytic formulations of the role of the analyst. Most agree on the centrality of the therapeutic relationship, in both its transferential and its here-and-now aspects, based on Freud's (1912) formulation that 'effigies cannot be destroyed in absentia'. For example, in ISTDP the therapist aims to engender clients' problematic affect (anger, intimidation, avoidance) in relation to the therapist, making these feelings available for examination and transformation. Verbally expressed meanings in therapy are evocative as well as denotive, performative as well as declarative. We don't just talk *about* love or anger or envy or fear with our clients – we/they experience it, directly or vicariously, as therapeutic conversations proceed.

Self-psychology and relational psychoanalysts accept the inevitability and desirability of the therapeutic relationship as new experience. They see neutrality as an impossible ideal, with the unconsciousnesses of both therapist and patient brought into play, while enacting different roles (Aron 2000). Limited self-revelation on the part of the therapist is encouraged, helping to normalise client problematic experiences and exemplifying the skill of self-mentalising with which the client can identify and internalise.

The discussion of 'therapeutic action' briefly summarised above tends to have a distinctly theoretical ring. Gabbard and Westen (2003, p. 837) claim that the issue for contemporary psychoanalysis of

> what is therapeutic . . . is an empirical question which can no more be answered by logic and debate than the question of whether one or another treatment for heart disease is more effective.

Gabbard and Westen's (2003) somewhat disingenuous formulation glosses over the fact that there *are* questions of logic and debate at stake. According to Gustafson (1986) [drawing on Bateson (1972), who based his ideas on Bertrand Russell's 'theory of logical types'], psychic change invariably entails taking a perspective at a *meta-level, or 'higher logical type'* from the problematic behaviours or experience that have led the sufferer to seek help. 'Mentalising' – 'thinking about thinking' or 'mind-mindedness' (Meins 1999) – clearly fulfils the Gustafson criterion. Moving from action and impulse to reflecting on one one's own and others' mental states is crucial to therapeutic action in psychoanalytic psychotherapy, and perhaps the psychotherapies generally (Allen 2008).

Paradox and change in psychotherapy

The organising principle of the oedipal triangle and its resonance in the transference guides each psychoanalytic approach to change, albeit in differing ways according to theoretical predilection. For Malan and Della Selva (2006), therapist, patient and significant other (T, P, O) play out the roles of mother, father and child. Finding a connecting pattern enables the therapist to bring all three together in a 'complete interpretation'. For the neo-Kleinians the child's capacity to tolerate parental intercourse – and in its 'translated' version, the therapist's separateness – is a first step towards objectivity and the ability to think and see situations from many sides. This can be seen in Bion's terms as 'intercourse' between thoughts; its obverse, 'attacks on linking', as the envious denial of procreativity.

For Ogden (1989) and relational psychoanalysts such as Benjamin (2004) the 'analytic third' is not so much an oedipal constellation as the analytic relationship itself, distinct from either participant, which, as a novel creation, is a first step towards the restoration of generativity in psychic life. In attachment terms the combination of 'maternal' security and empathy (which can equally be provided by the father) and 'paternal' mastery (which can just as readily be provided by the mother) facilitates the liberation of playfulness and companionable interaction.

By placing Oedipus at the kernel of psychotherapeutic meta-psychology, an inherently paradoxical view of psychic life is implied. We are often our own worst enemies; perversely we bring about the very dangers and disasters we most wish to avoid; what we want is what we most fear; those we love may also be those we most hate; we are frequently strangers to ourselves. The aim of therapy, in this view, is to replace this tragic vision with an ironic acceptance of fate and our unruly child-like selves (Schafer 1983).

People turn to the paradoxical promises of psychoanalytic therapy when common-sense solutions to their problems have failed. Poacher turned game-keeper, psychoanalysis uses paradox to outflank the inherent perversity of psychological disturbance. It is assumed that the presenting symptom will manifest itself in the therapeutic relationship, which then occupies the central focus of the work. Paradoxically also, the intensity of the therapeutic relationship is both 'real' – the client may develop an intimacy with his therapist more intense than any previously experienced in adult life – and 'unreal' in that it remains encapsulated within the ethical and physical confines of the contract and the consulting room. Ultimately the therapist is a quasi-secure base rather than the real thing.

Other therapeutic modalities also implicitly or explicitly use paradox as therapeutic techniques. 'Milan' family therapy (see Gustafson 1986) offers families a 'no change' message and 'prescribes the symptom' ('we suggest that Caroline go on starving herself since she believes that the family would fall apart were she to stop being such a worry and regain normal weight'). This strategy recognises the power of stasis and defence, as well as subtly making therapeutic 'failure' impossible, in that such injunctions either reinforce the influence of the therapist if they are adhered to or, if not, stimulate healthy rebelliousness and autonomy. Similarly, dialectical behaviour therapy (Linehan 1993; Linehan et al. 2006) gives its borderline clients a poised change/no-change message, simultaneously validating the client's symptomatic behaviours as a way of coping with intolerable mental pain while encouraging them to find less self-destructive ways forward.

Fonagy's account of the mentalising-fostering aspects of psychotherapy can also be seen as 'paradoxical'. Bleiberg (2006) suggests that mentalising is an essential social skill for group living. Being able to mentalise or to read the intentions of the Other was a vital 'friend-or-foe' appraisal as small groups of hominids learned to collaborate and to cope with competition. However, once the Other is identified as unthreatening, mentalising is inhibited. With the appraiser's guard down, psychic energy is available for other uses. Extreme instances of this are seen in intimate relationships between infants and their mothers, and romantic partners. Brain patterns in the two are similar, with inhibition of the neuroanatomical pathways subsuming mentalisation (Zeki 2008). This releases psychic energy from the appraisal task, and perhaps explains the necessary idealisation inherent in such relationships ('my baby/lover/mum is the best baby/lover/mum in the whole world'), in which negative features are ignored or discounted.

A similar sequence may apply in psychotherapy, as the client begins to imbue the therapist and therapeutic situation with secure base properties, and to relax (literally so if lying on the couch) into a comfortable state of held intimacy. However, while encouraging the development of trust, the therapist will also insist that the client examine his feelings about the therapist and the therapeutic relationship – to acquire, activate and extend mentalising skills. A psychotherapy session is *recursive* in the sense that it loops back on itself in ways that normal relationships tend not to, except perhaps when repair work (i.e. an everyday form of 'therapy') is needed. To take a commonplace example, there is often a tussle between therapist and client – especially if a deactivating one – about reactions to breaks. The client may insist that it is perfectly all right for the therapist to have a holiday ('everyone needs time off, especially in your sort of work'), while the therapist relentlessly probes for signs of disappointment, rejection and anger, sometimes much to the client's irritation. The client is made to mentalise in the service of therapeutic change.

Seen this way, psychoanalysis puts the client in a 'benign bind'. In Bateson's classic formulation of the double bind (1972), the potentially psychotic adolescent is given an approach/avoidance message from his 'schizophrenogenic' parent; this triggers a psychotic response as the only possible escape from an intolerable crux. While this etiological model has been conclusively disproved, it lives on in Main's (1995) approach/avoidance model for disorganised attachment. A positive feedback loop is initiated in which a child feels threatened by the very person (i.e. the parent) to whom he would naturally turn for succour when faced with threat. The more attachment behaviours are activated, the more he seeks out a secure base, but as he approaches the 'secure base'/source of threat, the more threatened he feels, and so on. The bizarre self-soothing manifestations of disorganised attachment, such as furling into oneself, rocking and head-banging, can be seen as attempts to 'solve' or escape from this impossible dilemma.

But because it leads inevitably to change of *some* sort, a 'double bind' can also foster positive developments. Therapy puts the client in a paradoxical 'change/no-change', 'inhibit mentalising/mentalise' bind, forcing the emergence of new structures, and extending clients' range of interpersonal skills and resources. Clients are 'forced' to think about feelings and identity in ways that would normally be dealt with by repression, avoidance, acting-out or projection. This theory is potentially testable, given that attachment and mentalising are subsumed under distinct neuroanatomical pathways (Jurist and Meehan 2008) – attachment pathway 'A' involving the middle prefrontal lobes, while pathway 'B', the 'theory of mind' route (of which mentalising is an example), relates to the amygdala. Normally these are kept separate and are mutually excluding. This approach predicts that in therapy both are activated.

A clinical approach consistent with this comes from Lear's (1993) extension of Strachey's (1934) classic 'mutative interpretation' hypothesis. Lear sees transformational transference as a three-stage process whereby the therapist first enters the client's pre-existing internal world – with its assumptions and preconceptions and linguistic manifestations (the shared associations and meanings that develop in the course or a therapy, or 'idiolect'). Once 'in', secondly, the therapist begins to disconfirm transferential expectations, neither colluding with the client's preconceptions nor allowing herself to be discounted as alien, irrelevant and expellable. The client is thus in a bind. His internal world has been 'colonised' by therapy, but the therapist neither conforms *nor* accepts 'de-colonialising' expulsion. Thus, thirdly, the patient is forced to revise his expectations, assumptions and schemata about intimate relationships. In so doing, as his perceptions of himself, the therapist and their relationship become 'de-transference-ised', he becomes more realistic in his appraisals and more skilful in managing them.

Linking this perspective with the tripartite insecure attachment typology, we see how the pressure of paradox may produce sudden 'flips' from one attachment style to another. This is perhaps most commonly seen when a previously deactivated client suddenly becomes flooded with panic and anxiety and demandingness, becoming temporarily 'hyperactivating' (Eagle and

Wolitzky 2008). Conversely, from a psychoanalytic perspective, 'hyperactivation' can be seen as a hysterical defence in which the client, estranged from her true feelings, displays not the real thing but a simulacrum of emotion, often via envious identification with the parental couple (Britton et al. 1989). The sudden realisation by the client that, despite *Sturm und Drang*, 'I actually don't really feel *anything*' may mark the beginning of a less self-estranged inner life. Deactivation/hyperactivation thus become not immutable traits but alternative epigenetic pathways, in which one predominates, but that may, if challenged and reorganised via therapeutic paradox, open up to new and less maladaptive neural networks and external relationships.

All this remains speculative, but is consistent with 'chaos theory' (Gleick 1987), a mathematical approach appropriate to the unstable and fluid world of interpersonal relationships. Chaos theory suggests that injecting energy into closed but unstable systems – chemical reactants or weather systems, for example – leads to the emergence of new and more complex chemical or meteorological structures. Change in psychotherapy can be thought of in an analogous way (cf. Scharff and Scharff 1998).

How many interpretations does it take to change a Lucho?

As a fictional quasi-clinical illustration of the ideas put forward in this and the preceding two chapters, consider the Peruvian author Mario Vargas Llosa's 'magical realist' masterpiece, *Aunt Julia and the Scriptwriter* (Llosa 1983). In true postmodern style it contains a number of 'stories within a story'. In one, Lucho, a travelling drug rep whose wife of three months is pregnant, is involved in a horrendous road accident. A child suddenly runs in front of his car; he stops; while examining the moribund child on the highway he is himself run over by a juggernaut whose brakes have failed. The child is killed and he badly injured.

He makes a full physical recovery but develops appalling post-traumatic stress disorder (PTSD), and is unable to sleep, concentrate, relax or contemplate travelling in a car. His wife has a miscarriage, the marriage breaks down and she returns to her parents. Eventually his company sends him to a renowned psychotherapist, Dr Acémila: a middle-aged, cultured woman with a formidable reputation.

Her first move puzzles Lucho: she asks him not about his problem, but his constipated bowels, and immediately prescribes regular use of prunes with his breakfast. Only then does she say (p. 180):

> You may [now] tell me what's troubling you. But I warn you beforehand that I shall not castrate you of your problem. I shall teach you to love it, to feel as proud of it as Cervantes of his useless arm or Beethoven of his deafness.

Here we see her skilful management of Lucho's attachment anxiety. Like a parent in the Strange Situation, by distraction and physical soothing she reduces his panic to manageable proportions. She offers a positive connotation and soothes his fragile ego by linking it with famous men (neurologists comfort people suffering from epilepsy by reminding them that Julius Caesar and Dostoevsky were similarly afflicted). Lucho is now ready to explore his feelings.

Once the story is told she immediately moves to meaning-making, offering a seemingly shocking interpretation (p. 181). She explains that: 'so-called accidents [do not] exist; they [are] merely subterfuges invented by men to hide from themselves how evil they [are]':

> You *wanted* to kill that little girl . . . And then, since you were ashamed of what you'd done and afraid of the police or of Hell, you *wanted* to be hit by the truck, as punishment for what you'd done or as an alibi for the murder.

Her formulation is inherently mentalising. She communicates to Lucho that, unremarkably ('Your story . . . is so banal and stupid it bores me'), there is a part of his mind inhabited by murderousness. Unacquainted with this aspect of himself he is horrified, so relentlessly punishes himself with mental pain.

Attachment and meaning-making now accomplished, Dr Acémila moves on to her change-promoting prescription. The working-through she suggests entails a change of attitude, and a homework task. She gives him a written prescription: 'exercise for learning how to live sincerely'. If he is to live authentically he has to accept his hostility towards children, see how demanding, difficult, and time- and money-consuming they can be. He must get in touch with his aggression and feel able to dislike child-beggars, the whining, puking children of his friends, and the ways in which they destroy women's beauty and detach them from their menfolk. In addition, he is asked to re-enact the scene of the accident by building a model of it with children's toys – to bring the trauma, in Winnicott's terms, into the realm of omnipotence (Casement 1985).

Lucho is now in a bind that can only lead to cure. If he disobeys Dr Acémila and becomes loving towards children, his good feelings have returned; if he submits to her prescription, his crippling guilt is undermined and his sense of helplessness lessened.

One day he frightens himself by thinking he might actually physically attack a child. In a blind panic he orders a taxi and rushes to Dr Acémila's surgery. Suddenly he realises that he has travelled to her without a second thought in a once-dreaded automobile. He is 'cured'. He is reconciled with his wife, and she becomes pregnant again. But Lucho is worried that his hatred of children may return in relation to his own child, whether he is to be an 'infanticidal recidivist'. Dr Acémila replies (p. 190): 'Have no fear: you'll recover before the fetus grows eyes'. As befits a postmodern tale, however, the concept of 'cure' remains in doubt; we are left wondering whether Dr Acémila's certitude is to be trusted, or whether she is madder than her patients – or her 'friends', as she prefers to call them.

Due allowances must be made for poetic licence. Dr Acémila's combination of nutritional therapy, Kleinian interpretation and CBT cannot be routinely recommended (I once saw an advertisement in a Los Angeles newspaper for 'psychoanalysis and colonic irrigation: first session free'). Nevertheless, the moral of this tale is germane to my argument. Her triad of attachment, meaning-making and change-promotion gets results. And the literary genre of magical realism itself is paradoxical. The novel rests on the questionable premise (based on Llosa's own life) that an 18-year-old can transcend the oedipal incest taboo and happily marry a 32-year-old. The reader is poised between vicariously enjoying the transgressive aspect of sexual love (see Chapter 9 below), and knowing that in reality it is doomed to failure. But by imaginatively exploring the extent to which fantasy can invade 'real life', the contact barrier between the conscious and unconscious minds is strengthened – a precondition for psychic health.

Outcomes in psychoanalytic psychotherapy

The principal focus of this book is psychoanalytic psychotherapy *process*, and the attempt to weave together attachment and psychoanalytic ideas in order to strengthen the theoretical base from which to practise effectively. But the very use of the word 'effective' raises the spectre of *outcome* research (e.g. Malan and Della Selva 2006; Parry et al. 2005; Leichsenring and Rabung 2008). Yet the fundamental question, beloved of third-part funders and liable to strike fear in psychoanalytic practitioners, especially if working in publicly funded settings – 'does psychoanalytic psychotherapy work?' – cannot ultimately be evaded. In the final section of this chapter I shall briefly survey this theme.

A number of versions of psychoanalytic psychotherapy have been shown, via randomised controlled trials (RCTs), to be effective in a wide range of conditions. These include mild to moderate depression (Shapiro et al. 1994), personality disorders (Bateman and Fonagy 2004, 2008; Abbass et al. 2008), panic disorder (Milrod et al. 2007), somatisation disorders (Guthrie et al. 1991) and eating disorders (Dare et al. 2001). There are several cost–benefit studies (Gabbard et al. 1997) showing that psychoanalytic psychotherapy, while resource-intensive, 'pays for itself' given the savings in revenue – less time spent in or visiting hospital, fewer medications consumed, reduced time spent on benefits, return to work and therefore generating tax revenue – compared with 'treatment as usual'. However, compared with CBT, the evidence for psychoanalytic psychotherapy is generally less impressive: smaller numbers of trials, based on fewer patients, less replicated, and confounded by inevitable allegiance effects (Roth and Fonagy 2006).

In brief, there are three main ways in which psychoanalytic psychotherapists tend to respond to this critique (Gabbard 2005), and especially the unfavourable comparison with CBT. The first argues that psychoanalytic psychotherapy is inherently less easy to research than other forms of treatment. Randomisation is contrary to the spirit of psychoanalytic psychotherapy, in which motivation and finding the 'right therapy for the right client' are fundamental principles. Psychoanalytic therapies tend to be long-term, which means that generating adequate research funding is problematic. Given this, compared with brief therapies, intervening variables such as adverse life events are more likely to confound the impact of therapy. Thirdly, the aims of psychoanalytic psychotherapy go beyond symptom relief to structural changes in personality that are inherently more complex, time-consuming and expensive to study.

The argument here is essentially that, given sufficient time and resources, psychoanalytic psychotherapy can and will be shown to be as effective as other modalities of therapy, if not more so, and that its unique indications are gradually emerging: absence of evidence does not equate to evidence of absence. Leichsenring and Rabung's (2008) meta-analysis of long-term (defined as more than one year) psychoanalytic psychotherapy (LTPP) supports this. Compared with short-term psychoanalytic psychotherapy (in which relapse post-therapy is common) and treatment as usual, LTPP patients showed effect sizes of around 1.8 (a very respectable figure, higher than the average antidepressant) for target problems, overall effectiveness and personality functioning. Ninety-six per cent of LTPP patients were better off than comparison groups. Although only around 10 studies met their stringent criteria, they estimate that more than 350 studies showing contrary findings would be needed for their conclusions to have arisen by chance alone.

An example included in their analysis is the Bateman and Fonagy (2004, 2008) borderline personality disorder project, an intensive programme that shows impressive reductions in suicidality, use of medical services and psychiatric consultation rates up to five years post-therapy (cf. Chapter 10). These findings are especially important given the possibility that usual therapies (including short-term psychoanalytic therapy) with this diagnostic group may actually make patients worse, and the failure of cognitive approaches to show maintenance of gains once therapy comes to an end (Levy 2008).

In contradiction of the latter point, a second defence of psychoanalytic psychotherapy revives the famous 'dodo-bird verdict' of equal outcomes irrespective of therapy modality. On the whole, head-to-head studies show few major differences in outcome for psychoanalytic psychotherapy compared with CBT (e.g. Shapiro et al. 1994), although those differences that do arise tend to favour CBT. The argument here is that the impact of 'common factors' such as the therapeutic alliance and remoralisation far outweigh the technical contributions of specific therapies (Wampold 2001). The weakness of this tack for psychoanalytic psychotherapy is that it can be used to justify cheaper, briefer therapies that require less training and therapy-time than psychoanalytic work. However, there is good evidence – the 'dose–effect curve' – that better outcomes from all forms of therapy result from longer treatments (Seligman 1995). Also, the most significant of the 'common factors' is the therapeutic relationship, including the ability of the therapist to instigate rupture repairs, which are key areas of expertise for psychoanalytic psychotherapists.

A third argument, ironically closest to the heart of psychoanalytic psychotherapy yet least likely to cut ice in the public arena, is the argument that the project of outcome evaluation is fundamentally misguided and contrary to the spirit of psychoanalysis, which is concerned with idiographic individual life stories, not nomothetic, instrumentalist, 'best buys'. This applies particularly to 'full' psychoanalysis (e.g. five times a week for five years), which has never been, and perhaps never will be, subject to an RCT, although various methodological modifications can be used to evaluate its outcome – these, on the whole, tend to be favourable (see Sandell et al. 2000). While this appears at first sight to be an untenable 'backwoods' defence, there are growing hints of a wider dissatisfaction with over-technologised and compartmentalised healthcare, and an emerging interest in qualitative studies of narrative-based medicine (Greenhalgh and Hurwitz 1998; Avdi 2008), with which psychoanalysis might usefully ally itself. This brings us to the topic of our next chapter: power and psychoanalysis – what kinds of power it exerts, and how this manifests itself in the consulting room.

Chapter 6

Empowering

Most clients seeking psychotherapy feel disempowered in some way: uncertain of themselves, unable to achieve their goals in life, no longer in command of their lives and their feelings, weak, marginalised, irrelevant – 'a waste of space' as it is sometimes so piteously described. (Representing his self-imposed futility and impotence, a patient dreamed of an interloper named Nils Borrodoss who had 'squatted' his house – a 'nothing', a 'borrower', 'dossing down' in his 'citadel'.)

Chambers Dictionary (1972) defines power as follows: *the capacity for producing an effect; strength; energy; right to command; authority.* Therapists hope that treatment will enhance their clients' 'capacity for producing an effect' – their efficacy, having a strengthened sense of self, fostering the ability to be an 'author'-ity in the sense of knowing oneself, of being an 'author' of one's own life. But how does psychotherapy empower? In some forms of therapy empowerment is an explicit focus – in assertiveness therapy clients are given homework tasks: to return faulty goods to a shop, or stand up to their spouses when they are feeling oppressed or bullied. In this chapter an attachment and relational perspective is used to think about the ways in which psychoanalytic psychotherapy empowers its clients.

The power dynamics of the therapist–client relationship

Parents are in a position of power over their children. So too, at least at a symbolic level, therapists wield power over their patients. The analyst sets the terms of the relationship, prepares the room, dictates – albeit by negotiation and contract – the frequency and duration of meetings, and decides how best to intervene, or not, in the clients' lives. Theoretically the patient can dispute the contract, or walk away from therapy at any time, in ways that a baby cannot (cf. Holmes and Lindley 1997). But, unconsciously or otherwise, being a patient means laying one's vulnerability and powerlessness at the feet (or in the lap) of the analyst's knowledge and strength.

All being well, by the end of therapy, the tables are reversed. The analyst's powerlessness beyond the confines of the consulting room contributes to empowerment of the patient, who departs from therapy to lead her own life, while the analyst, momentarily at least, is left bereft.

The argument of this chapter runs as follows.

1   There is an implicit ethic within psychotherapy that contrasts authentic empowerment with pathologies of power – the latter usually taking the form of being either underpowered or overpowering.
2   Power relations have been somewhat ignored in the psychoanalytic litera-ture, Adler being an honourable exception.
3   Attachment theory provides a developmental context for theorising how empowerment and disempowerment arise.
4   Mentalising, emerging from secure attachment, is a crucial factor in the empowerment that analysis offers.

The ethic of empowerment

Power is intrinsic to social relations – society controls its citizens by wielding not just physical power via the apparatus of the state, but psychical power over their minds. This power can be used for good or ill, captured in a series of binary oppositions: tyranny vs. democracy; heteronomy vs. autonomy; master/slave relationship vs. contractual relationships freely entered into; power *over* vs. power *to*; conformism vs. agency; omnipotence/impotence vs. limited but real potency. Psychoanalysis allies itself with the positive side of this ethic, seeing empowerment as coming about primarily through enhanced self-understanding. *Scientia potentia est*: knowledge is power. But knowing extends beyond knowing oneself – it entails knowing oneself-in-relation-to others, others-in-relation-to-oneself – or, as defined in Chapter 2, mentalis-ing. To know is to be in touch with reality – to be able to differentiate 'things as I and others perceive/feel them' from 'things as they truly are'. Empowered by the ability to make that distinction, one's chances of successful adaptation to the physical and social world are enhanced.

Psychoanalysis and power

Implicit in the list of binary polarities above are contrasting scientific and social definitions of power. For Freud, schooled within a nineteenth-century scientific paradigm, power equates with the quasi-material energy of a drive, whether libidinous, aggressive or death-seeking. In his model of psy-chic determinism, the power of untamed, ungrasped, unconscious forces pushes us like billiard balls (or planetary bodies) towards unhappiness and neurosis.

Tom: Confusion and clarification

Tom, mentioned in the previous chapter, was depressed and lost. His wife had had an affair. Without really discussing their feelings, Tom insisted that she leave the marital home, leaving him with their two young children. He felt utterly confused – unable to work out what was happening to him or what to do next, feeling guilty and impotent. He felt that the marriage had been irreparably damaged and that *he* should leave, but felt powerless to do so, and hoped that the therapist would somehow 'tell' him what to do. He had been born during the Second World War; his father had been seriously injured in the fighting and returned to the UK for a convalescent period lasting several months. Tom's mother left him with her parents to be at her husband's bedside.

The therapist suggested that his current confusion over the marital breakdown was a replay of this childhood trauma. Tom had been 'dumped' by his wife when she had her affair, just as he had felt dumped by his mother, and, in pushing his wife out of the marital home, the tables were turned: he was now 'dumping' her. But, having been dumped himself, he knew how horrible an experience it was. Hence his guilt and confusion.

In the sessions he was obviously avoidant – barely able to discuss his feelings or, if so doing so, employing a detached, affectless, unelaborated style. He was especially out of touch with feelings of anger at his wife's betrayal. The therapist suggested that it was as though he had 'switched off' feelings – especially rageful – early in life. Perhaps that was what had driven his wife to her affair, seeking a warmth and presence lacking in her marriage. 'So you are suggesting that in some way I *engineered* her betrayal . . .', he replied. 'Yes, your unconscious keeps "returning to the scene of the crime". In this case your childhood trauma.' Curiously, this explanation seemed to take some weight off his shoulders. Seeing how he was at the mercy of unconscious forces unbeknown to him made Tom feel *less* powerless. Now better able to mentalise, empowered by that understanding, with sadness he did leave his marriage, able to acknowledge responsibility for the pain he had caused but no longer so overwhelmed by narcissistic guilt.

Adler (Ansbacher and Ansbacher 1985), a forerunner of relational psychoanalysis, was interested in the social aspects of power. Power relations are inherent in all human relationships, from the nuclear family or imperial Rome. Who has power over whom, and how is that power wielded? The power of the baby's cry is pitted against that of the – ultimately – potentially infanticidal parent (Hrdy 1999). People cannot be separated from their social context – we are embedded in concentric rings of relationships, from mother, father, family, through work and friendship groups, to wider society and the myriad power relations that exist within each niche of that matrix. From this quasi-sociological perspective the power aspect of the analyst–patient relationship needs to be examined as objectively as the drives, including the putative 'drive to power'.

The unwritten British constitution differentiates 'powers spiritual' (the clergy) from 'powers temporal' (monarch, parliament, executive bureaucracy, etc). Ethnically excluded from the 'corridors of power', Freud aimed to make inroads on powers spiritual. Freud (1921) conceptualised group power relationships as essentially regressive, infantile and malign. The power of the leader mobilises primitive oedipal wishes and fears. Psychoanalysis struggles to this day to establish itself as an equal player among the 'powers temporal'.

But there is no escaping the social dimensions of power, even in the privacy of the consulting room; still less within the fervid atmosphere of psychoanalytic politics. In any power relationship there is a need for an absolute authority, a 'final court of appeal', to settle power disputes. Democratic and authoritarian tendencies coexist within psychoanalysis. The authority of the founding fathers (and mothers) and the apostolic succession to senior analysts is still a significant feature, bringing inevitable fissures and splits. But open discussion and listening to opposing views is also intrinsic to the psychoanalytic ethos, difficult though this often is in practice (Tuckett et al. 2008). For Freud an appeal to 'reality' was the ultimate arbiter of psychic health, and neurosis always a 'turning away from reality' (Freud 1917). Psychoanalysis is a power relationship whose aim is to deconstruct power relations. I shall argue that via triangulation and 'co-mentalising', psychoanalysis is an interpersonal *methodology* for finding the truth rather than a set of specific truths or interpretations.

Power is indispensable to health, psychic and physical (poverty – economic powerlessness – is associated with excess morbidity and mortality). Power provides access to the resources needed to survive, reproduce and live well: security; material, sexual and social 'capital' (esteem, recognition, popularity, etc.). Ultimately perhaps, the purpose of power is, as Freud saw it, 'love' – the survival and multiplication of selfish genes. Under normal circumstances cooperation and mediated power strategies are more likely to be successful than the Machiavellian exercise of naked power (Dawkins 1978). The search for unbridled power as an end in itself is ultimately self-defeating. Most political careers end in failure. Shelley's Ozymandias invites future generations to 'look on my ruins and despair'. The great king had 'lived forwards, understood backwards'. Mentalising provides an opportunity to 'understand forward' and thereby reduce one's chances of failure and despair.

Attachment theory and power

From an attachment perspective, power and security are closely linked. The weak seek out those with power for their protection, both individually and collectively. The 'secure base' provider has the power to make the vulnerable individual feel safe. A secure individual is not only safe, but also empowered – to explore the world and to find her own inner power and security.

In secure attachment the secure-base provider provides the mastery needed for psychological growth to proceed. In contrast, in insecure attachment the power aspects of the care-giver/care-seeker relationship predominate, inhibiting exploration: power remains problematic for the care-seeker, rather than being effortlessly transferred as appropriate from care-provider.

Deactivating and hyperactivating children are engaged in mild power struggles with their care-providers. The deactivating, insecure–avoidant individual (Main 1995; Mallinckrodt et al. 2008) tends to have had a care-giver, however 'loving', for whom power predominated over sensitivity. He therefore diminishes his felt and expressed needs in order to achieve a modicum of security – saying, in effect, 'if I am not too demanding will you look after me?' Later, when he enters school, he may 'identify with the aggressor' and become a 'bully'. In contrast, the hyperactivating, insecure–ambivalent individual is likely to have had a protean care-giver whose attentiveness could not be taken for granted. In order to ensure attention, she exaggerates her dependency needs, thereby learning to wield 'weak' or victim power: 'I'll make such a fuss so you have no choice but to notice me'.

In disorganised attachment the care-giver is either powerless (helpless/frightened) or compensatorily power-hungry (intrusive/self-referential) – balancing her own extreme powerlessness and vulnerability by wielding power over her child, sometimes in perverse ways (Welldon 2009). Power comes to predominate over all other aspects of relationships. In the case of the frightened care-giver there may be subsequent role-reversal, where the child becomes inappropriately powerful *vis-à-vis* her mother. The intrusive/hostile pattern leads to an even more pronounced identification with the aggressor, in which the abused may himself/herself become an abuser. In sado-masochistic relationships the master always has a willing slave at hand as a receptacle for his projected inner weakness and vulnerability; the slave always has a master to protect her, however much she has to sacrifice her potency to achieve that.

Adler's notion of 'organ inferiority' can be seen as a precursor of the concept of insecure attachment (Ansbacher and Ansbacher 1985). The 'will to power' is a response to that insecurity: 'never again will I feel powerless if I become master and enslave others as containers for my projected helplessness'. For Freud, Oedipus' fate is intrinsic and intrapsychic: his blindness to the pulsive power of the 'Oedipus complex' means that he is phylogenetically condemned to desire his mother and hate his father. For Adler, Oedipus can be understood relationally, and in terms of lived experience. He compensates for his 'organ inferiority' – the damaged/swollen foot that gives him his name – with the 'drive to power'. Abandoned on a mountain top without protective parents, to face and accept his vulnerability as an adult would be to relive that trauma. His draws on his intuitive knowledge of handicap to 'read' the Sphinx's message – he understands the tottering transience of man's upright gait. He is blind not to his sexual and aggressive drives but to his weakness, or, to vary the myth, his Achilles' heel. His infantile helplessness metamorphoses into a tragic drive for power rather than mentalised empowerment. If he can 'marry' his mother he will have an ever-ready secure base; by killing his father and usurping the Theban throne he wreaks revenge for his weakness, thereby evading his vulnerability and ultimate mortality.

Example: Spielman and the can of pickled gherkins

Mentalising is not necessarily benign. Totalitarian regimes, like poets and psychotherapists, know that no man or woman is an island. They are experts in the psychology of attachment and its destruction. They use the power to break up families; separate parents from their children, children from their parents, spouses from their husbands and wives; forcing migrations that sever the ties between people and their familiar environment; stripping people of their possessions, clothes and roles – these are the tried and tested means to destroy the very essence of what it is to be human.

Even brutality can be a form of relatedness. There is a degree of security in sado-masochism: if someone wants to hurt you, at least they want you; if you have the power to hurt another you ensure that you are not quite so alone in the world. First destroy all attachments, and then offer a hook to a bleeding hand and be certain that it will be held on to. That way children become terrorists, regimes enslave their populations and, even in the midst of democracy, psychosis and trauma are born.

Humans cannot not relate. Without another there is no self. Like chemical free radicals, the unattached state is utterly unstable. Starting in babyhood, the attachment prerogative asserts itself imperiously. We must find someone or something with which to be connected. Almost anything will do, even if it means making a part of the body into an 'other'.

In *King Lear*, Poor Tom, homeless on the stormy heath, is the 'thing itself' . . . the 'bare forked animal' grasps at the wind in the hope of a relationship. Even a fork implies a 'difference' that can allow for a relationship. Hand can grasp hand, leg twine round leg. Konrad Lorenz's geese made a mother out of a cardboard box on the end of a string. Genitals have a life of their own and so are available for comfort.

Roman Polanski's film *The Pianist* is based on the true story of the musician Wladyslaw Szpilman (Spielman in the film), who survived the German occupation of Poland and the Warsaw Ghetto. Szpilman's entire family is deported to the gas chambers; he has no friends he can trust; occasionally he stays in an empty apartment with a piano but does not dare play for fear of giving himself away. A compulsively gifted communicator, he is tragically condemned to silence.

He moves from place to place, utterly alone, until finally he hides in a derelict burnt-out building near the Nazi headquarters. Starving, he searches everywhere for food and finally finds a tin of pickled gherkins, overlooked by earlier scavengers. How is he to open it? He cradles the tin like a mother with her baby, clings to it like a child with a favourite toy. In a fireplace at last he finds a makeshift poker and hammer with which to open the tin (an ironic reference to a piano's hammers, perhaps). But the noise he makes is his undoing. A Nazi official hears him and he is discovered. Fortunately this man is a music lover – he makes Szpilman perform on a miraculously undamaged piano, and the sheer beauty of his Chopin-playing saves his life. The Nazi brings him some food and Szpilman survives until the Russians arrive – only to arrest and deport him. He dies in the Gulag a few years later.

Despite being stripped of all connections, Szpilman's life is saved by his attachments – to the tin of gherkins, to music, even to his Nazi 'saviour'. For the spectator, the pattern and beauty implicit in great art help transcend enmity and war. Understanding is a step towards forgiveness and reparation.

How does psychoanalytic therapy empower?

For Freud, understanding that one's unhappiness is self-generated, albeit unconsciously and unwittingly, liberates. Knowledge enables Plato's chariot-eer to control rather than be controlled by the 'horse-power' of the unconscious. A Kleinian perspective holds that analysing projective processes in the transference leads to reclamation of previously disowned or inaccessible parts of the self (Britton et al. 1989). Winnicott's (1971) model of analysis as 'learning to play' implies accessing the power of the imagination.

From an attachment perspective, the power relationship between patient and therapist is both real and imaginary (i.e. transferential). To repeat our key theme yet again, a fundamental attachment principle is that a person in distress – at whatever stage in their life-cycle – seeks out a stronger, wiser, secure base in order to alleviate anxiety. Exploration, including thinking itself, is inhibited until attachment needs are assuaged. Secure-base provision is the 'real' power that the therapist has to offer her patient. Wielding that power judiciously will empower the client to discover her authentic story, while at the same time fostering the acquisition of mentalising skills.

Paralleling this real power relationship, 'transferential power' comes into play: the projection of absolute power onto the therapist, and its counterpart or 'reciprocal role' (Ryle 1990), the assumption by the client of weakness and vulnerability, often arising out of sub-optimal attachment patterns in the course of development. The patient may enter therapy longing for total secur-ity and protection and understanding. Discovering the limitations of that vision puts him in touch with reality – and is in itself empowering.

Therapy explores the dialectic between real and transferential power rela-tions. Minute to minute, the therapeutic relationship is clouded by transferen-tial mist, seen through a glass darkly; for a while it clears and in a 'window of opportunity' the client can grasp the *Ding an sich* before the fog descends once more. As therapy draws to its close, the transference, with luck, begins to dissolve more permanently (see Chapter 13). The client sees herself and the therapist for what they are, their strengths and weaknesses. Empowerment is both a discovery of true potency and a counter-omnipotent acknowledgement of limitations.

Triangulation

Cavell (2006), a philosopher/psychoanalyst, has developed Davidson's concept of 'triangulation' to unravel Kant's paradox: how, despite the fact that reality is always filtered through the mind, do we come to appreciate what is real, what imaginary? For Cavell the clue lies in the notion of 'triangulated referencing'. A baby reaches out towards a cup. The mother 'refers' to the cup, verbally and visually, by looking at it 'with' the baby. She says '*cup*', lets the child hold and feel and smell it. She 'references' it: the baby looks at the cup; looks at the mother looking at the cup; and looks at the mother looking at him looking at the cup. A triangle is formed: mother–child–cup – two selves face to face with reality. Parent and child are both looking at the same real cup, similar but not identical, each with their own unique point of view – the angle subtended on each of their retinas by the cup differs by a few degrees.

Now the child begins to compute the *reality* of the cup, fixed via language, and appreciating the overlap of his own experience with that offered to him by his mother's imaginative identification with his own. We differentiate a perception from a hallucination using this same mechanism: 'did you hear a noise just then?', we ask. If the answer is negative, we know we must be 'hearing things'. Where this referencing/checking is unavailable, either developmentally or because the perception of the other is suffused with fear – that way paranoia lies.

The example above refers to a physical object, a cup – perhaps too to a 'symbolic equation' in which cup equals breast. The same principles apply to emotional understanding. The security-inducing care-giver presumes that the child has a mind, different from but comparable with her own. Despite their differing perspectives, there is a shared cup 'out there'. It is real; the cup is an objective fact; it is the case that it exists. Similarly, if the child is happy, or upset, the mentalising mother attributes desires and intentions to a sentient being immersed in his/her own experiential world, and, via 'mirroring' and naming, helps the child to begin to 'see' his/her own feelings, which are no less real than those of the objective world.

In psychotherapy, the 'cup' becomes the patient's feelings. The triangle now comprises patient, therapist and the patient's lived life-experience. The reality of the last of these is what is at stake. The more the patient can recognise his feelings and the contexts in which they arise, name them and appreciate the asymmetry between them and 'reality', the more empowered he will become. Transferential feelings are essentially those in which the external referent is archaic rather than contemporary. These 'archaic' feelings may relate to the need, for security's sake, to maintain proximity to a powerful object. Differentiating those feelings from what is really the case is empowering.

Madelaine and the credit crunch

Madelaine had worked in financial services since leaving school. Married but childless, she had planned to retire at 50 on a large bonus so that she could pursue her passion for breeding and riding horses. The world economic downturn put paid to all that and she became depressed. That in turn led to a recurrence of a life-long secret, a shameful preoccupation that had started in adolescence. She became convinced that her face was covered with unsightly hair, and would spend hours in front of the mirror examining it. She withdrew socially and became semi-reclusive.

She was a fatherless child whose flamboyant mother had married when Madelaine was five. She had two half-siblings, and had always felt that her step-father favoured these sisters. She reported that she was happily married and that she and her husband never rowed. She used the word 'shame' several times in her early sessions – saying that she was ashamed to show her face and also ashamed that she had succumbed to her depression and preoccupation with hirsutism.

I suggested that perhaps her sense of shame looped back to the lack of a father, which made her feel different from other children in the rather conventional and restricted village where she grew up. She had felt, I suggested, vulnerable and powerless in the absence of a 'real' father, and her pursuit of money and success were an attempt to compensate for this. The financial crash had parachuted her back to her child-like feelings of 'illegitimacy'. Behind the smiling face she turned to the world lay feelings of envy and rage that had to be kept at bay at all costs. Her worries about what was emerging from beneath her skin were a manifestation of this.

A CBT approach might have asked Madelaine to research facial hirsutism, and to rate her own hairs on an objective scale of 1 to 10 compared with normal. Here the triangulation is like the cup described above – with the visible world of objects. The focus in psychoanalytic psychotherapy is not with the 'objective' presence or absence of hairs, but with the emotional states that lie beneath them. Madelaine was able to resonate with the suggestion that feelings of envy were important, and to talk about the colleagues who had received their bonuses despite the crash and how unfair she felt this was, and to connect this with her feelings about her half-siblings as a child. When a family illness meant that I had to postpone her session, this gave her the opportunity to vent some anger at me. She said that getting cross felt very strange to her, but was able to relate it to her feelings *vis-à-vis* her half-sisters:

obviously my family was much more important to me that she was, just as they were to her step-father. Triangulating, we looked together at an event in our relationship and tried to unearth the truthful feelings – contemporary and transferential – evoked by it.

Anderson's fairy-story child who exclaimed *but the emperor has no clothes* was deconstructing the prevailing transferential misperception of the all-powerful emperor as dressed in regal garb. A mentalising prodigy, he was able to triangulate (a) his perception of the emperor ('*I* can see no clothes'), (b) his mentalised presumption of others' perceptions ('*they've got it wrong*, because for various transferential reasons they *need* to get it wrong – the emperor's narcissism, the courtiers' dependence on his power'), and (c) 'reality' ('on the balance of probabilities, *the emperor has no clothes*').

Both classical and 'relational' models of psychoanalysis veer towards a binary rather than a triangular model of empowerment. In the classical model the therapist helps the client find the known truths of which he is the guardian. Relational psychoanalysis (Aron 2000) rejects the 'classical' model of an all-knowing, all-seeing analyst who gradually transmits knowledge to the client, replacing it with a 'co-construction model' to which client and therapist's conscious and unconscious minds contribute. The first is 'Platonic' – the client finds his true self in the mind of the therapist, once resistance is overcome (Bion 1962, 1967). The second is 'postmodern' – there is no absolute truth, just stories that are more or less coherent (Spence 1987). By contrast, the attachment-informed model offered here is 'Popperian' (Popper 1959): the truth can never fully be apprehended, but untruths can be identified through falsification. The patient says 'No, that's not quite it . . .'. Therapy offers the client a laboratory in which he can explore the reality of himself and his life with the help of a referent, the therapist. A 'true' story is assumed to exist, even if our mental models, however coherent, can only approximate to it. Via 'polysemy' the therapist is in touch with the variety of meanings that the imagination can conceive; with the help of triangulation the one that corresponds to the client's experience is selected. Polysemy proposes; triangulation disposes. These could also be seen as 'masculine' (facetiously, polysemy could be translated as sowing one's wild semantic oats), while triangulation rests on a 'feminine' best fit of intuition.

Bringing together an attachment and a psychoanalytic perspective suggests that if a child can tolerate temporary exclusion from the parental couple he gains freedom. He begins to develop his own 'point of view' and capacity to think for himself, liberating him from dependency and fostering empowerment. The child, as it were, says to himself: 'I can see mum and dad want to be alone together; that doesn't mean that I am forgotten or unimportant. True, I envy them, and wish I could have mum all to myself, but I know that's just a feeling and will soon pass; if I'm really upset and call for comfort, they'll be there for me; my mum seemed to know what I was feeling when I was a baby, I am beginning to see that she has feelings too; sometimes I want to spend time with my dad, and mum doesn't seem to mind being left out, in fact she positively encourages it, so it's probably OK me feeling left out right now; I can let them have their power temporal, me my power spiritual, rather than having to try to wrest power from them with my screams and hatred, or self-hatefully despise my own powerlessness.'

This idealised reconstruction imagines the beginnings of mentalising skills in the healthy child. Attachment theory sees those skills as having their origins in the mother's capacity for mentalising, now internalised by the child; in her ability to provide a secure base from which the child is able to explore his feelings; and to make the move into the wider world, provided and guarded by father (as before, the sexist implications of this model are acknowledged). The child's power to think about thinking, and to 'move' freely, has its origins in the secure base. Where the base is insecure, reflexive thought and movement are compromised. Where there is no empowerment, then, paradoxically, power becomes a salient feature of relationships.

Example: Edward's doubts

Edward's dilemma was that he knew he 'ought' to go ahead with marrying his long-term and highly suitable and compatible girlfriend, Miriam, but whenever the reality of moving in together loomed, he panicked and felt that he couldn't do it. Tolerant as she was, she was becoming impatient, and Edward, himself now in his late thirties and not getting any younger, knew the present situation could not last for ever. An attractive, intelligent and likeable man, the early sessions were interesting and stimulating. We talked, perhaps in a rather superficial way, around Edward's problem. Was it a case of 'once bitten twice shy?', he wondered, his first marriage having come to an end when his wife left him for another man. Edward had behaved like a 'gentleman' over this, but not far beneath the surface we unearthed enormous hurt and anger. Was he afraid of the inevitable loss of absolute control – the 'hostage to fortune' – involved in a marriage? Single, he could do what he liked when he liked, and avoid exposing himself to the possibility of being rejected yet again.

As the weeks went by, nothing much changed. Stimulating conversations continued, but there was no progress with Edward's dilemma. I tried a few half-hearted cognitive-type interventions, asking him, like Charles Darwin, to write down good reasons for marrying and those for staying single. The former far outweighed the latter, but still no movement or decision was forthcoming. I tried paradox: 'maybe you are just not the marrying kind, and need to remain a happy bachelor, having superficial but enjoyable relationships, and preserving your independence and control' – no, came the emphatic response, that wasn't right at all!

My initial formulation of a highly deactivating attachment style was confirmed by Edward's admission that whenever he thought about his girlfriend, much as he liked her, there was a heart-sinking reminder of 'the problem', quickly dispelled by concentrating on work or one of his many hobbies. Our conversations were similarly stimulating but somewhat affect-less. I found myself feeling increasingly irritated and excluded by Edward's impenetrable perfection – his highly polished shoes and impeccable time-keeping. Was there a narcissistic defence lurking beneath his apparent gentlemanliness? As a youngest 'afterthought' child he had basked in his mother's love but was mercilessly bullied by his brothers, and had decided in his teens that he would have to be 'better' than everyone else, in sport, study and financially, albeit in the nicest possible way.

Not before time, I felt I must invite Edward to 'triangulate' reflexively what was going on between us. There seemed to be a parallel, I suggested, between *our* relationship and that with his girlfriend – we got on well, had interesting sessions together, but fundamentally nothing changed. My sense, I went on, was that were he to allow my comments and interventions 'in', his fear was that he would be taken over, lose control, would be thrown back once again to being the vulnerable, bullied little boy, prey to domination by his brothers and abandonment by his wife. There was a stunned silence, a mini-epiphany; Edward then started laughing, almost uncontrollably: 'are you suggesting that I might be *frightened* of getting too close to Miriam? That's rich! She'd *love* that idea!' More laughter. 'Well, perhaps you're *right*, maybe she *is* stronger than me in some ways. But I'm not frightened of anything! I am a rock-climber. Or maybe inside I *am* . . . Maybe all that macho stuff is a way of persuading myself I'm not chicken . . . Oh dear, I'll have to talk to her about all this.' (He did. They moved in together a few months later.)

This example illustrates a number of points germane to this book. First, Lear's (1993) model in which the therapist enters the client's world but refuses to conform to it: at the moment of my intervention Edward was forced to listen to what I was saying without immediately dismissing it out of hand. Second, his temporarily confused speech pattern was an indication of psychological reorganisation *à la* chaos theory (Gleick 1987). Third, he was reciprocally contingently marking (Gergely 2007) my comments in the way that a care-giver habitually does to a care-seeker. Finally, we were together triangulating (Cavell 2006) his affective response to my intervention – and he was, reluctantly, tentatively able to concede – 'yes, perhaps I *am* frightened . . .'.

A final point relevant to power emerges from this story. Winnicott argues that an infant needs both to discover and to feel that the primary object can withstand his envious attacks: 'hello object I just destroyed you' – he is angry with the breast for not being there just when he needs it, but, despite his rage, needs reassurance that it is still intact and ready to feed him. Comparably, in adolescence, children need to square up to parents who are reassuringly stronger but who also acknowledge the children's growing power, and concede that they will eventually have to give way to the next generation. In

Edward's case, as his mother's 'favourite', he did not have to out-fight his father. But this short-circuit to oedipal conquest was ultimately a Pyrrhic victory. He did not have to go out in the world and 'win' a girl. His realisation that he might be frightened of his girlfriend put him in touch with a vulnerability he needed to 'triangulate' if he was to escape from his narcissistic fortress.

Conclusions

From a theoretical perspective it would be comforting, and consistent with psychoanalytic convention, to argue for a single theoretical construct underpinning therapeutic action – in this case triangulated mentalising, via its capacity to put one in touch with reality, as the unique agent of empowerment. However, the real world of therapy is far more complex and multifaceted than theory-builders would have us believe (cf. Gabbard and Westen 2003). I suggest that psychotherapy empowers in one or more of the following ways:

- *fostering mentalising-skills*, and therefore greater appreciation of what belongs to reality, what to transference
- the attunement and attention of the therapist communicates to patients that, in contrast to the dictates of low self-esteem, they have the power to *evoke responses* from intimate others
- *challenge* – giving the patient a sense of having the strength to survive robust well-meaning questioning on the therapist's part, and being seen to be able to 'take' such a challenge
- *rearranging the oedipal triangle*, with the therapist rather than the patient now occupying the excluded 'powerless' observing apex
- *humour and playfulness* – giving the patient a sense of vitality and significance
- *fostering autonomy*, so that patients feel more able to make their own life-decisions and choices
- relinquishing the need of underpowered, hyperactivating individuals to use 'down-power' to achieve their goals, and therefore evoking *assertiveness*
- helping 'overpowered' hypoactivating people to be *less frightened of their vulnerability*, and to see that it doesn't necessarily compromise genuine potency
- *rupture repair* (Safran and Muran 2000) in which the patient's genuine complaints about the therapist are listened to and taken seriously.

This last item is the theme of our next chapter.

Chapter 7

Repairing

I have suggested that empathic ruptures and the capacity to repair them are ubiquitous features of intimate relationships – whether between mothers and babies, romantic or spousal partners, or therapists and their patients. In this chapter I shall develop this idea, and in particular look at the relationship between mentalising and the capacity for rupture repair. I illustrate this with a detailed description of a psychotherapy session with a borderline patient, and how efforts at restoration of a ruptured alliance were initially thwarted but, in the end, rewarded. A discussion of the psychoanalytic notion of reparation follows.

Repair and the 'psychological immune system'

At least since Freud's early (and later rejected) theory of sexual seduction in the origin of hysteria (Breuer and Freud 1895), psychotherapists have been prone to the fallacy of *ex post facto* or *post hoc, ergo propter hoc*: using patients' histories to 'explain' in a causative way – rather than to help understand or throw light on – their current difficulties. Adverse developmental experience, widespread in the population, is habitually seen as a sufficient explanation for difficulties in later life. However, the resilience literature suggests that people vary in the extent to which they succumb to childhood adversity. The presence of a supportive family member (e.g. grandmother or aunt) or sympathetic adults such as a teacher; personal qualities such as good looks, sense of humour, sporting or artistic talents; and in adolescence and early adulthood forming a stable romantic relationship – all these protect people from the psychological ill-health that might be expected to be the consequence of childhood adversity. It seems that it is not so much adversity *per se* that is pathogenic as the way in which difficulties are, or are not, mediated, initially with the help of care-givers and later intrapsychically. Resilience is thus closely liked to reflexive function; mentalising is a crucial determinant of the outcome of adversity.

An early study pointing in this direction was Fonagy et al.'s (1991) finding that subjects classified as 'unresolved' (i.e. with respect to loss or trauma) on the Adult Attachment Interview (AAI) did not appear to have an excess of traumatic events compared with those not so classified, but, rather, lacked the 'reflexive function' needed to process such trauma. Subsequent researchers have investigated the links between the unresolved category on the AAI and the development of disorganised attachment in their infants. Discussing the association between 'frightened or frightening' behaviour on the part of a care-giver and disorganised attachment in the child (Lyons-Ruth and Jacobvitz 2008), Solomon and George (1999) suggest that the impact of frightened/frightening behaviours on infants may be moderated 'by the degree to which care-givers *repair* their relationship with their infant after frightening' them (emphasis added) (Cassidy and Mohr 2001, p. 283).

Slade (2005) has further explored the relationship between maternal capacity for mentalising and disorganised attachment using Lyons-Ruth and Jacobvitz's (2008) measure of mother–infant communication, AMBIANCE. This indicates how mothers successfully, or otherwise, respond to their infants' distress on separation. AMBIANCE is based on in the Strange Situation but, unlike traditional measures, looks not so much at the infant's as the mother's response to disruption of the mother–infant affective envelope, and *how she sets about repairing it.*

There is a strong negative correlation between maternal reflexive function as measured via the Parent Development Interview (PDI, an offshoot of the AAI) and maternal behaviour *vis-à-vis* her infant as measured by AMBIANCE. Disorganised infants had mothers with very high AMBIANCE scores – i.e. grave deficiency in the ability to 'read' infant distress and to maintain a strong parental role, resorting instead to withdrawal or aggression towards their distressed infants. Mothers' capacity to respond reparatively to infant distress appears to be a crucial determinant of infant security or insecurity and especially disorganised attachment. Secure attachment arises out of a mother's ability (a) to intuit her infant's state of mind, seeing it as meaningful rather than wilful or irrelevant, and (b) to respond accordingly with stable and soothing manoeuvres. As mentioned in previous chapters, the research literature calls these functions 'mirroring' and 'mastery' respectively. Put differently, mothers must be sufficiently sensitive to see that something has gone or is going wrong, and sufficiently confident to be able to put it to rights.

In an earlier attempt to theorise this theme I postulated a 'psychological immune system' (cf. Holmes 2001) comparable to its physiological counterpart, whose function is to support psychological integrity by putting adverse experience to good effect, via 'tear and repair' strategies (Safran and Muran 2000), and to maintain continuity in the face of the inevitable disruptions and distortions of intimate relationships. Initially this immunity is provided in the context of a parent–child relationship (comparable to the antibody-rich colostrum provided by mothers in the early stage of breast-feeding); later it becomes internalised as an autonomous psychological function.

Psychological difficulties can be seen in terms of relative under- or over-reactivity of this system, or as a more radical inability to activate appropriate self-protective manoeuvres through seeking help and learning from experience.

Repairing alliance ruptures in psychotherapy

If rupture-repair is ubiquitous in intimate relationships, we would expect it to play a role in psychotherapy. The original CBT formulation of depression was in terms of an excess of 'depressive cognitions' leading to depressive affect. However, recent findings suggest that the issue is not simply a quantitative matter. Depressed thoughts are as common in non-depressed subjects as in those with depressive illness (Kuyken et al. 2005). The current CBT view is that depressive illness is characterised not so much by the quantity of negative thoughts as through *the ways in which those thoughts are experienced and handled* intrapsychically. Rather than pushing depressed thoughts to one side, or seeing them for what they are – 'just thoughts' – depressed people tend to enter cycles of rumination in which the depressive cognitions become more and more 'real', and any counteracting protective thinking is seen as flimsy and unconvincing. In the face of negative thinking, non-depressed people, with intact reparative mechanisms, manage to negate negative thoughts, or even put them to good use ('I'll try to do better next time'), and maintain a core sense of self-worth in spite of them.

Looking at this in the context of psychotherapy, Safran and Muran (2000) studied the process of alliance rupture and repair in the consulting room. Psychotherapy research consistently shows that a strong therapeutic alliance is correlated with good outcomes in psychotherapy, and that a weakened ('ruptured') alliance presages drop-out and poor outcome. Asking clients to describe their feelings immediately post-session, they found that patients often harbour unexpressed negative thoughts about therapy and their therapists.

They also found that therapists, even if psychodynamic and therefore theoretically attuned to such 'negative transference', are often unaware of the extent of clients' negative thoughts about therapy. There is always a core of real here-and-now failure on the part of the therapist onto which prior experiences of being let down are then transferentially projected. Even when therapists do pick up on negative transference, it does not necessarily bode well. Piper et al. (1999) found a paradoxical positive correlation between numbers of transference interpretations and drop-out in therapy. One possible explanation is that as the alliance deteriorates therapists resort to defensive 'interpretations', which may be 'heard' by clients as blaming them, and lead in turn to further alienation and poor outcome.

However, the news is not all bad. When therapists and patients, together, 'take action to repair weakened alliances' (Safran et al. 2001, p. 408), the result is a stronger alliance than before. Safran et al. go on to suggest that 'dealing effectively with alliance ruptures ... may actually be an intrinsic part of the change process' (p. 408).

Safran and co-workers have developed a 'process model' of rupture and repair that includes (a) attending to 'rupture markers', (b) exploring the negative feelings underlying such a marker, (c) exploring why it has been avoided, (d) looking at the underlying wish that has led to the negative feelings.

These researchers concentrate mainly on gross or macro-level 'rupture markers' such as missing sessions or confrontation, i.e. escalating disagreement, in which the therapist becomes defensive in the face of patient onslaught. Here is a somewhat inglorious but not entirely atypical example.

The missed appointment and the eight-mile round trip

Fred, a 35-year-old entrepreneur, entered therapy when his business and marriage failed due to alcoholism, followed by a serious suicide attempt. He was living in a dry house; debarred from driving, he walked the eight-mile round trip to therapy and back once per week. Therapy initially went well. His craving for drink diminished and he re-contacted his children and resumed some business activities.

Three months into therapy I found that I had 'inadvertently' double-booked his appointment and, deciding that Fred was the more robust of the two clients, rescheduled it. He failed to turn up for next two sessions due to 'flu'. When he did return I immediately raised the topic of the missed appointment and subsequent no-shows, apologising for my inefficiency and insensitivity. Initially he dismissed the episode, saying 'Oh I understand, these things happen ... I have done the same thing with clients myself'. Pressed, however, he admitted that he had felt hurt and angry, that the whole episode had been a setback, the journey home had taken him dangerously near a pub, and that his 'flu' could well have been a combination of a 'slip' in which he had started drinking again and depression. As we examined the episode in greater depth it emerged that it had triggered feelings very similar to those he had felt as a child when his mother had been admitted to hospital with depression. He realised that he was, in the end, on his own, and just had to cope as best he could without support. He habitually resorted to alcohol to help him deal with feelings of rejection and loneliness – from his mother or wife, and now me.

Here we have to add a countertransference enactment component to Safran et al.'s process model. The rupture was my double-booking. Whatever my unconscious reasons for doing so (perhaps inflicting a 'you will have to wait' punishment for his neediness, mirroring similar childhood experiences of my own), I was also unconsciously enacting the role of the inaccessible care-giver from Fred's childhood. Ruptures are thus shaped by two unconsciousnesses – the client's and the therapist's. Repair entails mentalising both arms of this process, which then becomes a possible opportunity rather than an inevitable failure.

Nevertheless, my mistake with Fred's appointment was lamentable and, I hasten to add, a rare occurrence. An empathic attunement perspective as described in Chapter 3 suggests that micro-ruptures in sessions are equally important as these gross lapses, and much more common. These arise essentially from empathic disconnection, often marked by what Davanloo (Malan and Della Selva 2006) called 'strategic defences' on the client's part – avoiding eye contact, crossed arms and other defensive physical postures, abrupt change of subject, vagueness, rambling discourse, etc.

With both macro- and micro-ruptures the therapist will need (a) to attend to negative countertransferential feelings such as coldness, boredom, sleepiness, discomfort, irritation and inadequacy as pointers that 'something is going on' to which attention needs to be paid ('positive' feelings such as excitement, sexual interest, protectiveness, equally also need to be examined); (b) to disentangle 'induced' countertransference, in which she is being shaped by the patient's unconscious expectations to play the role of an inattentive or abusive care-giver, from her own 'classical' countertransferential preoccupations or distractions; (c) to acknowledge this process with the patient and (d) to find ways to think about or mentalise these various components.

Safran and Muran (2000) found that non-defensive behaviour on the part of therapists was especially important in resolving ruptures, a precept that is more easily honoured in the breach than the observance. It is difficult to stay non-defensive when under attack, but doing so pays therapeutic dividends. It is never a mistake to acknowledge faults and failings to one's patients and to say sorry. But in therapy, as in 'real life', the temptation is to add a 'but . . .', and turn the apology into a pseudo-interpretive counter-attack, which in turn will elicit further defensive manoeuvres, thereby negating its potential benefit.

Crispin and his unmentalising therapist

Let us turn to an extended clinical example, reminding ourselves of the precept that attending to a 'rupture marker' involves thinking about its meaning and aiming to explore negative feelings while combating one's impulses as a therapist to behave non-therapeutically. 'Repair' involves: restitution of a good working alliance in which therapist and patient are in tune with one another; looking back and trying to mentalise the states of mind of client and therapist that led to the rupture; and instilling a sense of hope that repair is possible.

Crispin suffered from borderline personality disorder – his intimate relationships were problematic, he abused alcohol, his sense of self was precarious, his moods fluctuating and unpredictable. Now in his late thirties, he had been a maths teacher but had lost his job due to ill-health. He was in his second year of twice-weekly psychoanalytic psychotherapy, which he had sought after a physical and mental breakdown precipitated by addiction and admission to hospital with liver failure.

He had had an exceptionally disrupted and difficult childhood. His parents separated soon after his birth. He spent most of her childhood shuttling between his mother and step-father, his father and step-mother, and grand-mother – feeling unwanted and inadequate more or less wherever he was. The main redeeming features of his childhood were an intermittently good relationship with his grandfather, who sadly had died when he was 14, and his skills at maths and chess, encouraged by one male teacher whom he revered.

Here is a Monday session from our work together. It followed a turbulent period a week previously in which he had had a 'slip' and had gone on a drinking bout for two days.

The first thing that 'happened' – the vital opening move of the session – was that I found myself asking, before he had a chance to speak: 'How was your weekend?', rather than waiting, as I would normally do, for him to begin. This might be seen as an example of a minor boundary-crossing (Gabbard 2003), typical of work with borderline patients.

'How was *yours*?' came the riposte, quick as a flash.

Unable in the heat of the moment to mentalise that response (i.e. work out what state of mind it represented), I could more easily identify the anxiety that had prompted my question and decided to voice it: 'I think my asking you that question is a coded way of enquiring about whether you have been drinking this weekend'.

He said that Friday evening and Saturday had been really difficult days, and that he had indeed been within a whisker of taking drugs again, but that he had been able to distract himself by visiting a girlfriend and that this had somehow helped to ward off the craving.

At this stage I didn't know what to make of this, but felt that there was a radical lack of emotional connection between us; so, following the psycho-analytic precept of 'when in doubt, shut up', I remained silent.

Next he said that he was thinking of taking driving lessons. Asking for clarification, while wondering countertransferentially if he was looking for a more effective 'instructor' than myself, I said 'I thought you already had a driving licence . . .?'

'Oh, you really *have* got a crap memory . . .'. My supposedly poor memory is a well-worn theme between us in which he accuses me of not getting the details of his complicated network of cousins, step-siblings, half-siblings, etc. straight. I had already noted in myself a typically defensive response. I had offered a possibly valid, but definitely unhelpful, understanding of this in terms of an absent reflective care-giver as a child leading to an inability to turn his family constellation into a coherent narrative in his own mind, with this confusion then spilling over, projectively, into me.

Next he mentioned that his sister had once had an old tape-recording of their father talking, but had got rid of it in a garage sale. 'I heard it once: he starts off being nice and then ends up shouting at me. If only I could get that tape back it might hold the key to my problems. He was my hero and yet could be so cruel . . .'.

Now I began to sense that he was angry with me, and that this somehow connected with what had happened, or failed to happen, in the previous week's session: he told me that he had wanted to drink immediately after the session; that I had a crap memory; and talked about someone who was a 'cruel hero'.

In the reference to the tape-recording there is a theme about the contrast between dead, mechanical memory versus the living hopeful 'remembrances' of a story. That gave me enough material to fly a transference-interpretive kite, although at that stage I didn't really know what it was I had done 'wrong'. I said, 'Perhaps you felt that *I* was being cruel in some way last week . . .'.

Now, for the first time in the session there was a feeling of a moment of meeting. Together patient and therapist were looking at an episode of failed relatedness – a rupture marker and its meaning. He said emphatically: '*Yes*, you put me down, telling me I needed an alcohol counsellor as well as a therapist. Also, I felt you were really preoccupied, not *with* me at all.'

I looked back to the previous week, trying to mentalise my state of mind at that time. It was true that I had thought it would be useful to have someone to monitor his drinking in parallel with the sessions with me – a therapeutic 'mother' and 'father' who, unlike his real parents, could be seen to be working together for his benefit. It now occurred to me that he might have experienced this bit of benign 'acting-out' on my part as one more rejection – being bundled off to an alcohol counsellor just as he had been parcelled off to various unwilling care-givers as a child.

Then I recalled what might also have been going on, and decided on a further bit of self-revelation (another example – I persuaded myself – of judicious boundary-crossing): 'Mmmm . . . you could well be right; it's true I had family members staying from abroad and could easily have been a bit distracted by that . . .' (I work from home and so had been peripherally aware of our visitors' presence during the session).

He said: 'I nearly didn't come today I felt so bad . . .'. My admission of failure had enabled Crispin to connect with his own bad feelings.

Now that our attachment needs – his to feel safe, me to provide security – were at least partially satisfied, I could begin to explore Crispin's opening salvo: 'How was *yours*?'. Based on my theoretical knowledge that children with disorganised attachment in infancy often demonstrate role reversal with care-givers later in childhood (Lyons-Ruth and Jacobvitz 2008), I surmised that he was telling me that my insensitivity had forced him to reverse roles and think about me; that I hadn't been doing my job properly, which is to think about *him*.

I said: 'Your antennae last week were more sensitive than mine. I didn't actually realise at the time that I was distracted, but' – I repeated – 'I'm sure you are right. Once again you were subjected to a distracted, uncaring care-giver, on this occasion me. That is the moment when you turn to drink – when there is no one there for you, or they're there but unavailable, and you get forgotten. And *their* anger and cruelty gets played out inside you – you end up being cruel to yourself'. (Using here the idea of the frightening, non-mentalising, self-referential care-giver who becomes an alien internal presence urging self-destructiveness; Fonagy et al. 2002.)

This overlong speech, however, triggered another rupture. He was having none of it: however much it is longed for and needed, being understood can be problematic for the borderline patient, because it equates with control or abuse (cf. Chapter 10). 'I drove my girlfriend's children to the beach. We had a great time. I wasn't distracted at all . . .'.

I try to repeat my interpretation more succinctly: 'You feel rejected and powerless, and long for comfort, that's when you turn to drink . . . but you discovered that you have got some inner resources to draw on, visiting friends, helping them, being an attentive care-giver to others, even though I was unable to be one to you . . . maybe like you having to look after your mother when she was too depressed to care for you . . .'.

It's the end of the session. Tentatively he volunteers: 'Shall I come back next week? I didn't like you at *all* last week . . . Perhaps I *do* need an alcohol counsellor . . .'.

Finally we seemed to be in the same place at the same time. In the previous session, instead of me thinking about – mentalising – him, I was forcing *him* to mentalise *me* – to wonder what was going on that I should seem so dis-tracted: 'my therapist isn't really listening to me today – it's probably nothing to do with me, but I'm damned if I'm going to let that drive me to drink, and I'll show the bastard how people *should* be looked after when I take my girlfriend's kids to the beach'. As we jointly tried to examine what was going on in our own and each other's minds, and the links between them, we began, first via my countertransference and then by his confirmation of it, to identify and articulate his feelings of anger, abandonment and the need for comfort. These then could be accurately reflected first in my mind and then his, but not before a mentalising *process* was set up between us.

Borderline patients are handicapped because their feelings are not available to guide them towards positive experiences and help them to avoid negative ones. Feelings are either so overwhelming that they cannot be thought about or so radically repressed or split off that they are inaccessible. Mentalising is impossible without affect regulation – representing one's feelings to oneself vividly enough for them to be worked with, but not so powerfully that they blot out all else. In therapy, focusing on feelings in the absence of mentalisa-tion either has little effect or provokes an affective storm. Conversely, trying to mentalise without access to affect becomes mere intellectual game-playing. Only once this mentalising process was in operation was Crispin able to think about his feelings of anger and rejection.

Reparation

Let us return now to the theme of repair. A connection between therapist and patient was broken. In the course of the session the rupture was repaired. What does it mean to 'repair' an interpersonal rent of this sort? Metaphors come easily to mind: harmony is restored; the relationship is 'back on track', in step; therapist and patient are once more in tune (cf. Stern 1985). Recall the puzzlement and discomfort evident in videotapes of infants whose mothers are asked to 'freeze' their facial expression in the course of playful interaction, and the relief when the minute-long agony of inaccessibility is over (P. Hobson 2002). How can we best theorise the disjunction of rupture and the connectivity of repair?

From an attachment perspective one might say that a secure base had been re-established, thereby enabling exploration to continue. That formulation, however, fails to capture the mutuality – the two-wayness – of the process. Heard and Lake (1997) grope towards this when they write of 'companionable interaction' as an expectable outcome of security provision. Lyons-Ruth et al. emphasise the significance of repair of what they call 'now moments', based on 'implicit relational knowing': 'almost by definition the repair of a *failed* now moment will the lead the dyad into one or more new now moments' (Lyons-Ruth and the Boston Change Process Study Group 2001, p. 16).

This meeting, or non-meeting, of minds is the locus of repair: reparative activity starts from the therapist's capacity to mentalise his own mind, to reach out empathically to the patient, to think and articulate about 'we/us', 'what is going on' in the relationship itself.

Separation and loss, and the desire to restore attachment, are intrinsic to the attachment/separation dialectic of relationships rather than guilt-motivated attempts to repair the damage done by one's aggression. In Freud's (1905) famous *Fort und Da* story of his grandson's repetitive throwing of a toy on a string from his cot and retrieving it, he conceptualised this as the child's attempt, by transforming passivity into activity and control, to master his mother's unpredictable comings and goings. (A contemporaneous farcical version of this is to be found in Grossmith and Grossmith's 1892 *Diary of a Nobody*, in which the socially insecure Mr Pooter triumphantly announces his two friends – 'isn't it strange that Gowing is always coming and Cummings is always going?'.)

The cycle of repair and restoration in the fabric of endlessly broken and reformed communication is a crucial aspect of analytic therapy. Mentalising is fundamentally reparative in that it entails holding the living presence of another in mind when they are not physically present. In the next chapter, which stands as an interlude between the theoretical and applied parts of this book, I shall develop these ideas in relation to psychotherapeutic and poetic creativity.

Chapter 8

Poetising

In an attempt to establish strengths as well as pathology, my routine history-taking includes asking patients what they are interested in, and what their idea of an enjoyable activity might be (note that the use of the conditional is already a step into the 'active imagination' brought alive by both therapy and poetry). Rarely, if ever, does reading or writing poetry come as the answer. Poetry is definitely a minority interest. Nevertheless, at times of emotional intensity, whether painful or joyful, people turn to poetry, trite or great, as a means of containing and expressing their feelings. Since those moments are central to what we do as psychotherapists, if we wish to enhance the depth and quality of our work, it is perhaps worth listening to what poets have to tell us. There is evidence there, albeit of the experiential variety.

In this chapter I look at a particular poem and, based on the case presentation in the previous chapter, outline some formal similarities between poetry and psychotherapy. I shall also compare the Kleinian concept of reparation (Segal 1991) with an attachment perspective.

Poetry and psychotherapy have a surprising amount in common. Both regularly arouse suspicion and incomprehension, yet people often turn to them when in states of heightened emotion – love, elation, despair, confusion, loss and bereavement. We come, once again, to mentalising: the capacity to 'think about feelings' or to be 'mind-minded'. Finding 'the best words in the best order' (Coleridge's famous definition of poetry) is a crucial skill for therapists (and their patients) as well as poets, since the appropriate image or metaphor can mirror or evoke feelings in the listener in a way that facilitates empathic attunement. If sorrow can be given words, feelings shared and objectified, their power to distress or overwhelm is mitigated. Poetry and psychotherapy are both concerned with repair of the endlessly rent human experiential and communicative fabric.

We can never have direct access to another's feelings. Metaphors are an indispensable means by which we reach into another's inner world. We ask: 'what did it *feel like* when your mother died; your partner abandoned you; you wanted to kill yourself . . .?'. Matte-Blanco (1975) translates Freud's (1911) 'two principles of mental functioning' – the one logical, classifying,

verbal; the other emotive, image-based, in which contradictions can be tolerated – into what he calls asymmetrical and symmetrical thinking. The mind,
probing, understanding, classifying and manipulating its environment, is
constantly comparing one thing with another, symmetrising ('my wife is just
like my mother') and asymmetrising ('my wife is the very opposite of my
mother'). Metaphor is a symmetrising device: it shows how one thing is
always *like* something else. When a patient uses metaphor or simile to
describe his depression – 'it's like being in a dark room and not being able to
find the way out' – a window is opened into his inner world. We begin to put
ourselves into his place, to see what it might be like to *be* him.

Poetic metaphors are of course just one sort among many. There are psychotherapeutic lessons to be learned from a life drawing class, in which a
combination of empathic identification with the body to be depicted and
objective appraisal of its lineaments is required. If your passion is golf,
teeing up, getting lost in the rough, holing in one, etc. will serve to describe
the ups and downs of a typical psychotherapeutic day. But since metaphor is
central to both poetry and psychotherapy – finding the best words in the
best order to communicate an affective experience – I suggest that poetry
may have a special contribution to helping understand how psychotherapy
works (cf. Ogden 1999).

Poetic and psychotherapeutic parallels

Let us go straight to a specific poem, and see how unravelling its meaning and
mechanics may help illuminate what psychotherapists get up to. I have chosen
'Dinner with My Mother' by the contemporary British writer, Hugo Williams
(1994). Biographical information on the author would no doubt help illuminate aspects of the poem, but the reader is invited to consider the poem as a
self-sufficient 'subjective object', just as it is sometimes desirable to respond
to an account of a psychotherapy session as an 'unseen translation' in its own
right without the obscuring impact of excessive life-history data (Padel 1975,
personal communication).

Like a case history, my hope is that the poem provides qualitative evidence
of the power and relevance of poetry. I have chosen it, from an infinite
number of possible examples, because it is accessible, short, 'good' (i.e. in my
judgement, emotionally authentic and well crafted), and describes a seemingly
everyday event but with the strong emotional overtones that might crop up in
a routine psychotherapy session. The title and content are self-explanatory.

Dinner with My Mother

My mother is saying 'Now'.
'Now', she says, taking down a saucepan,
putting it on the stove.
She doesn't say anything else for a while,

so that time passes slowly, on the simmer,
until it is 'Now' again
as she hammers out our steaks
for Steak Diane.

I have to be on hand at times like this
for table-laying,
drink replenishment
and general conversational encouragement,

but I am getting hungry
and there is nowhere to sit down.
'Now,' I say, making a point
of opening a bottle of wine.

My mother isn't listening.
She's miles away,
testing the sauce with a spoon,
narrowing her eyes through the steam.

'Now,' she says very slowly, meaning
which is it to be,
the rosemary or tarragon vinegar
for the salad dressing?

I hold my breath, lest anything
should go wrong at the last minute.
But now it is really 'Now',
our time to sit and eat.

Let us suppose that part of the impulse to write a poem, or to consult a psychotherapist, comes from the need to make sense of, or do psychic work on, something that seems painful, confusing or troubling in the subject's mind. Can we learn something about the minutiae of the reparative process by looking at the poem from a psychotherapeutic angle? What was Williams' protagonist wrestling with in this poem, and what conclusions can we draw about him/her, his/her feelings about his/her mother and their relationship? I select seven aspects where parallels might be drawn between poetising and psychotherapising.

Finding a space for mentalising

The writer Doris Lessing (2007), in her Nobel acceptance speech, asks:

have you found that space, that empty space which should surround you when you write? Into that space, which is like a form of listening, of attention, will come the words . . . inspiration.

The therapist's 'frame' (consistency of place, room, time, technique) and poetic form (the bounded 'empty space' of the blank page, the 'form' of stanza, rhyme and rhythm) are the therapeutic analogues. Williams uses the space provided by his poetic form to explore the difficult emotions aroused in him by both wanting to please and get close to, but also being irritated and controlled by, his mother. For mentalising to operate there has to be a safe space, both literally in the therapist's room and also an 'internal' space in his or her mind.

The search for emergent meaning

In both a psychotherapeutic session and a poem there is a dialectic between expectable form and the infinite possibilities of new or 'emergent' meanings (Margison 2002). The structure of a session is formalised and familiar, yet neither patient nor therapist knows in advance what is going to happen during the 50 minutes of their session/sitting, other than that there will be moments of both meeting and missing, of rupture and repair. Similarly Williams' poem, with its careful arrangements of groups of four lines and steady metrical beat, has a formal structure that allows for the containment of uncertainty and tension – we don't know at the start if that meal is ever going to get onto the table! The 'subject' of both poetry and psychotherapy is the processing of difficult feelings. Such feelings are liable to trigger attachment behaviours – seeking out a secure base – which is inimical to exploration and mentalising. The holding and security provided by the therapeutic situation, and by poetic form, assuage attachment behaviours, allowing for the emergence of playfulness and exploration.

Recursiveness

A therapy session, like a poem, being bounded, has a beginning, a middle and an end – but not necessarily in that order: as in Eliot's (1986) oft-quoted second quartet, *East Coker*, 'in my beginning is my end'. There is a recursive aspect to a poem and a psychotherapy session. Therapists need to attend closely to the opening and closing features of a session, since, under the pressure of anxiety, they contain in compressed form much of what is to come and what has been.

Crispin's opening remark in the previous chapter – 'How was *yours*?' – finally made sense when contextualised by what later emerged as his feelings of not being listened to, and reverting to a borderline-type role reversal. Contrariwise, what happened in the rest of the session made sense in the light of his opening remark. Williams' deceptively simple poem loops back on itself while its sense emerges slowly only on careful second and third readings. The repeated 'Now' turns from an initial verbal mannerism into a philosophical statement of the value of two people being present to one another and, finally, perhaps, in the same place at the same time. Unravelling the meaning of a psychotherapy session in supervision is often helped by looking back at the opening moments in the light of subsequent developments. A casual remark about the weather as the patient enters the therapy room may, as it turns out, reflect her underlying emotional tone. A patient who comments that he is late because he has 'had difficulty in parking' may be wondering if the therapist really has sufficient space to accommodate his neediness, and so on.

'Action replay'

Wordsworth (1802) famously defined poetry as 'emotion recollected in tranquillity'. Both lyric poetry and psychoanalytic work have the capacity to focus on tiny fragments of experience and replay them, tracing their emotional links backwards in time and 'sideways' with other sets of experiences and emotions. Subjecting one's experience to this type of slowed-down close reading is synonymous with mentalising. Williams attempts to take his mother's monosyllabic 'Now' and, frame by frame, put it under the poetic microscope. Similarly, attending to the minute particulars (P. Hobson 1985) of sessions – small fragments of interaction – is an essential part of therapeutic and supervisory work. Noticing a non-verbal response of averted eyes and slight blanching to an interpretation, the therapist might ask: 'What happened just now when I made that comparison with your relationship with your father?'. The patient might say 'I was shocked; I felt you had no right to say that', and so on. Supervision can similarly home in on a small segment of therapeutic interaction and, holographically, reconstruct an entire relational constellation.

Somato-sensory experience

Action replay focuses on the component parts that make up, and contain within themselves, an elusive whole. But in responding to a poem, and a patient, we need to oscillate between the 'minute particulars' and the overall feel of the patient/session/poem. The latter might be called 'dreaming the patient' – allowing the therapist's unconscious to resonate in an unfettered way to that of the client – as Freud recommended, with 'evenly suspended attention'. The devil is in the detail, the minute particulars, but also in the overall contour of one's response. We need to be able to find eternity in a grain of sand, but to dream the whole dune too.

A poem and a session are somato-sensory experiences grasped through 'reverie', i.e. the reader or therapist's 'day-dreams, fantasies, ruminations, bodily sensations, derivatives of unconscious inter-subjective constructions' (Ogden 1989, p. 76). For Bollas (2007) and Ogden, the capacity to weave conscious and useful thoughts out of these dream-like elements is the crucial contribution of psychoanalysis to the achievement of psychic health.

Although the medium of communication is primarily verbal, the therapist's starting point is often corporeal. In the session reported in the previous chapter, I 'sensed' – i.e. had some sort of physical awareness – that things were not right with Crispin from the outset of our encounter on the Monday morning. His face and posture followed by the verbal 'attack' (in the musical sense) of 'how was yours?' must have communicated this subliminally, leading no doubt to my own perceptible bodily discomfort at being in the presence of someone who was unhappy and angry, although initially I would not have been able to put words to those feelings.

A supervisee reported that in the course of a session her patient had described a friend as having 'passed away'. The use of this conventional term jarred (note physicality of the metaphor, albeit one that is near-defunct!) on her consciousness, although she could not initially say why this was so. Further exploration revealed that in fact the friend had committed suicide, and thinking about that had been unbearably painful for this patient whose mother had similarly killed herself when the patient was a child, so much so that she had to wrap up the event in a euphemism.

There is a dialectic in which the use of a word or phrase triggers off non-verbal, or perhaps more accurately 'pre-verbal' – 'language of thought' – reactions in the listener, leading to a return to the linguistic realm, and further exploration of what it denotes in terms of the utterer's inner unformulated experience. Comparably, the music of Williams' poem – its steady, almost stately metre, the repetitions and dreamy rhythms interrupted by the abruptness of phrases and words like 'hammers out' and staccato 'steaks' – enables it to penetrate, to be physically absorbed into our body/mind, and, once inside, for us to be able to think (or in Ogden's sense 'dream') about it and its multiple meanings. In both poetry and psychotherapy there is a constant interplay between feelings and language. As suggested, identifying and then finding what initially may be no more than a vague 'shape' for these feelings leads on to the attempt to find words to describe them and, via the process of mentalisation, to begin to delineate meaning. The therapist's task is to 'read' the 'text' that the patient brings, 'back-translating' words into affective/bodily experience. She does this by the reverse process within herself, 'reading' her physical and emotional responses ('countertransferences') and then finding words to capture them.

These interpersonal physiological sensations invariably have a temporal aspect – they are 'feelings in time', and this is often a pointer to their meaning. This is manifest in both poem and session by the balance between tension and its resolution. Psychoanalytically the poem could be compared to the struggle of an infant at the breast gripped by hunger, longing to 'latch on' to a slightly distracted and self-preoccupied mother. One reading of 'Dinner with My Mother' might imagine a final moment of bliss when breast and nipple come together via the 'let-down reflex' and the milk begins to flow: 'our time to sit and eat'. An alternative take on the poem's 'high level ambiguity' (Zeki 2008; see also Chapter 10) might view the bleakness of the non-meeting of preoccupied mother and son continuing right through to a miserable end: the protagonist in the poem needs to open a bottle of wine if he is to tolerate his mother's mild narcissistic self-preoccupation. In both accounts the story is one of rupture and attempt at repair, successful or unsuccessful.

Self-referentiality

According to Eagleton (2007, p. 21) poetry:

> is always at some level language which is about itself. There is something circular or self-referential about even the most publicly engaged of poems. The meaning of a poem is far less abstractable from its total process of signification than is the meaning of a road sign. This is not to say that you cannot give a summary of a poem's content . . . [but] the resumé is likely to be less informational. Poetry is something which is done to us, not just said to us. The meaning of its words is closely bound up with the experience of them.

As McLuhan (1964) famously put it, 'the medium is the message' – a statement equally applicable to psychotherapy. Poetry and psychotherapy are 'ono-matopoeic' in the sense that their form and content are indissolubly linked. A psychotherapy session has an intrinsically self-referential quality that sets it apart from 'ordinary' discursive discourse – whatever the client brings pro-vokes the therapist to ask herself 'Now what, apart from its self-evident conno-tations, might all this have to say about "us"?'. When Crispin in the previous chapter starts talking about needing to find a driving instructor, the therapist immediately wonders if he is looking for more guidance than he feels he is getting in the therapy, and how this links to his absent father in childhood.

Similar considerations apply to humour. A humorous, albeit somewhat rarefied, example of what I am calling 'onomatopoeia' comes from Holt (2008). The Oxford philosopher J. L. Austin was giving a lecture in New York to a group of fellow philosophers. In it he raised the question of double negatives. 'In some languages', said he in his precise Oxford voice, 'a double negative yields an affirmative. In others it yields a more emphatic negative. But I know of no language in which a double affirmative yields a negative.' From the back of the hall came a drawling professorial Brooklyn accent: 'yeah, yeah'. Here, once again, the medium is the message – the content and form of the point being made were coextensive.

The psychotherapeutic analogue of a 'poetic moment' is a 'moment of meeting' (Lyons-Ruth and the Boston Change Process Study Group 2001) – or indeed of non-meeting – between therapist and patient, and attempting to follow the chain of associations this conjures up. Something 'happens' in the session: therapist and client then look together at what it is that has happened and try to understand it. The transference/countertransference matrix is the force-field that evokes such emotion-laden unconscious memories. Every story, reaction, feeling, and experience brought to the session is examined in the light of the therapist–patient relationship. The very act of understanding is not exempt from that scrutiny, just as the philosopher's interjection *was* the very point being made.

Eagleton suggests that poems contain explicit or covert reference to the act of poetry-making itself. Williams, like his mother, is 'hammering out' something in his poem – using words and the patterns they create to make sense of an experience. The poet has to choose his words as carefully as finding the right dressing for a salad. The poem, like the meal, is 'simmering' in his mind; nothing is said, until the 'Now' moment, when it can be written down, arises. The capacity to 'think about thinking' implicit in this self-referentiality is a key feature of mentalising. The mentalising mother is able to feel her feelings towards her infant – overwhelming love, protectiveness, anxiety, frustration, fury, etc. – and at the same time be *aware that she is feeling these feelings*, and use them to repair interruptions in the continuity of their relationship.

In the previous chapter Crispin arrives in a state of discomfort instantly replicated in the therapist. He 'holds on' to that feeling, waiting to see where it will lead, just as the poet lets his words hold the feeling of hunger. Tension rises. The therapist offers a tentative interpretation – perhaps Crispin is angry about last week. Crispin confirms this and adds detail. The therapist in turns expands on Crispin's comments, generalising, objectifying, mentalising. This pattern between them is understandable as part of a general pattern of need, distraction, and turning to comfort, just as the protagonist in the poem needs to open a bottle of wine in order to tolerate his mother's self-preoccupation. Crispin confirms the therapist's hunch by telling him how he 'hated you last week'. In this moment of meeting, momentarily, client and therapist are at one, sharing understanding, mutually mentalising – just as one might say 'that's a good poem' or 'that works for me'.

Objectification

As an artefact, the poem itself is present to the reader over and above the events and objects to which it refers. That is what gives it its objectivity and general relevance. Williams' poem is not just an account of a mother and son preparing supper – it is about mother-love, filial love, unmediated oedipal love, the gulf between the generations and much else. The poem 'reads' us – in that it evokes particular feelings and memories in its readers – just as much as we read it. Poetry presents our feelings to us in an objectified way – it mentalises them for us. It presents a constant interplay between our verbal representation of reality and the experience that representation seeks to instate. The poet is always in a dyadic relationship to his 'material'. Out of the 'nothing' of the blank piece of paper she/he creates an *other*, with whom she/he begins to have a conversation – the nothingness of which could be construed as an ultimate rent in the continuity of existence. What finally emerges as the poem is the poet's attempt to make sense of that 'conversation with himself'. The therapist's role can likewise be thought of as helping the patient to have a conversation with himself or herself – a 'duet for one'.

Attachment and repair

Crispin and I were 'reading' one another throughout our session, or trying to do so. In fact, in the previous session he read me better than I was able to read myself. There was, as always in an analytic session, both understanding and confusion/misunderstanding. As in the poem, there was a dialectic of intimacy and disconnection. As a session finishes and the next is anticipated, the never-ending movement between absence and presence, loss and recovery, is the grist of psychotherapy. A poem is a device for turning subjectivity of feelings into sharable objectivity. A psychoanalytic session, via its focus on the relationship between therapist and patient, is a device for exploring and containing the *Fort und Da* of relationships. The objectification of the inevitable misunderstandings, exploitations, absences and failures of communication is an essential step in the process of repair, of returning the *Da* back to *Fort*. Both poetry and psychotherapy can be seen as reparative in this sense.

Bion (1987) saw thinking as arising out of absence – as his analysand Samuel Beckett might have put it: 'no breast, imagine a breast'. In a more restricted sense mentalising can be viewed as enabling us to cope with the inevitable breaches, lapses, lacunae, failures, narcissistic self-preoccupations, disruptions and potential traumata of everyday life. To mentalise is to construct a reparative bridge over the chasm of loss.

The Kleinian perspective sees reparation making good the psychic devastation wrought by aggression unleashed in the face of deprivation and absence. The murderous and murdered 'bad breast', full of projected hatred, is brought back to life through the creative process (Segal 1991). Aggression and reparation are indissolubly linked. By contrast, attachment theory sees mentalising as a built-in repair mechanism helping us to survive the inevitable and 'objective' separations and losses that are the reverse side of the attachment coin. Gross disruptions of care in childhood compromise mentalising in ways that link to the symptomatology of borderline personality disorder (see Chapter 10). Tragically, the bigger the rent, the more mentalising skills are needed to withstand it. Children who can articulate their perception of their care-givers as stressed, intoxicated, depressed, etc. are protected against disorganisation of their attachment representation compared with those who cannot make that judgement (Fonagy et al. 2002; Slade 2005). Similarly the ability to recognise one's own feelings of rage or aggression or despair for what they are – ultimately 'just thoughts' – is a bulwark against self-destructive acting-out. Most therapies for borderline patients, whether behavioural, dialectically Buddhist, transference-focused or Kleinian, aim to foster this capacity, or skill.

Where does poetry fit in with this viewpoint? There is a powerful link between poetry and loss – people turn to poetry at moments of great joy or great sadness, either because there is an intrinsic awareness either that happiness cannot last for ever, or in an attempt to re-establish the fabric of existence ruptured through death or separation. The business of poetry is to generate truthful and beautiful images, i.e. feeling-toned mental representations of experience, through which the 'lost object' can be 'reinstated' (Segal 1991) in the mind. The external object is lost, but mental continuity still maintained. Poetry has the power to conjure up images in the internal world in a way that keeps the ongoingness of reality intact in the face of loss. By creating language that 'onomatopoeically' represents and recreates experience, the poet reaches out across the chasm of loss to a listening other.

Words, when used poetically, through rhyme, rhythm, metre, tempo, tone and assonance, re-establish connection and continuity despite the fact that they also oedipally cut us off from the primal flux of existence (Lacan 1977). This connectivity of poetry – the way that rhyme, pulse, images get 'into' us – is comparable to the 'scaffold' of the psychotherapeutic session. The poem becomes a living thing that 'holds' us for the duration of our attention to it. Similarly, a held child/patient can use mentalising to overcome despair, and thus himself hold hope in mind. We habitually try to avoid, blot out or kill the pain that life, especially when traumatic, inflicts on us. As Ogden (1999, p. 992) puts it:

> we turn to poetry and to psychoanalysis ... with the hope that we might reclaim (or perhaps experience for the first time) forms of human aliveness that we have foreclosed to ourselves.

Poetry and psychotherapy have a part to play in that ever-renewing process of, metaphorically, 'staying alive'; sometimes, as we shall see in Chapter 11, literally so.

Part II

Practice

Chapter 9

Loving sex

As the reader may by now have gleaned, I am by nature an integrationist – a 'lumper' rather than a 'splitter', a symmetriser rather than an asymmetriser. My project has been to find points of similarity, complementarity, overlap and translation between attachment and psychoanalytic ideas. But the time has now come to confront a topic of possible radical divergence between the two theories: sex and sexuality.

Contemporary psychoanalysis has, it seems, gone off sex. In a broadside against psychoanalytic pluralism, Andre Green (2005, p. 630) bemoans the current emphasis on the 'role of attachment which supposedly replaces infantile sexuality; the conceptions of memory based on neuro-scientific findings rather than repression, and so on'. Meanwhile, Fonagy and Target (2005) chart the waning number of publications on sexuality in psychoanalytic journals, and Budd (2001) notes the curious reversal in which sex, for Freud the latent theme concealed in every psychiatric symptom and dream, is now viewed merely as the manifest content of patients' difficulties, concealing 'deeper' issues such as maternal deprivation and other attachment-related themes.

In one sense Green's concern is justified. Infantile sexuality and the Oedipus complex are central planks of psychoanalytic theory – take them away and what remains? It is also true that attachment theory was devised by Bowlby in part to provide an account of parent–child relationships in which security, rather than sex, was the central theme. In this chapter I shall suggest that attachment theory does indeed offer a radical challenge to the theory of infantile sexuality. The attachment perspective sees security-seeking as the key to understanding parent–child relationships. Sexuality is viewed as a distinct behavioural system, with restricted salience in infancy and young childhood.

Despite this, given that secure attachment arises out of mutually pleasurable care-giver–child interactions, the two approaches are not necessarily incompatible. As a bridging concept I propose the notion of *hedonic intersubjectivity*. By this I mean a playful, self-affirming, interactive sensuality – which can, however, only tendentiously be described as sexual. This in turn links with the *erotic imagination*, a concept with Winnicottian over-tones, which has its origins in the 'transitional' phenomena of hedonic intersubjectivity.

In the early psychoanalytic days latent homosexuality was to be seen lurking under every stone. An unresolved Oedipus complex meant a failure to separate fully from the mother, to make the move towards identification with father for boys, or to take him as a libidinal object for girls. In both cases, lingering attachment to the mother was seen as a manifestation of 'homo-sexuality'. Homosexuality is no longer seen as a sign of pathology: there is as much potential for healthy love in homosexuality as in its heterosexual coun-terpart, and equal potential for 'perversity' in the latter. I hope, therefore, despite writing from a predominantly heterosexual and male angle, that my contentions are equally applicable to female and same-sex perspectives.

Theorising sex

Freud's theory of infantile sexuality had two main building blocks: (a) his view that adult patients' neurotic problems could ultimately be traced back to sexual trauma and repression, and (b) a developmental perspective that saw early childhood experience at the kernel of adult mental life (Freud 1905). If adult neurosis is essentially sexual, and this reflects a developmental con-tinuity from childhood into adulthood, *ergo*, sexuality must be as salient for infants and children as it is for adults. As we shall see, attachment theory sees this neat syllogism as fatally flawed, flying in the face of the fundamental facts of life. In this chapter I shall argue against the binary drive to reduce all affect to Eros and Thanatos, and that sexual love, romantic love and maternal love are distinct, albeit related, psychological and neurological (see Zeki 2008) states.

Classical psychoanalytic theory sees attachment relationships as a mani-festation of the sexual instinct and its vicissitudes. Infantile sexuality – initially the oral pleasure derived by the infant from sucking at the breast – is the glue that binds children to their parents. Libido continues, through the develop-mental pathway from polymorphous perversity to genital sexuality, to be the fundamental force that both holds human society together and, with the inherent ambivalence of the oedipal situation ('the mother whom I love is possessed by another'), contains the ever-present possibility of disruption.

Freud saw the psychological vulnerability of humans as arising from the contrast between physical immaturity and 'adult' psychological impulses (love, hate, the desire to possess and be possessed) together with their physical manifestations (excitation of the various body parts). To oversimplify, the little boy cannot fully 'possess'/'have' his mother because he is not big enough to do so, nor strong enough to defeat his father in a battle for her. Love and hate, attachment and separation can ultimately be traced to infantile sexual desire and its inescapable emotions of envy and castration-anxiety.

Attachment theory, by contrast, as an ethological account of security provision and protection from threat, sees the prime motivational force holding families and societies together as the need for security: together we stand; divided we fall. Attachment and sexual behavioural systems are distinct and separate, each with their own releasers, timing and, to use Freud's terminology, aims and object.

Attachment theory starts from the need for parents and other care-givers to provide security for their helpless infants in the face of a hostile and potentially predatory environment. Like Freud, Bowlby saw the helplessness of the human infant as a crucial developmental factor. Attachment theory might well agree with psychoanalysis that the ultimate biological purpose of life is reproduction. But rather than instating the sexual impulse as omnipresent throughout the life-cycle, attachment theory encompasses sexuality through the fact that infants need to *survive to sexual maturity* in order to be able to reproduce. Physiologically, sex hormones and the immune system have little in common, but unless the immune system is intact there will be no one for the sex hormones to drive towards mating. The same applies to the 'psychological immune system' provided by attachment relationships (Holmes 2001).

'Successful sex' has a number of components: (a) optimum mate selection – finding as 'good' a partner as one's own 'social capital' will allow; (b) therefore being able to 'read' another's intentions and qualities successfully based on mentalising; (c) 'proximate' skills, to be elaborated below, which release pleasure in oneself and one's partner with consequent enhancement of both successful reproduction and (d) long-term bonding, needed for successful child-rearing because of the prolonged helplessness of the human infant, itself a result of the human 'big' (and therefore mentalising-capable) brain.

While Bowlby was insistent that attachment and sexuality should be seen as distinct systems, he also acknowledged the close links between them (Bowlby 1971). The difficulty in disentangling sex and attachment is that although they demonstrably involve separable behaviours, emotions and constructs, it is clear too that they are intimately and bidirectionally related. In adult sexuality, as courtship proceeds, sexual attraction ushers in attachment feelings; once established, a close cohabiting attachment relationship between adults provides the usual context for quotidian sexuality. For established couples, sex and attachment are usually mutually reinforcing. The 'bonding' hormone, oxytocin, is released during sex, but also in non-sexual activity such as hugging (Zeki 2008).

Sex, even between one couple, takes many and varied forms. From an attachment perspective one might speculate that for each of the defined patterns of attachment there could be a corresponding pattern of sexuality (Feeney 2008; Hazan and Shaver 1994). Perhaps securely attached couples make love freely, spontaneously, safely, excitingly, harmonically, tenderly and empathically; couples when enmeshed clingingly, desperately, reassurance-seekingly, endlessly; when avoidant, couples' sex might be distant, mechanical, emotionless, violent, inconsiderate and infrequent. Disorganised couples might make love controllingly, inconsistently, dissociatedly, self-destructively. At the extreme ends of human behaviour attachment is clearly neither necessary nor sufficient for sex: rape represents sex devoid of attachment; the reverse applies in unconsummated or post-sexual marriage.

Sexual and attachment arousal: A source of confusion

There is an ever-present possibility of confusion surrounding sexual and attachment arousal. In order to become sexually aroused, couples, especially the more vulnerable and necessarily biologically more choosy female partner, need to feel safe. People almost never make love in public. In a hostile savannah, a couple having sex would have been vulnerable to predation, and in a modern environment they are subject to envious and judicial censure.

The incompatibility of exploration and attachment-seeking applies to sex, and therefore, since every act of sex is an exploration of one's own and the other's body and mind, if anxiety or threat has triggered attachment pathways, sexual arousal will be compromised. The picture is complicated, however, in that sexual behaviour and attachment behaviours may look very similar from the 'outside', even through they feel very different from the 'inside'. If one partner feels unsafe she or he may seek out the other's proximity in a way that may be misread as wanting sex. A classic source of resentment in couples is the scenario where 'she' seeks a reassuring hug, while 'he' takes this as a go-ahead for sex. Equally, 'he' may be in search of security, but only able to express this via sexual need, while 'her' sexuality may, given continuing social repression of women's sexuality, get lost in the search for intimacy.

This in turn may lead to various forms of dissociation, benign or self-destructive, to be explored further in the clinical section below. 'Good sex', perhaps especially for women, is predicated on secure attachment – a combination of extreme excitement and absolute relaxation and trust. This theoretical and experiential view is supported by neuroimaging studies which show that orgasm in females – but *not* simulated orgasm – involves deactivation of hippocampal regions of the brain associated with anxiety (Bartels and Zeki 2004). Comparable neuroimaging data for males have thus far been less informative.

Attachment versus infantile sexuality

Are these attachment-derived ideas compatible with the psychoanalytic notion of infantile sexuality? From an attachment perspective it makes little sense to use the word 'sexuality' to characterise the physical proximity of care-giver and infant: (a) because its purpose is primarily security-providing rather than reproductive and (b) because the genital aspects of the contact are usually fairly insignificant. Freud gets round the latter objection via the concept of 'polymorphous perversity' – but from a philosophy-of-science perspective (Lakatos 1970) this is an arbitrary addition of a supernumerary concept to buttress a fundamentally unsound theory. Is it really helpful to think of as 'perversity' the fact that infants and young children derive sensual pleasure from the whole body surface?

Pleasurable, touch-mediated interaction between care-giver and infant is clearly central to good care-giving. While the experience for mother and infant of lusty breast-feeding may be in some ways *analogous* to (rather than a homologous antecedent of) enjoyable love-making, pleasure is inescapably the appropriate word to apply to kissing, cuddling, tickling, holding, mutual gazing, stroking, playing, patting and all that goes on to cement a secure attachment bond between parents and their infants and small children. What makes a secure base secure is in large measure its physicality: the warmth, holding, feeding, reassuring heartbeat, soothing words, gentle touch which proximity to the parent gives to the infant – and that is something *desired* by both child and parent. The experience of bodily pleasure, in a playful, respectful interpersonal/intersubjective environment, makes for secure attachment; conversely, secure attachment makes such playfulness pleasurable. Bodily stimulation that *lacks* interpersonal sensitivity quickly becomes unpleasant – an everyday example would be when tickling gets 'out of hand'. Similarly, there is something essential missing from an unembodied verbal or visual relationship with a held-at-a-distance infant. A tamagotchi is no substitute for a real pet.

If all pleasure is seen as essentially sexual then infantile sexuality survives to live another day. Here Freud's view of word-representations as 'switches' between different associative chains or networks leads to an elisis, a glossing over, a symmetrisation, rather than clarification, since the German word for pleasure of all types – non-sexual as well as sexual – is *lust*, which in English has clear sexual connotations, as does the word 'libido'. Infants and children clearly have desires and feel intense pleasure and unpleasure, but arguably it is neither helpful nor necessary to view these as sexual.

From a relational-attachment point of view, while the classical psycho-analytical concept of infantile sexuality is questionable, there are clearly possible links between in infant's capacity for pleasure and adult sexuality. Widlocher's (2002) 'hedonic capacity' is a building block in infancy for later sexual enjoyment. In addition, *relationships*, usually thought of in rather abstract terms, are in fact psychophysical phenomena, mediated by an inter-active bodily 'dance' – whether this be patterns of eye contact, posture, gesture, voice timbre or touch. As Lakoff and Johnson (1980) convincingly show, here is a physical concomitant to the metaphors used to describe emotions and relationships: we feel close or distant, in tune, in or out of touch, on the same wavelength, can't keep our hands off each other, are sparring all the time, etc. The 'regressive' aspect of adult sexuality 'back-translates' sophisticated adult feelings of interest, attraction and excitement into the language of the body.

Fonagy and Target (2005) preserve the idea of infantile sexuality by considering the contribution made by the *parent* in this infant–care-giver 'dance'. While the infant is sexually naïve, the parent necessarily brings sexual resonances into the relationship. These include the sexual feelings described by some, but by no means all, women while breastfeeding, and a father's occasional erections while dandling his infant. There is thus a potential disjunction between the parent and the infant's experience of mutual bodily interaction. This is similar to Widlocher's (2002) suggestion that infantile sexuality and attachment are associated in the child's mind only in retrospect, via *nachträglichkeit*. Fonagy and Target argue that the infant senses in some indefinable way the aura of sexual mystery surrounding physical intimacy with a parent, suggesting that the inherently disturbing aspect of adult sexuality has its origins here.

Both Oedipus and 'primal scene' need to be rethought from this perspective. The Oedipus complex as much describes an adult male's feelings towards his child as vice versa. A father may envy his partner's maternal preoccupation and his relegation to the role of provider and distant supporter in the early months of a child's life. There may be murderous feelings towards the child. Here adult feelings have been split off and projected into the putative infantile sexuality of the child. Conversely, the 'primal scene' viewed as the foundation of a person's view of themselves and of intimate relationships arises more likely from an extrapolation from a child's relationship with her care-giver than from any appreciation of adult sexuality in reality or phantasy.

Fonagy and Target (2005) focus, as does Freud, on the incest taboo and its relationship to childhood sexual development. Freud encapsulates men's sexual difficulties with a famous aphorism – where men love they cannot desire, and where they desire they cannot love. A successfully negotiated Oedipus complex means being able to feel comfortable with the transgressive aspect of sexuality. The arousal associated with breaking a taboo contributes to sexual excitement. Sexual desire carries us over the gulf between parental and spousal attachment – encapsulated in the symbolic significance of the husband carrying his wife over the threshold into their bower, with its physical connotations of penetration. Feeling safe enough to 'risk' penetration or being penetrated means, to reverse the Bellocian (1907) phrase, 'letting go of nurse', while not afraid that one will 'find something worse'.

Apropos the incest taboo, Fonagy and Target (2007) argue in an exception-that-proves-the-rule fashion that, unlike all other affective experiences in healthy development, a child's nascent sexual feelings are *unmirrored* by the parent. A little girl who habitually proffers her bottom or a boy who brandishes his erection will, in Western cultures at least, likely be studiously ignored or severely reprimanded by otherwise attuned and loving parents. This non-mirroring, Fonagy and Target suggest, sows the seeds of the mysteriousness of sex and, once adolescence is reached, the search for a partner with whom a mutual mirroring response *can* be established.

It is worth noting here that Freud, in his discussion of the sexual basis of hysteria, acknowledges that symptoms derive as much from 'the patient's *phantasies* (or imaginary memories) mostly produced during the years of puberty . . . which were built up out of and over . . . childhood memories' (Freud 1905, p. 75; emphasis in original). In my reading, this is tantamount to acknowledging that what in retrospect is seen as 'infantile sexuality' is in fact an amalgam of infantile *sens*uality overlayered with adult (or adolescent) *sex*uality.

From drive theory to intersubjectivity

Classical psychoanalytic drive theory focuses on the individual and her inner world. Object relations incorporates the object and the self's relationship with it, but still as played out with*in* the psyche, rather than *between* psyches. Winnicott's ideas form a bridge from Kleinian object relations towards an interpersonal perspective, and between attachment theory and mainstream psychoanalysis. His seminal paper 'The capacity to be alone' (Winnicott 1971) centres around the image of a securely attached child happily playing 'alone in the presence of the mother'. The mother's background presence as a secure base allows the child to be (with) himself or herself. Winnicott explicitly includes sex as an adult analogue of this situation, but remains intrasubjectivist rather than intersubjectivist in the sense that, while he movingly conceptualises each participant in sex as needing, post-coitally, to be able to 'be alone in the presence of the other', he does not address the mutuality of sex itself.

Yet 'good sex' is hard to conceptualise other than from an intersubjectivist perspective, albeit one that can usefully incorporate Winnicottian notions. When sex 'works' (the repeated quotation marks are an acknowledgement of the normative implications of what is being conveyed) each partner incorporates (literally, as well as psychically) the other's body into his and her inner world and makes it his and her own. The pretend/equivalence mode distinction (see Chapter 2) – the separation between phantasy and reality – is temporarily obliterated. The contact barrier between self and other and between fantasy and reality is in abeyance. Each partner is, momentarily, both alone and fused with the other.

Sex, with its necessary 'regressive' aspects, here becomes a form of everyday creativity. In Winnicott's model, a mother anticipates her child's needs so that the infant has the temporary illusion of having 'created' the breast, which appears, as though by magic, just at the moment that he or she begins to imagine it. Similarly, in satisfying sex, each partner 'knows', before the subject herself or himself is aware, just what feels good – and not so good.

This view of the developmental origins of sexuality suggested here is a mirror image of the Kleinian perspective put forward by Britton (2005). Attachment suggests a sequence running: (a) secure, playful, psychophysical, mutually mentalising interaction with care-giver in infancy, (b) fostering general imaginative competence, (c) providing a developmental basis for the capacity for erotically imaginative adult sexuality. By contrast, Britton sees a phantasy of a good 'primal scene' – i.e. an inner imago of satisfying parental sex – as the *pre*condition for (rather than the outcome of) the imaginative function itself, including, presumably, sexual imagination. From an attachment perspective good sex follows from and is a manifestation of imaginative freedom; for Britton imaginative freedom is only possible in the context of a 'good' primal scene – a phantasy of parental intercourse neither obliterated by splitting nor damaged by envy.

The erotic imagination

Hedonic intersubjectivity can now can be linked to what Denman (2004) calls 'the *erotic imagination*'. Like all imaginative activity, erotic imagination can be seen as a form of 'free association', expressed not in words but in the image/emotion/sensation/proprioceptive amalgam that comprises sexual experience. There is a need to theorise the difference between 'masturbatory' sex (whether practised alone or with a partner) and 'good intercourse'. Both involve the imagination, albeit in pornography in a debased and potentially harmful form (via exploitation of those whose images are depicted). Devoid of the mutual excitement inherent in 'good intercourse', the need for stimulus in masturbatory sex becomes more and more extreme, and ultimately grotesque. The protective barrier between phantasy and reality remains unpenetrated, the post-orgasmic outcome inevitably a vacuous tristesse.

'Good sex' is characterised by the interplay of two erotic imaginations, feeding, playing, sparking, gyrating off one another. Good sex is 'thinking with the body' – in tandem. When a couple's sex life works well, each partner can freely follow his or her sensual/sexual feelings with the help of the other's body, which becomes a medium, each to each.

Good therapy has a similar quality – what Malan (1979) calls 'leapfrogging', where the patient's association sparks off a thought in the therapist, whose interpretive response enables the patient to leap one place further, and so on. Just as in sex the partners adopt different and often mutually exchangeable roles – containing/contained, exploratory/subsuming, fierce/tender, etc. – so too in therapy the different roles of patient and therapist facilitate the associative process. The rather surprising therapeutic implication of this suggests that learning to associate freely in therapy might enhance sexual capacity, just as we imagine the foundations of enjoyable sexuality to lie in the hedonic intersubjectivity of parent and child in infancy.

What are the possible barriers to the full expression of the erotic imagination? From an attachment perspective, a crucial impediment is the lack of a sense of security, since, in the absence of a secure base, exploration and imagination, including the sexual imagination, are necessarily inhibited. It is impossible to trust the object fully if there is an ever-present fear of losing it, and good sex is predicated on trust. In insecure attachment the avoidant child never fully locks into the mother because if he gets too close he runs the risk of rejection; ambivalent infants cling to mothers whose inconsistency activates fear of losing their attention. In these organised forms of insecurity the object at least *exists*, albeit one with whom ambivalence is never fully overcome. In disorganised insecurity the object as a separate entity with a life of its own cannot be fully formed in the mind (Fonagy et al. 2002), making mutuality even more problematic. Here survival strategies such as controllingness, dissociation, exploitation or malevolent aggression come to occupy the interpersonal field. In each case hedonic intersubjectivity is compromised.

Psychoanalytic approaches to sexual difficulties

Before moving into clinical accounts of sexual difficulties from an attachment perspective, I briefly list some well-established, and in some cases already mentioned, psychoanalytic conceptualisations of unconscious and defensive aspects of compromised sexuality as it manifests itself in the consulting room.

- *Difficulty in expressing 'healthy aggression'.* Psychoanalytic writers (e.g. Stoller 1979; Green and Kohon 2005) emphasise the importance of aggression in sexuality, perhaps because they wish to preserve Freud's binary concept of life and death instincts as primary, and bring both into play in eroticism.
- *Fear of 'transgression'.* Oedipally, the mother 'belongs' to the father and therefore to explore her body is to excite paternal wrath and potential castration. Feminist psychoanalysts have revised the female version of Oedipus, which is no longer seen as a mirror image of the classical oedipal situation with the sex roles reversed. A girl does not have to abandon her link with her mother in order to find her sexuality. Nevertheless she needs to feel that her father adores her and finds her beautiful, while at the same time seeing her sexuality as sacrosanct, and that she has her mother's blessing for this 'platonic' love affair with her father.
- *Physiological difficulty in tolerating mounting excitement.* The mother's ability to regulate her infant's affective storms via containment and mentalisation might be a prototype for the combination of excitement and security needed for satisfying sex.

- *Fear of engulfment.* Successful sex requires the ability to allow the self to merge into another, secure in the knowledge that a trusted other will not harm or control or enslave the yielded self. 'Smother-mothering' might be a precursor of this sort of anxiety.
- *Inability to tolerate separation.* Both Winnicottian and Kleinian perspectives imply that the capacity to tolerate loss is, paradoxically, an essential ingredient of intimacy. To 'have' an object inevitably implies the possibility of losing it. Losing the intimacy of sex must, post-coitally, be tolerable.
- *Fear of rejection by the object.* Narcissistic anxiety means that intimacy may be avoided for fear that one will be found wanting, unable to please the other.
- *Failure to differentiate healthy and unhealthy regression.* Sex is necessarily 'regressive' in the sense that it involves a move from mind to body, from rationality to emotion, from verbal to physical communication. If regression is felt to be dangerous (e.g. a fear of not being able to recover oneself intact), or conversely addictively alluring (a fear of returning to the mundanity of 'normal' life post-coitally) then sexuality may be inhibited or over-valued.
- *Lack of a good 'primal scene' imago.* Ultimately, for successful sex there needs to be a sense that coupling is 'good', and procreation productive – that they are infused with love rather than hate and destruction. This in turn links with the oedipal idea that in successful resolution of the oedipal situation the child has to be able to 'allow' her or his parents to have sex, and not to feel unbearably excluded or frightened when faced with a closed bedroom door.
- *Failure of healthy idealisation.* Money-Kyrle (1956) argues that there needs to be a sense that the embodied other remains beautiful and intact despite one's angry or envious attacks. The healing quality of sex is testament to this process, although sometimes it may lead to an unhealthy cycle of rows and rages followed by reparative sex, only to be followed by further disillusionment following the temporary bliss of pleasurable sex, more rows, etc.
- *Difficulty in accepting one's bisexual nature.* Rycroft (1985) links psychological bisexuality with creativity in that most artists combine in some form 'feminine' receptiveness with 'masculine' creative potency. Sexual empathy involves imaginative erotic identification with one's partner, drawing on and not being afraid of one's sexual shadow self.
- Eagle (2007) argues that there is an *inherent tension*, especially for males, between sexuality and attachment – between, in Freud's terms, love and desire. Sexuality is associated with excitement; attachment with safety and security and diminution of arousal. Long-term sexual object-choice involves a compromise or trade-off between these two contradictory needs; the predominance of one or other pole is associated with instability and pathology.

Clinical examples

Attachment-organised interactions provide a distinct, non-sexual 'platform' on which the fantasies associated with adult sexuality are built. The apparently abstract sub-categories of attachment can be seen as mentalised representations of physical relationships – characterised by fluidity, clinging-ness, distancing, or bizarreness of posture, and so on. Since the quality of parent–child interaction in infancy and childhood predicts the quality of young people's 'romantic relationships' (Grossmann et al. 2005), it seems likely that the nature of the early adult's sexual relationships will have been built on the foundations of childhood capacity for playfulness and mutually pleasurable physical interactions. Where this has been compromised, as it is in the differing patterns of insecure attachment, we might expect to find comparable difficulties in sexual life.

Contemporary psychoanalytic psychotherapy – in contrast to behavioural influenced sex therapy, or possibly to 'classical' psychoanalysis – does not focus on sex as such, but rather sees sex as part of the totality of a person's relationships. Those relationships may be more or less sexual, but unless the patient is specifically sexually dysfunctional, sex will be discussed mainly as a manifestation of relationships in general. Some patients talk a great deal about sex, others hardly at all.

In the hyperactivation pattern I suggest that attachment needs often masquerade as sexuality, and therapeutically the patient needs to be helped to differentiate one from the other. In deactivation the problem lies with either repression or exaggeration of aggression in relation to intimacy, both of which can compromise sexual relationships. The patient needs to be helped to healthy assertiveness, which in turn may have consequences for sexuality. In disorganised attachment, imaginative activity, including the erotic imagin-ation, is not clearly bounded off from reality, leading to either degraded or grossly inhibited sexuality. Here helping the patient to mentalise, and thus to differentiate action from imagination, can in time lead to less sullied sexuality.

Hyperactivation/mild disorganisation: Sex as an attachment 'hook'

Celia, 26, a US-born barrister working in the family division with divorce and child-care clients, had been depressed since student days and sought help, she said, to 'keep her going' through her stressful career choice. In addition, she had 'sexual problems' with her long-standing boyfriend. Sex was often painful, and she was subject to recurrent bouts of vaginal thrush. They had had behavioural 'sensate-focus'-type therapy for this, but with little benefit.

The older of two girls, she was the family high-flyer, a parentified child, keeping, as she saw it, the family in order. She strongly identified with her workaholic father, also a lawyer, and was, like him, an Ivy League graduate.

She saw her mother as a rather weak and insipid character, always trying to please others, with little identity of her own, suggestive of the frightened–withdrawn pattern of mothering seen in some children with disorganised attachment. She envied her younger sister who seemed to have escaped the family pressure to succeed. Celia was a self-appointed second mother to this feckless sibling, who, she felt, had found the elusive secret of enjoying herself and doing as she pleased.

Celia had been depressed at least since high-school days, and described how she would binge on chocolate while sitting for hours in front of the TV in a vacant state.

She presented in a mildly flirtatious way, as though saying 'I'm an attractive girl, in a bit of mess, please come and rescue me, I'm sure you would know how to overcome my sexual difficulties, unlike these inexperienced young men', while at the same time appearing quite unresponsive to my therapeutic interventions. It seemed as if, once she had 'got' me as a therapist, she could immediately distance herself from the process. She evinced in me a mild sense of rivalry and inadequacy.

A couple of months into once-weekly therapy she starting talking with worryingly clear plans about suicide when, having split up with her boyfriend, she almost immediately took up with another man, and once more developed a vaginal infection that prohibited sex. Before that she had been to several parties where she had, as she put it, 'pulled a bloke' – using macho vernacular of sexual liberation that somehow didn't ring true. As we explored this, it became clear that *the idea of being alone was insupportable to her*. Her only hope was to have a man, but, in her mind, the only way to keep one was to offer sex: no sex meant no man, which meant being alone, which meant that she would be better off dead.

Together we tried to formulate her difficulties.

1   Celia's fear of being alone was so great that that she was primarily in search not of sex, but of security. Her dyspareunia was a manifestation of her inability to trust her boyfriend as a secure base. Constantly fearful that he would find her wanting and leave her, she could not relax sufficiently to enjoy penetration. Her thrush, to the extent that it was a somatisation symptom, was also a way of testing whether her boyfriend could offer her the absolute security she craved without the reward of sex.

2   There were suggestions of disorganised attachment, and some 'borderline' features: her suicidality, and turning to food and the TV as substitute care-givers – typical strategies used in disorganised attachment to deal with an absent care-giver at times of threat and stress. Both soothe the self but at the expense of relatedness, and the possibility of secure exploration of her sexuality. Celia's controllingness was also a typical disorganised strategy in which, via role reversal, she managed her own

vulnerability by telling her mother, sister and legal clients how to lead their lives and loves.

3   Celia's sexual anaesthesia illustrates Britton's (2005) notion that in hysteria the sufferers vicariously identify with the parental couple from and of whom they feel so excluded and envious. Her own feelings got lost: in sex she *played the part* of a rapacious man or yielding woman, but was in reality self-estranged. Through sex she was able to make contact with the feelings of the other, as a substitute for being in touch with her own bodily sphere.

The main initial task for Celia was to develop a more trusting relationship with the therapist; this, it was hoped, would release her exploratory imagination as her need for security diminished. Her enmeshed/ambivalent attachment style meant that she had to hook me in via a kind of little-girl 'sexiness', probably without realising she was doing so. In the transference as in her external life, attachment needs were confused with sexual feelings.

Her borderline features, based on a putative disorganised attachment arising out of a frightened/withdrawn care-giver, meant that I needed to engage her actively through a combination of:

- *reassurance* ('If you are feeling really desperate you can ring me between sessions')
- *challenge* ('If he drops you just because you can't make love for a while, is he really worth having as a boyfriend?')
- *humour* ('Realistically, exactly what odds would you put on your ending up barren, loveless and in a nunnery?').

As therapy progressed Celia began to relax, and my uncomfortable countertransferential feelings of erotic manipulation and affective distancing receded. Her narrative competence (Holmes 2001) took off, and she began to talk more fluently, vividly and meaningfully about her feelings, including her sexual life. She was angry and sad when holiday breaks meant missed sessions – I became a person whom she missed rather than an object she needed to control. As she began to feel that her boyfriend cared about her as a person and not just a body, their sexual relationship improved and she was able to cope with her tendency to develop thrush infections without being plunged into despair.

I shall return to the initially worrying suicidal aspects of this case in Chapter 10.

Avoidance: Sex and aggression

Peter, a married teacher in his mid-forties, came for help with depression and a feeling that his marriage of 20 years was failing. He loved his wife and didn't want to leave her, but their sex life had waned and they seemed to have little in common these days.

Peter's father had left his mother soon after Peter's conception. His early childhood was spent alone with his hard-working mother, who frequently left him with child-minders, providing a safe but tough home routine in which there was little time for fun or cuddles. Later his mother married; Peter felt rejected by his step-father, especially when two half-siblings were born.

Peter was a friendly, apparently easy patient who nonetheless often left me feeling uncomfortable, as though something was missing from our sessions. It took him a long time to admit that he was having an affair with a woman, also married, whom he had met through work. Tentatively, he spoke about their exciting sexual relationship, but was clearly bothered by his need to 'dominate' and feelings of triumphant aggression while they were making love.

Two related themes came through in our work together. The first was his lack of identification with a strong father, and therefore his difficulty, despite his unequivocal heterosexuality, in asserting his masculinity. Somehow he saw both his wife and his lover as dominant – he had to fit in with their demands, whatever they were. Peter equated assertion with aggression, which he saw as impossibly destructive.

As suggested earlier, to achieve healthy assertiveness a boy needs to be able to hate and wish to eliminate his father – and for the father to survive and remain loving and proud of his son. This played itself out in therapy as Peter tentatively, and with encouragement, revealed his anger and disappointment with me at my various failings, particularly when, in an egregious rupture, I 'inadvertently' missed a scheduled session while on holiday – perhaps enacting my assigned role as an absent father or an overburdened mother.

Second, Peter's brusqueness and mild aggression were typical of those with avoidant attachment states of mind. Peter felt safe with his mother, but had always felt held at a distance by her. In his sex life his avoidant strategies had become eroticised in dominant–submissive sexual fantasies and enactments. As he was more able to allow himself to become appropriately angry with his therapist, but also with his wife for her withdrawal and preoccupation with her work and the children, his need to confine his anger within the walled-off world of his sexuality with his lover diminished.

Eventually Peter broke off the affair and told his wife about it. A huge amount of turmoil inevitably resulted, but they managed to stay together. Peter agonised over whether he and his wife could ever achieve the closeness he so desired, or whether he was doomed, as with both his parents, always to take second place. In one session he spoke about how in an attempt to repair things between them he and his wife had spent the weekend on an organised botanical ramble: a love of natural history was something they had in common. He then described how the tutor had focused on lichens and their biology – explaining that they were a symbiotic evolution from fungus and algae, which eventually results in the emergence of a new free-standing organism. Linking this apparently unimportant detail to his presenting problem, I suggested that this beautifully symbolised his situation: if he and his wife could allow themselves to get truly close, and be able to trust the outcome, then something genuinely new in both their lives could arise.

He reported in the next session how he had told his wife of my remark, and how they had laughed at my convoluted 'off the wall' interpretations. Looking back on my spontaneous comment I wondered if this was an attempt to invoke a 'combined parent' emerging into the psyche of this boy who had never had a mother and father who were close for any length of time, a manifestation of the mutuality of secure attachment. The imaginative leap from botanical expedition into bedroom and/or nursery was pleasurable both to me and to Peter and his wife. All three of us were caught up in hedonic intersubjectivity, harking back to an all-too-infrequent childhood playful interaction between Peter and his mother – the relationship with whom, incidentally, he reported had become more relaxed and less constrained recently.

Severe disorganisation: Sex as a perverse route to attachment

People suffering from personality disorders at the severe end of the spectrum almost invariably have concomitant disturbance in their sexual life. The self-destructive behaviours of people suffering from borderline personality disorder, which sometimes include risky, debased, unpleasurable, perverse or shame-inducing sexual activity, can fulfil a number of roles.

1   It may be a way of engaging the Other, albeit by resorting to dominance/ submission rather than mutuality – being a victim ensures a role, and some sort of protection, at the expense of pleasure or self-respect.
2   Any routine is better than total chaos.
3   Bringing together of sex and aggression means that the sufferer at least feels something – even if it is pain – and so escapes from feeling-less dissociation.
4   The shame of vulnerable neediness is re-enacted through degraded sex in a repetitive way, giving the subject an illusion of mastery.

These phenomena can be conceptualised in attachment terms as follows. A developmental precursor of borderline personality disorder (BPD) is disorganised attachment. Severe disorganisation is associated with a frightened/ withdrawn or intrusive/self-referential care-giver. The bizarre posturing and dissociative responses to stress seen in these children can be seen as attempts to create some sort of coherent strategy for self-soothing, often involving splitting of the self into a distressed 'part' and a care-giving part (Fonagy et al. 2002, cf. Chapter 10).

All this was evident for Andrea, an unemployed, single, childless woman in her mid-forties who came for help wanting to overcome her drug addiction and lack of a positive direction in her life. She had had a pitiful childhood history of care-giver neglect and abuse. As with many resilient children exposed to adversity, her saving grace had been a female teacher at school, on whom she had developed a 'crush', who had spotted her intelligence and potential and encouraged her to go to university. Once there, however, she succumbed to a drug culture and her twenties and thirties were characterised by frequent moves and sexual relationships with both men and women, including several episodes of rape and sexual exploitation. She described a relationship with a man whom she had loved from a distance for many years – and her hope that if only they could 'get it together' all would be well. Eventually they did go to bed, only for her to experience intense disappointment that the longed-for feelings of intimacy and happiness once more eluded her: she realised that, for him, 'it was just sex'.

She soon developed a 'crush-like' attachment to therapy, and gradually and very painfully began to describe the ways in which she had been sexually harmed. She found it hard to relax, often experiencing the sessions as an ordeal to be endured and from which to emerge unscathed by painful feelings, rather than an opportunity for safe exploration – rather like her experiences of sex. Any sense of hedonic intersubjectivity was painfully elusive. Typically for borderline patients, she could play with her beloved pet rodents – she had a large collection of rats and guinea-pigs – but not with the unpredictable and panic-inducing propensities of people.

One day she confessed that she 'loved' her therapist, and then clumsily blurted out 'I haven't had sex for four years now' (roughly the length of time she had been in therapy). I tried to respond to her comment in terms of attachment security as the necessary precursor of sexual enjoyment. I said 'Perhaps that is the length of time it has taken for you to begin to feel that to be close to someone would not inevitably mean a descent into misunderstanding, exploitation and degradation'.

For such people sex is a stark manifestation of self-negation – a sacrifice of oneself in the service of some sort of survival. Therapy will be about 'the negation of the negation' – holding back from the lure of self-destructiveness. In her statement Andrea was affirming at least the *possibility* that she could feel safe and sexual at the same time and this could be seen as a degree of progress. Eventually she did find a partner through the drug-reducing programme she attended, and their relationship had positive qualities of mutual support – their sexual life was restricted and rarely pleasurable, but at least non-exploitative.

To summarise the main points of this chapter, attachment theory makes a clear distinction between healthy and vulnerable developmental pathways, including problematic and non-problematic sexuality. I have questioned the psychoanalytic notion of infantile sexuality from an attachment perspective.

Nevertheless there is a mutually pleasurable aspect to the infant–care-giver relationship that I characterise as 'hedonic intersubjectivity'. I suggest that securely attached couples elicit one another's 'erotic imaginations' in ways that cement their relationship. That in turn has sexual-reproductive implications in that closely bonded couples provide a more efficient nurturing environment for their offspring than those that are insecurely attached.

For hyperactivating individuals sex can be a hook to establish attachment. Deactivating people may have difficulty in either bringing aggression into play in sex or keeping it at bay. In mild cases of disorganised attachment sex may be used as a way of activating dissociated feelings, often via the other's sexuality. In severe borderline personality disorders and disorganisation sexual pleasure is almost always compromised, and degradation and exploitation provide means of supplying a meagre degree of security.

Conclusions and coda

Attachment theory makes a clear distinction between normal, sub-optimal and potentially pathogenic developmental lines. Psychoanalysis paradoxically 'normalises' pathology by suggesting that perversion is a persistence of normal polymorphous perversity into adult life. In the Freudian worldview 'we' are all to a greater or lesser extent neurotic, and this applies especially to sexual life, since all have to negotiate the incest taboo and therefore the inherent ambivalence of the oedipal situation. Fonagy and Target (2005) continue this line of thinking with their suggestion that sexual relationships and 'borderline' personality disorder have in common an encounter with an unmirrored – and therefore potentially 'alien' – part of the self leading to a craving for, but also fear of, a mirroring other

Continuing with this contrast, I end this chapter with a poem by the happily married Georgian poet Edward Thomas. In my reading, it is a meditation on the delights and difficulties of conjugal sex.

After you speak

After you speak
And what you meant
Is plain,
My eyes
Meet yours that mean,
With your cheeks and hair,
Something more wise,
More dark,
And far different.
Even so the lark
Loves dust

And nestles in it
The minute
Before he must
Soar in lone flight
So far,
Like a black star
He seems –
A mote
Of singing dust
Afloat
Above,
That dreams
And sheds no light.
I know your lust
Is love.

Psychoanalytically the poem might be read as follows. Our highest feelings – love, the capacity for poetry and song, the sublime – cannot be divorced from the baseness of lust and dust: Freud accused Jung of trying to obliterate the importance of the 'bottom story' in the house of the psyche. Aron (2008) tells the story of how as a young analyst he was ribbed by a Freudian colleague: 'Oh you relationalists, you don't want to fuck! You just want to hold hands'. Fonagy and Target (2007) might suggest that, despite the comfortable domesticity of conjugal sex, there are questions nestling in the kernel of the poem – does the protagonist's 'you' *really* love him (or her); is theirs a lust that could be satisfied by any man (or woman)? The unanswerableness of this leaves the poet in the dark (Thomas suffered from serious depressions). No light can be shed on the question: when it comes to sex, he is no better off than the pre-borderline infant, deprived of a mirroring Other.

An attachment reading of the poem starts from the security of a good marriage: the fact that the poet *knows* his wife, nestles with her. This enables his poetic and sexual imagination to be released. His feet are on the ground; dust is the secure base from which he soars to explore his feelings. Their marital sexuality is as much 'above' as it is 'below'. Instead of an impasse that confuses and conflates attachment and sexuality, sex and love are two sides of a coin – held together, like a kite, by the ego of its earthbound flyer. They are linked each to each in a fluid, three-dimensional, flexible, interchangeable way, releasing the sexual and poetic creativity that comes with secure attachment, arising out of good developmental experiences or, when necessary, psychotherapy.

Chapter 10

Borderlining

One of John Bowlby's prime motivations in developing attachment theory was to bring scientific ideas to bear on what he saw as the intellectually sequestered world of psychoanalysis. There are analogies between the world of intimate relationships that is the object of psychoanalytic work and other unstable fluid systems such as weather formation, traffic flow and economic activity.

Recent thinking in those fields suggests that there is a reciprocal relationship in such systems between flux and 'information', using the latter term in its most general sense, and that smooth movement depends on information remaining in step with flow (Julian Hunt 2009, personal communication). Where they become disconnected, turbulence, or damming up, followed by violent discharge is likely to occur. A smoothly flowing river accommodates itself to changing contours by its sinusoidal and enveloping changes of current direction: 'Big Hole River talked with the land as it wound its way through the valley, collecting creeks as it went, quietly taking the path of least resistance' (Larsen 2009, p. 4). Traffic 'automatically' adjusts its speed according to the prevailing density of vehicles. But suddenly encountering a rapid decline turns a gentle river into a cascade. An unpredicted halt in traffic flow due to a crash 'backs up' and leads to stasis or further accidents. In these cases information and flow are out of step. In human affairs mentalising is the informational half of the action/reflection dialectic. Sudden catastrophic psychological events can likewise be traced to the disconnection between action and reflection. Nowhere is this more relevant than in the psychology of borderline personality disorder (BPD), where fragile mentalising capacities are regularly overwhelmed by sudden surges of affect.

Disorganised attachment and borderline personality disorder

The standard 'insecure' attachment patterns originally described by Ainsworth are not in themselves associated with psychological ill-health. They are better seen as vulnerability factors, which, taken with adversity, including genetic predisposition, can precipitate psychopathology. The links however between disorganised attachment and psychopathology are relevant and robust. Deactivation and hyperactivation of the attachment system can been seen as adaptive responses to sub-optimal care-giving. Disorganised attachment is, by definition, non-adaptive, and therefore a potentially pathological response to inadequate care-giving.

In this chapter I connect evidence about disorganised attachment with the clinical problems presented by people suffering from BPD. I look at the ways in which individuals whose attachment patterns are disorganised attempt to create some sort of security for themselves, however degraded, simplistic, distorted or self-defeating this may be. I also draw on attachment theory's capacity to discover meaning in the detailed analysis of minute segments of behaviour and to make interpersonal sense out of them.

I start by a brief recapitulation of the literature on disorganised attachment in relation to adult psychopathology, and BPD. 'D' was first described by Main and Solomon (1986) after reviewing a series of Strange Situation tapes of a group of infants previously categorised as 'unclassifiable'. The D category appeared to be stable over time, to be unrelated to temperamental factors, and to appear not infrequently in relation to one parent but not the other. The prevalence was relatively low in middle-class samples (14%) but Van Ijzendoorn (1995) found much higher figures in low socio-economic status groups generally (24%), and in maltreating samples the figure reaches 60%–70%.

Cortisol levels are higher in D infants than in controls, and these infants show decelerated development compared with controls even when maternal IQ is controlled for (Lyons-Ruth and Jacobvitz 2008). This suggests that we are looking here at a stressed and potentially disadvantaged group of children. D classification coexists with the other three attachment categories. The largest proportion of D infants showed ambivalent attachment (46%), while only 14% were secure and 34% avoidant. Crittenden (1985) sees in D features of mixed avoidant and ambivalent characteristics.

If D is a valid entity two questions arise: under what circumstances does the D pattern occur, and what are the long-term implications for the child of D classification? As previously discussed, one way of approaching the meaning of D is to see it as a response to an *approach–avoidance dilemma*, intrinsic to the very nature of attachment (Main 1999). Attachment theory postulates that a threatened or frightened child will turn to an attachment figure for comfort, security or reassurance. But if that attachment figure is itself the very source of the threat the child is presented with an insoluble problem. No consistent behavioural strategy will relieve the threat. There is no equilibrium point comparable to the situation in avoidant attachment in which the child gets close to the mildly rebuffing secure base – but not too close; or in ambivalent attachment, where the child clings to an inconsistent attachment figure.

What parental characteristics might lead to this approach–avoidance bind? The adult analogue of D is the 'unresolved' category on the Adult

Attachment Interview (AAI). 'Unresolved' is coded when the respondent shows 'signs of disoriented disorganisation when discussing potentially traumatic events' together with 'lost awareness of the discourse context'. Main's (1999) idea is that the care-giver – usually a lone mother – of a potentially D child is herself the subject to unresolved loss or trauma. This disrupts her capacity to focus on her care-giving role, which triggers painful memories from her own childhood. The care-giver is not just frightening, but frightened. She cannot maintain affective continuity in her own inner world, and so lacks the capacity to provide buffering for her infant's affective peaks and troughs. Hesse (2008) emphasises the 'dissociative' aspect of D in both child and care-giver, seeing the child as dissociated from the immediate environment and the insoluble fright/flight dilemma itself. In this model, the care-giver is triggered into a frightened state herself by the child's distress, dealing with this again by dissociation, thereby making herself all the less available to the child as a secure base.

Studying parents of D infants with the AAI, a meta-analysis of nine studies involving 548 subjects showed high correlation/effect size between parental unresolved attachment and child D status (Van Ijzendoorn 1995). Lyons-Ruth and her co-workers specify a range of care-giving behaviours likely to be associated with D, including: role confusion (parent uses child as surrogate parent); negativity; intrusiveness; disorientation; asynchronous mother–infant exchanges ('not being able to get on the same wavelength'); and apparently unmotivated emotional withdrawal.

The next piece of the jigsaw comes from follow-up studies of children classified as D at one year. Two such prospective studies have shown that there is a strong link between D and *controllingness* of children with their mothers and peers at age six or seven (Lyons-Ruth and Jacobvitz 2008). These children insist on role reversal with their care-givers, in which they make executive decisions, and are unable to engage in 'democratic' play. George and Solomon (1996) have further studied these children using picture completion methods and found that these controlling children find it hard to resolve frightening scenarios, responding with total silence, or stories illustrating passivity or catastrophe.

We thus can speculatively begin to build up a developmental picture of links between D and adult psychopathology as a series of stages:

1   parental unresolved/traumatised states of mind
2   the D infant caught in an approach–avoidance bind, with no secure base refuge when threatened either from without or by her own unmodulated feelings
3   The controlling six-year-old who has eventually found a security strategy based on role reversal and providing a pseudo-secure base for herself
4   repressed terror and inability to repair interpersonal discontinuities and loss, as revealed by picture completion studies

5   in adolescence and early adulthood an individual who is controlling, aggressive, unable to self-soothe when faced with emotional turmoil and loss, liable to dissociation, and unable to extricate herself from pain-producing relationships

6   compromised mentalising skills: overwhelming affect drives out the ability to mentalise, and not having been seen or treated as sentient beings by their care-giver means that such people find it difficult to 'read' their own or others' feelings

7   finally, a diagnosis of borderline personality disorder. Hobson and colleagues found that a group of patients suffering from BPD (as opposed to major depressive disorder) were almost entirely classified as unresolved/preoccupied on the AAI (P. Hobson 2002). This can be seen as a mark of non-mentalising in that they were unable to process emotional trauma, neglect or loss.

Note that at each stage there are possibilities for reversibility. The capacity for mentalising is likely to be a crucial component of resilience in the face of adversity, and a key objective in effective therapies in BPD.

Borderline personality disorder: Can attachment-informed psychoanalytic psychotherapy help?

Publicly funded psychoanalytic psychotherapy currently stands or falls by its capacity to help people suffering from long-term, complex and borderline personality disorders. It is clear that short-term treatments for BPD are ineffective. As discussed in Chapter 5, there is gradually accumulating evidence that long-term therapy can be beneficial. There is, however, some suggestion that 'standard therapies' (i.e. 'unmodified' medium-term therapy) may even make things worse (Fonagy and Bateman 2006). A starting point is to analyse why conventional and 'treatment as usual' approaches are potentially iatrogenic with such clients. Using the tripartite heuristic laid out in Part I, difficulties arise in each of three of the main therapeutic arenas.

Therapeutic relationship

Applying the Main (1999) conceptualisation of disorganised attachment to borderline patients, the sufferer, when faced with the possibility of intimate relationship, finds herself in an unresolvable dilemma, from which he or she 'escapes' (i.e. achieves temporary self-soothing and a degree of control over a chaotic inner and outer world) via pathological solutions such as withdrawal into a 'psychic retreat' (Steiner 2002), dissociation, bizarre experiences or self-injurious behaviour.

This goes some way towards explaining some of the difficulties BPD patients have in forming a therapeutic alliance. Attachment needs in such people are highly aroused, but difficult to assuage. Need is overwhelming, but meeting it seems impossible. Help is viewed with extreme suspicion, leading to either resisted engagement ('centrifugal' type) or excessive dependency ('centripetal' type). The patient finds it hard, particularly in the early stages of treatment, to adapt to the rhythms of attachment and separation inherent in the therapeutic process. Faced with this, therapists may find themselves enacting patterns comparable to those identified in mothers of disorganised infants (Lyons-Ruth and Jacobvitz 2008): fearful withdrawal ('this person keeps missing sessions, they're not really motivated and it's a bit of a relief if they drop out; to be honest they scare and confuse me'), or self-referential interpretations ('the patient is projecting his own aggression and despair into me, and insists on extra sessions as a way of controlling me'). Unsurprisingly, therapists are often viewed by their clients as unconcerned, abandoning, hostile or intrusive.

Meaning

Similar difficulties beset the elucidation of *meaning* for BPD patients. Clients are typically invited to think about *why* they did or felt such and such – 'what is going on' in relation to the therapist or therapeutic situation or significant other – and/or to listen to the therapist speculating about these issues and their putative developmental origins. For BPD patients such questions, however valid, may be experienced as either persecutory or incomprehensible. Like Miriam in Chapter 4, 'why' questions make the patient feel 'put on the spot', activating attachment anxiety, triggering withdrawal or thoughts of self-soothing via alcohol etc. They are anti-mentalising in the sense that they raise anxiety to a point at which it is impossible to describe or reflect on experience. The lapses of mentalisation identified as characteristic of the care-giver of a disorganised child mean that the BPD patient lacks the experience of 'the fundamental need of every infant to find his mind, his intentional state, in the mind of the other' (Fonagy and Target 1997, p. 683). Being understood, rather than leading to a sense of relief and deactivation of attachment, and triggering of exploration and companionable exploration, equates to having one's thoughts and feelings invaded, stolen or dictated. Interpretations may be experienced as 'mad', denigratory or pointless.

Change promotion

Thirdly, the idea of *change* itself is far from straightforward in BPD. Linehan (1993) argues that for such sufferers invitations to change habitual patterns of behaviour, however apparently self-defeating, are likely to be ineffective. Deliberate self-harm, the temporary comforts of substance abuse, the vicissitudes of chaotic relationships, affective oscillations between blissful fusion and feelings of fear and loathing, all serve a psychological purpose. They attempt to reproduce, albeit in pathological and partial form, some of the physiological aspects of a secure base: warmth, oral comfort, being held (Holmes 2001). Death or oblivion is sought as an all-accepting safe 'bourn', albeit one from which no traveller returns. Less self-defeating alternatives may appear to offer little more than a void or an impossible dream. Linehan's (1993) 'dialectic' involves offering patients a paradoxical 'change/no change' message. This ensures that self-esteem is maintained by acknowledgement of their having achieved a modicum of psychological survival, while at the same time inviting them to consider different methods of affect regulation and the development of the self-awareness needed to learn from experience.

Mentalisation-based therapy

Two of the best-known evidence-based treatments for BPD – dialectical behaviour therapy (Linehan 1993) and mentalisation-based therapy (Bateman and Fonagy 2004, 2008) – are stand-alone, tailored approaches based on, but markedly different from, their parent therapies, behaviour therapy and psychoanalytic psychotherapy respectively. Each, in different ways, attempts to solve the problems of alliance building and maintenance, of achieving stable 'meaningful' meanings, and of promoting change without undermining existing methods of survival.

   Bateman and Fonagy's (2004, 2008) psychoanalytically informed partial hospitalisation programme has produced impressive results. Their mentalisation-based therapy (MBT) approach has been strongly influenced by attachment theory. Initially it was thought that BPD clients lacked mentalisation skills, and therapy was focused around the need to foster these, with a strong emphasis on 'rupture-repair work' focusing on the therapeutic relationship itself and encouraging clients to think about what may or may not have been happening in their mind and the mind of others in potentially therapeutic 'living-learning' incidents (arguments in the day hospital, missing sessions, violent episodes, getting drunk or drugged, risky sexual activity, etc.). However, the evidence suggests that disorganised children do not entirely lack mentalising skills, although the development of them is delayed compared with secure children (Gergely 2007). It seems, rather, that in BPD sufferers arousal is often so overwhelming that it inhibits fragile mentalisation capacities, and it is this underlies the relational turbulence so typical of this diagnostic group (Jurist and Meehan 2008). Therapeutic strategies therefore need not just to incorporate mentalising skills training, both formal and opportunistic, but also to help sufferers with self-soothing and other strategies needed to reduce arousal ('pressing the pause button', mindfulness exercises, etc.).

Meaning out of chaos

BPD is a social/psychological construct rather than a diagnosis in the sense that 'diabetes' and even 'panic disorder' are diagnoses. It is bestowed when there is a confluence of psychological dispositions and social disruption – abrasive interpersonal relationships, maladaptive contact with professionals, etc. A sociological as well as a psychological perspective is needed. The ability of care-givers to provide security for their infants connects with the capacity – or lack of it – of society to care for its members. Social configurations such as endemic racism create fear in victimised minorities, and that fear transmits itself via attachment relationships to oppressed people's children. The salience of absent or abusive fathers in the life-histories of people diagnosed as suffering from BPD should not be seen merely at the level of individual psychology. The social seedbed for these negative male roles – colonialism and consequent immigration, educational disadvantage, the move from manufacturing to a service economy – needs also to be acknowledged, and if possible worked with as part of a historical/social understanding that clients can build up in course of therapy. Enhancing mentalising skills in BPD sufferers aims not just to help them better understand their own psychology, but also to raise consciousness of the choices and dilemmas faced by their progenitors in previous generations.

Attachment theory can be criticised for its over-emphasis on the role of mothers in fostering or failing to foster security and autonomy in their children. Many of these women are themselves victims of abandonment and abuse by males – fathers, step-fathers, spouses – whose contribution, direct or indirect, to psychological illness in their children needs to be acknowledged. A systemic perspective is needed if the complex matrix of relationships whose resultant is individual suffering is to be fully understood and mitigated.

When the Holocaust survivor, psychiatrist and founder of logotherapy Victor Frankl was asked in an interview about the meaning of his life, he replied 'The meaning of my life is help others find meaning in theirs'. But what does it mean to 'find meaning'? Psychotherapy approaches meaning from two different directions. First there is the religious/aesthetic sense of finding value and beauty in life and the world – a life worth living. Second, in the medical/scientific sense meaning implies a purposeful – whether useful or perverse – relationship between structure and function. In physical medicine the meaning, say, of chest pain on exertion may be a narrowing of the coronary arteries – but the angina sufferer may also come to value life more deeply as a result of his brush with death.

Psychotherapy similarly helps patients find meaning in their difficulties, in this case an individual, ideographic, personal meaning or life story. For example: 'I keep having difficulties in my relationships with women: based on my very mixed relationship with my mother, I simultaneously crave closeness and resent feeling controlled and so push my partners away'; 'I was terrified of commitment until the age of 30: my father died when I was five, so I am convinced that anyone I get close to will leave me'; 'The reason we have such difficulty in getting our daughter to go to school is that we don't operate as an executive couple'. In each case there is an implicit assumption of an underlying psychological structure that determines the functional difficulty – controlling care-giver, fear-of-loss schema, conflicted family executive, and so on.

Attachment theory, firmly rooted in a scientific perspective, likewise represents a quest for meaning, seeing distorted function in terms of underlying structures. But with its emphasis on language – and especially narrative style – as a mark or indicator of underlying attachment patterns, attachment theory also has an aesthetic/ethical aspect. As argued in Chapter 6, language cannot be reduced to its purely denotive function. There is an aesthetic dimension to the succinctness, relevance and appositeness that comprise 'Grice's maxims' upon which the Adult Attachment Interview is based (Hesse 2008).

Deidre in the PD clinic

Deidre was a twice-divorced woman in her middle forties. She had lived with her third main partner, Geoff, for the past 11 years. She had four children: the eldest, a daughter from her first marriage, with whom she has no contact; a boy and a girl in their late teens from her second; and a nine-year-old daughter by Geoff. She had been employed in the past as a care assistant but was currently unable to work because of depression and anxiety. She was referred to our personality disorder clinic by her community care worker because of worrying outbursts of rage and violence, and in particular an episode in which she attacked her husband with a brass candle stick, causing quite extensive, although superficial, head injuries.

She arrived at the clinic with Geoff, and clearly found it hard to separate herself from him the waiting area when invited to come to the consulting room. He was a large, reassuring man, obviously younger than his partner. I perceived her as petite, slightly overweight, with dyed black hair. She asked immediately for a glass of water before she was able to start the session. With some encouragement, she then told her story: a dismal childhood, her (according to her mother) violent and useless father having disappeared when she was two, leaving her with a mother who quickly remarried and had two further children. Deidre felt *de trop* from the start, and more so when her step-father began to abuse her – physically in public, and sexually in private. She left home as soon as she could and married the first man who would have her, who promptly got her pregnant and left her. She then met her second husband, which led to ten years of beatings and rape before she found the courage to leave him.

I shall focus on two key moments in the assessment interview. The first came after about half an hour. Deidre was describing the fact that she found it hard to go out of the house. Asked why, she let slip (or so it seemed) 'I keep catching glimpses of myself in shop windows – I hate mirrors'. At this point her bottom lip began to quiver. 'What is it about them that you find so difficult?' I asked. Silence. I let the silence hang for a few moments. She looked terrified, glancing at the door, and imploringly at me, as though she wanted to be let off the hook, released from some nameless horror. I tried to keep her on track. 'When you look in the mirror you see something frightening, something difficult to put into words', I suggested. 'I . . . don't . . . recognise . . . myself . . . who . . . am . . . I?' – the words came falteringly. We had established earlier in the interview that she looked like her father – when she asked her mother what her father was like, the only reply she could extract was 'look in the mirror – you're his spitting image'. 'So what you see reflected is a terrifying part of you that in your mind is like your father', I suggest. She nods, with a mixture of relief and despair.

The conversation then moved into less threatening territory and after a few minutes I suggested we bring in her husband, whom I then went to collect, leaving Deidre with my colleague who was the supervisor and observer in the interview. The moment I returned with Geoff she leapt to her feet and buried herself in his arms, sobbing furiously. They left the room for a few minutes to hug and cuddle until she was calm enough to resume.

How can we make meaning out of this story? Some of it is relatively straightforward. Bowlby maintained that the need for a secure base was not something we outgrow – seeing development in terms of a move from immature to mature dependence. At times of extreme stress we turn to our secure base whatever our age. The stress of the interview activated attachment behaviour in Deidre and, like a child in the Strange Situation, she needed physical comfort and reassurance from Geoff before she was able to face the threat posed by the team. She had in fact already signalled from the start, via her request for a drink of water, her vulnerability and bid for nurturance.

How would we characterise Deidre's attachment style? Her need for physical proximity to Geoff and difficulty in calming suggest a hyperactivation pattern, and this is consistent with her narrative style in the interview, which is rambling, discursive and overwhelmingly affect-laden. What about the story of the mirror and her difficulty in talking about it? Here we see the coexistence of a disorganised/incoherent pattern with hyperactivation. Her thoughts are confused. She finds it difficult to stay on track. She is in a state of extreme terror out of proportion to the context, and she describes quasi-psychotic and dissociated feelings – she doesn't recognise who she is and wonders if she is seeing her father rather that herself in the shop windows.

We can speculate that 'behind' this incoherent (in the technical sense) speech pattern there may lie unprocessed trauma (her mother's aggression, her father and second husband's abuse) that my insistence on keeping her on track (which in my countertransference felt quite abusive and bullying) may have activated. In order to avoid the eruption of this potentially disorganising constellation of thoughts and feelings, she narrows her behavioural repertoire and seeks the physical proximity of Geoff to provide the external secure base that she lacks internally.

What about the outbursts of uncontrollable rage towards Geoff, which have brought her for help? There are perhaps three aspects to this. First, like Harry Harlow's Feli (Fischer-Mamblona 2000), a goose deliberately reared without attachments that showed inexplicable episodes of aggressive behaviour when faced with fellow geese, they represent 'displacement activity' in someone who lacks a consistent behavioural strategy for dealing with problematic intimacy. She wants to be close to Geoff, but proximity triggers feelings of extreme panic in her; attack is a way of escaping from that dilemma. Second, in a more straightforward way she is punishing him for not being with her at all times – a standard attachment-influenced interpretation of interpersonal aggression, similar to our understanding of deliberate self-harm when faced with an 'attachment crisis' (cf. Chapter 11). Aggression here is essentially a negative reinforcement schedule designed to re-establish a compromised attachment bond.

A third aspect concerns the characteristics of spouses of people suffering from BPD. Many or most BPD sufferers manage to drive partners away, and instability of relationships is part of the diagnostic criteria for this group. Those whose relationships do survive often are married to people who are phlegmatic in the extreme, and usually highly emotionally avoidant. The attack on Geoff was both a desperate attempt to elicit an emotional response and at the same time an attempt to reassure herself that however outrageous her behaviour, he would stand by her.

Psychoanalytically, one could argue that when Deidre attacks Geoff the unconscious meaning of these actions is to be found in rage at the step-father who abused her, the father who abandoned her, the terrifying mother who failed to assuage her fears. Her outbursts could be seen as the desperate attempts of an exploited, ignored, overlooked woman to communicate her need to be seen, acknowledged, given due attention.

A final point concerns Deidre's emotional 'collapse' when talking about the shop windows. Her tears and quivering lip here were quite different to what happens when, for instance, someone is talking about a bereavement or loss in their life. There was an incongruity and suddenness with which the overwhelming feelings erupted. Compare this with the sudden change of mood that might be seen in a two-year-old, happily playing 'alone in the presence of the mother', when the care-giver goes out of the room without warning – to attend to a chore or go to the lavatory, for instance. The child may suddenly dissolve into tears and the narrative envelope of her play collapse no less instantly that it might for the audience if a fire-alarm went off in the middle of a theatrical performance. In Deidre's case and that of the child there is no sustaining internal care-giving presence – or mentalising function – that can soothe and smooth affective fluctuations. These un-buffered emotional states or failures of self-soothing are part of the core diagnostic profile of borderline conditions.

Psychotherapeutic implications

Psychotherapeutic work with patients suffering from BPD is notoriously difficult. Therapeutic effectiveness of dynamic psychotherapy is based on two main clinical tools. First is the therapist's countertransferential capacity to use her own emotional reactions in the service of the sufferer. Second, the ability to put those feelings into words – to create a 'language game' of shared meaning with the patient. Both can be compromised when working with borderline patients.

The eliciting of powerful countertransference is in itself almost diagnostic of borderline states. Anyone who has worked with such patients will recognise feelings of rage, anger, exasperation, murderousness, intense pity, desire to rescue, erotic arousal, wish to extricate themselves from the relationship and many other intense emotional reactions in themselves. These feelings are usually understood in terms of projective identification, and in the Klein–Bion model represent the projection of the patient's primitive unmodulated feelings which have failed to be metabolised by care-givers and therefore cannot be re-introjected by the individual in a transmuted form.

Adding to this an attachment framework, we can postulate that an interpersonal situation akin to infancy is recreated in the consulting room in which the supposed care-giver (the therapist) is potentially distracted from her secure base function by powerful, preoccupying and potentially terrifying emotions. The trauma of a non-mirroring care-giver is reproduced in the therapist in the thrall of strong feelings and so unable to reflect accurately the patient's state of mind – despite the fact that those feelings were evoked by the patient. The pressure on the therapist to 'act out' – to enact her controlling, angry, loving, rejecting or all-embracing feelings in some way – is insistent. Like the D care-giver, therapists become frightened by their own fear and seek to evacuate it through action, or become subject to role-reversal pressures and try to use the patient as a receptacle for their own intolerable countertransference feelings. There is an attempt to impose pseudo-organisation on a chaotic situation, thereby deepening the split in the patient's inner world between control and the unmodulated chaos and terror that lie beneath.

A similar dilemma exists with the use of words in working with BPD patients. Clearly words are fundamental to organisation and resolution of painful feelings. The human voice in itself can be soothing; a bedtime story sends us to sleep safely until morning; telling the history of a life provides objectification and verification, imposing meaning on seemingly inchoate events and feelings. But for the BPD patient words are also a threat, arousing painful memories, counteracting defensive strategies and threatening to lay bare naked fear and panic. As suggested in Chapter 2, this can be understood in terms of the BPD patient operating within 'equivalence' as opposed to 'pretend' mode. In equivalence mode a word directly *evokes* an experience rather than being a *representation* of it, and therefore is associated with over-whelming affect, rather helping to process and master feelings.

Somatisiation and the failure of mentalising

A further vignette illustrates this point. Annabelle was a middle-aged woman referred for psychotherapy after she had had a series of fits for which no neurological basis could be found. She told me that the fits were very worry-ing to her because she believed she was having some sort of stroke, that the right side of her body was becoming weaker and weaker, and that she would be unable to carry out her role as carer for her disabled husband. She described his progressive rheumatological condition, and their son who had had a very bad motor bike accident recently, and her daughter who was involved with an unsuitable man. She made it clear that she and her husband never argued and that it was important to her to have a placid family life since her childhood had been so dominated by conflict.

When I then asked her about her upbringing and her parents there was the typical change in breathing patterns and eye-glazing of the 'unresolved' attachment pattern. She suddenly blurted out the story of how her father had murdered her mother and had been in jail for 10 years, that she had been ostracised by her siblings because she refused to believe that he had done it, and how after his release from jail he had threatened her, so that she had decided to have nothing further to do with him either.

At this point I tried to summarise the situation by saying that I thought she had suffered a huge amount of trauma and loss in her life and that it was entirely possible that this was what underlay her 'turns', since the body has strange ways of making its feelings known. No sooner had I said this than she began to 'fit'. Her eyes because glazed; she started to shake, especially on the right side of her body; her lip curled upwards; and she appeared inaccessible. The episode lasted for about a minute, after which she seemed drowsy and slow in her movements.

From a neuropsychiatric point of view, this was probably a 'pseudo-fit'. From an attachment perspective it was a psychosomatic response to what felt like a psychological assault, one that activated a neural network established on the basis of previous trauma. As Van der Kolk (2003) puts it, 'the body keeps the score'. From the point of view of our discussion it had some of the features of disorganisation described by Main and others in D children in the Strange Situation – bizarre posturing, stereotypical behaviour, incongruent affective response. This response emerged immediately after a com-ment from me trying to link disparate and inexplicable events – an attempt to move towards organisation and meaning. The patient was in an approach–

avoidance dilemma: the move towards meaning has the potential to increase her sense of security and continuity, but at the same time the words themselves arouse terrifying memories of trauma.

What then is to be done? How can we prevent 'D dilemmas' from reproducing themselves in therapy? The answer, if an answer there is, lies in mentalising, or 'thinking about thinking', and its differentiation from 'pretend' and 'equivalence' modes. In the case of overwhelming countertransference feelings the therapist has to be able to contain them – i.e. to recognise them for what they are without suppressing, dismissing or acting on them. To do so requires a high degree of affect regulation and mentalising capacity – the very skills that psychotherapy training aims to enhance in its students, via personal therapy and supervised practice. The therapist has to be able to see countertransference feelings, and the actions they stimulate, not as 'real', but as symbolising a need or inner state of the patient, and to be able to put this conjecture into words.

Let us say that a therapist is working with a patient who has been severely sexually abused, and that the patient is able to describe the 'facts' of what has happened, but without attendant feelings, and that the therapist finds herself experiencing disgust and rage and starts to imagine offering to accompany the patient to confront her abuser. To do so would, I suggest, simply evoke the typical D response in the patient – panic, embarrassment, dis-empoweredness and a wish to regain control. Instead, the sensitive therapist might say something like 'It sounds like these are feelings that it is very difficult for you to face on your own, but that to do so with another person brings up huge feelings of shame – so you are damned if you do, and damned if you don't'. The therapist takes her own responses as reflecting, representing or symbolising the emotional state of the patient. By introducing a 'conversation about conversation' the therapist is initiating the BPD sufferer to the possibility of a shared language of intimacy.

The patient needs to be offered not just words or meanings, but words about words, and meanings of meanings. Rather than in an *ex-cathedra* way suggesting that the patient's fits represented her unresolved trauma, it might have been better to have said something along the lines of 'We *could* talk about the pain and trauma you have been through, and this might help reduce the frequency of your fits, but it also might increase them because we would be approaching such painful topics which you have effectively buried for a long time'.

Helping on the borderline

PD (personality disorder) patients find it difficult to sustain a stable sense of the self and other as having beliefs, desires and intentions. This puts them at a grave disadvantage in interpersonal relationships, and may influence their problematic relationships with care-giving institutions. One of the functions of therapy with people suffering from BPD is to offer a 'thinking mind' that can plan, intervene, and take a perspective on them as persons, in which mentalising is a central component. But to do this on one's own is hard. Any organised *service* for people with difficult, complex or borderline disorders requires a *team* focused on mentalising and its related notion of *holding in mind*. The hope is that this 'holding in mind' function may eventually be internalised by the PD sufferer as a self-reflexive capacity that in turn will enhance their interpersonal life. What is being offered to these patients is continuity of care in its deepest sense. The nature of BPD means that it tends to vitiate attempts to create such continuity. The emphasis on engagement, consistency and long-term commitment is an attempt to mitigate the disruptive features that are so characteristic of the condition, and that tend to bedevil conventional psychiatric, psychotherapeutic and social service attempts to offer help to BPD sufferers.

Findings about care-givers of secure children (see Chapter 7) suggest that the secret of security lies in the combination of mentalising empathy and mastery. For the BPD sufferer an effective service will have: (a) clear lines of authority (e.g. deciding when a BPD sufferer needs a spell in hospital); (b) an unequivocal sense of who is 'holding the baby' at any given period; (c) demarcated role-distribution so that the therapeutic function (helping the client to understand and mentalise self-defeating behaviours) and the management function (helping the sufferer to cope with medical, financial, risk-assessing, housing, recreational, educational and other aspects) are kept separate; (d) good and regular communication between the various professionals involved, including the reflective capacity to examine countertransference and to see how the client's inner world of splitting and projection may be played out among the various team members. Without such an organised service psychotherapy on its own is likely at best to be ineffective, and may even make things worse. In such situations half a loaf may well be worse than no bread.

Before continuing with this topic in relation to suicide, an ever-present threat in the lives of those suffering from and working with borderline, I turn for a moment to another inescapable borderline issue – blame – starting with a trivial but, it is hoped, light-relief example of the ubiquity of this theme.

Blaming the victim

The 'Aga', that now ecologically unsound icon of British country living, is a kitchen stove designed by a Nobel-Prize-winning Swedish engineer, Gustaf Dalén. It is a robust and handsome machine that rarely goes wrong. When it does develop problems, however, the very fabric of middle-class rural life is undermined. Getting the thing repaired becomes an urgent necessity.

When ours started overheating, George, the 'Aga man', was with us in under an hour. 'No problem. We'll have that fixed in no time.'

Several hours later he was still struggling to get it relit. Eventually he succeeded, brushing his hands together as though to indicate that he was glad finally to be rid of us, and set off up the road in his van. Actually it had been a productive visit. I had learned quite a lot about the workings of the stove and he, in turn, discovering my profession, had chatted movingly about a recent bereavement in his family.

Two hours later the Aga had gone out again. George was phoned on his mobile and back he came to the rescue. More adjustments of oil-flow and electronic timing mechanism and he was off again, although this time I had detected slight cracks in his normally affable and helpful manner, as he muttered about worn screw heads and an inaccessible inlet pipe.

A hot bath that night was a delight and a relief, but by morning tragedy had struck once again, as we came down to a once more defunct stove. With trepidation, George was again recalled. He was friendly enough to us, but now, as he knelt before the four-square domestic goddess, his irritation turned to fury as he cursed first those who had installed it in the first place and then the machine itself, which he decided was inherently faulty, an obvious 'Friday afternoon' job at the factory, and a thoroughly typical example of overrated Scandinavian design.

It was at this point I decided that we had a 'borderline' Aga.

(George had done his best, but when, a few days later, the Aga stopped working again we turned to a different repair man, who finally got to the bottom of the problem – no more or less than a faulty thermostat.)

The term 'borderline' is much bandied about by psychotherapists, not excluding the present author. It has become synonymous with 'difficult' patients, suffering from 'personality disorders' – i.e. long-term difficulties in relating dating back at least to adolescence, and seeming to be deeply ingrained in the personality.

'Borderlines' can be problematic. They defy the rules of normal medicine – i.e. to cooperate docilely with what is offered, spend a defined amount of time being 'ill', and then gratefully recover thanks to the wonders of medical science. They are often described as 'disruptive', 'manipulative', 'antisocial', 'self-destructive', 'bad news', 'heart-sink patients'.

While there is no doubt some descriptive truth in some of these epithets, it is clearly an example of 'blaming the victim'. They have almost always had emotionally impoverished and/or abusive childhoods. This repeats itself when they come in contact with helping agencies such as psychiatric departments.

When something or someone – an Aga or a 'borderline' patient – fails to respond to our ministrations, we start, often subtly at first, to blame them, rather than examining our own contribution to the situation or looking objectively at what is happening. Being able to notice and think about that tendency is a necessary mentalising skill. Working in psychiatric settings with very difficult clients, I found that releasing feelings of frustration and impotence with colleagues prior to an encounter with clients often made for a smoother session than did a po-faced, ethically pristine, doctorly posture. Exploring one's 'hatred' in phantasy strengthens rather than breaches the 'contact barrier' between phantasy and reality, making one better able to empathise with the client's confusions. If George had vigorously complained to his wife about what difficult clients we were, he might have had a better chance of getting to the bottom of the Aga problem.

When I first went into psychiatry, 'schizophrenogenic mothers' were blamed for the major mental illness of schizophrenia. Such parents, it was claimed, were cold, unresponsive and a source of such confusing emotional messages, or 'double binds', that their offspring had little choice but to go mad. Similarly, mothers and fathers of autistic children were described as 'refrigerator parents'. Today we see the destructive effects of such attributions, and how they can only add to the huge pain of being the mother or father of a mentally ill child. We can also begin to see their origin in our own relative inability to understand intractable psychosis, and denial of objective factors such as genetics, just as George began to blame the Aga when his normal procedures failed to cure the problem.

I am not arguing against the need for holding oneself and others responsible when things go wrong. Working out who is to 'blame' is an important psychotherapeutic task. 'To understand all is to forgive all' may be a final state of wisdom to which all might aspire, but a lot has to happen along the way before such equanimity can be achieved.

Jean and the unforgivable

Jean had a horrible childhood in which she was brutalised and sexually terrified by her domineering and perverse father. Her mother was a weak bystander, unable to restrain her husband's cruelty. The early phases of therapy consisted mainly of gradually exploring the details of how he had hurt Jean, physically and emotionally. At one point we began discussing her father's background, and it emerged that he had had a very difficult time, both his parents having died when he was 10, and then more or less having to fend for himself at a time when facilities for orphaned children were nonexistent or riddled with exploitation.

When I gently, as I thought, suggested that 'We can begin to see what it was in your father's background that led him to treat you so badly', Jean was furious: 'Don't ever you dare to try to exonerate my father like that'. I realised that I had slipped into the role of the mother who had failed to protect her from her father, and that Jean needed to feel angry with her too, rather than, as previously, simply protecting and identifying with her.

I tried to use this rupture on my part to suggest that perhaps she was angry with her mother for staying with such a monster and not shielding her children from him. This in turn led Jean to be able to distance herself from her mother, with whom I felt she was rather over-involved.

Over the years Jean seemed to make slow progress in therapy, and for every step forward there would be one or two backwards. She was dependent on me, and her sessions, and led an unconventional, rather solitary life. I frequently had to restrain myself from expressing feelings of annoyance and frustration with her – probably unsuccessfully since Jean was highly sensitive to nuances of emotion. I had to learn to accept that her way of life was valid for her, even if it didn't conform to my imposed views about how a patient 'should' get better, i.e. be able to find a satisfying occupation, enjoy intimate relationships and eventually see a diminishing need to come to therapy.

In this I came to see the ways in which I was rather like her father, angrily and blamingly imposing a view of how his children 'ought' to behave and grow up, rather than accepting them as they were, and indeed seeing that cultivating quirky individuality was the only way to evade his tyranny.

Only several years later in therapy, and with the help of an aunt who told her that, whatever their later difficulties, her parents had been very much in love at the start of their marriage, was Jean able to begin to see things from her father's point of view (he had had a horrible time as a prisoner of war during the Second World War), and begin, partially at least, to forgive him.

Jumping to blame, labelling the victim, stigmatising and 'othering' – all of which are the everyday fate of the traumatised – is an ubiquitous and reflex defence, especially in response to the threats such people pose, either directly or to our sense of efficacy as professional helpers. As therapists it is important to recognise the subtle manifestations of the blame mechanism in ourselves, and to try to strike a balance between holding ourselves appropriately responsible for our failings and being able to forgive ourselves.

Although science seeks meaning in the sense of the causal connections, scientists also celebrate the intrinsic beauty and meaning in the pattern and form in nature that the search for causality reveals. Similarly, when patients struggle to lessen the disorder in their lives, both in the wider sense and at the micro-level of emotional regulation and interpersonal relationships, their appreciation of the value of life and its meaningfulness in the aesthetic/religious sense also seems to deepen. By putting us often painfully in touch with chaos and disorder, borderline patients help us to value connectedness and continuity, and to redouble our efforts to maintain them in the face of forces of disintegration and destruction.

Chapter 11

Suicide and self-harming

Suicide attempts and deliberate self-harm are commonplace in the lives of the borderline clients. They are also the actions most likely to cause alarm and concern in services aiming to offer help to them. Suicide is one of the most mysterious and most challenging of human behaviours, outside the usual range of expectable human behaviour.

As with infanticide (Hrdy 1999), an evolutionary perspective can help clarify what is at stake. In animal analogues of suicide in ground-nesting birds, an 'altruistic' outlier will endanger its own life by luring predators away from chicks or other vulnerable members of the flock. Evolutionary biology reconciles this apparently maladaptive behaviour by invoking the 'selfish gene' hypothesis, in which, based on 'rational' calculation, an animal will sacrifice its phenotype for the sake of its genotype, embodied in those to whom is related, thereby enhancing the overall chances of its genes surviving into the next generation (Dawkins 1978). As the great mathematical biologist J. B. S. Haldane is said to have replied when asked whether he would 'lay down his life' for another: 'yes, if he were an identical twin brother, or for two of my children, four of my grandchildren, eight of my great-grandchildren'.

The idea of altruistic suicide is firmly embedded in human culture, ranging from Graeco-Roman 'honour' suicide to Japanese kamikaze pilots and the wave of suicide bombings, not all Islamic, that is such a salient feature of modern guerrilla warfare. Genetic survival here is transposed to the social level, where the lives of one's fellows, whether genetically related or not, are at stake, thereby ensuring survival of one's group and its value-system. A key British end-of-empire narrative is Scott's 'failed' 1912 polar expedition, in which Scott's companion, Captain Oates, realising that his weakness was hazarding the entire mission on its homeward journey, left the tent for the blizzard, never to be seen again. His parting words – 'I'm going out, I may be some time ...' – are synonymous with heroic self-sacrifice in its Anglo-imperial guise.

In contrast to this evolutionary view, suicide is claimed by some as a uniquely human potential, an existential consequence of 'free will' (Camus 1955). This existential view of suicide founders in most instances on the fact that most people who commit suicide are not doing so in an autonomous state of mind, but in one compromised by psychiatric illness. 'Psychological autopsy' suggests that at least 90% of suicides occur in people suffering from mental illness, predominantly severe depression. People who kill themselves are not, it seems, exercising their human right to take their own lives, but do so 'while the balance of their mind is disturbed', as British legal phraseology has it.

Mentalising suicide starts from the crucial distinction between the *idea* of suicide and the act itself. 'The thought of suicide is a great comfort: with it a calm passage is to be made across many a bad night' (Nietzsche, quoted in Alvarez 1973); 'Suicide is the only thing that keeps me alive ... whenever everything else fails, all I have to do is to consider suicide and in two seconds I'm as cheerful as a nitwit. But if I could *not* kill myself – ah then I would' (Walker Percy, quoted in Gabbard and Westen 2003).

Thinking *about* suicide at difficult moments in one's life is existentially normal, and at times even helpful. By contrast, moving from suicidal thought to action is an act of destruction, the negative effects of which almost always far outweigh any putative crumbs of benefit. Suicidal people may feel that by killing themselves they will no longer be a 'burden' to their loved ones, but, except under exceptional circumstances such as intractable and unbearable terminal illness, the pain of bereavement from suicide far outweighs the temporary relief it may bring. At the moment of self-extinction suicide may appear to the sufferer to be the only possible exit from an impasse. But the unconscious is never still: as feelings fluctuate depression lifts. If suicide can be staved off, suffering in the trough of despair is almost invariably succeeded by lessened mental pain.

Underpinning the mentalising perspective is the implicit paradox that the capacity to think *about* suicide is likely to reduce its occurrence – even if the consequence of that thought is a form of denial, saying to oneself in effect 'I'm not under any circumstances going to go down that route'. Conversely, *not* being able to talk and think about suicide may make it more, rather than less, likely. Finding ways to develop a 'suicide narrative' enables death-preoccupied sufferers to talk about, rather than enact, suicidal impulses.

The concept of the suicide narrative is compatible with a number of different theoretical perspectives (cognitive, psychoanalytic, psychobiological), all of which view the suicidal act as the end-result of the impact on the mind of a chain of 'events', each of which may constitute a severe narcissistic blow (a row with or losing a partner, loss of a job, overwhelming mental or physical pain, the collapse of one's projects, bankruptcy) or 'non-events' (the missed letter in *Tess of the D'Urbervilles*, the telephone call that didn't happen). Reconstructing that narrative chain and the sufferer's psychological reactions – conscious and unconscious – to those events is the precondition for understanding the suicidal act itself. The suicide narrative attempts to find meaning in the inchoate life-experience integral to suicidality, to 'make sense' of incomprehensible and overwhelming negative affect (and perhaps even 'unbearably' positive feelings – knowing that intensity of feelings inevitably wanes, lovers say to one another at the height of passion, 'Shall we die right now?').

Therapeutic approaches to suicide aim to deconstruct the justification and pseudo-rationality of suicide as an 'answer' to a person's difficulties, but must guard against dogmatic imposition of another set of partial meanings. Each perspective tends to have its own favoured explanatory framework: psychoanalytic (suicide as a covert form of murder), cognitive (suicide as an over-generalisation from present hopelessness) or neurobiological (serotonin depletion). The mentalising perspective implies wariness about over-enthusiastic espousal of any specific theoretical approach.

In general, suicide can be seen as triggered by disturbance in, or collapse of, an individual's attachment network. With no one to turn to when threatened, one becomes, like self-blinded Oedipus expelled from Thebes, intensely vulnerable. Death is imagined as a preferable alternative to extreme emotional isolation. People whose attachments are compromised are ready targets for bullying and exploitation, thereby exacerbating existing feelings of non-belonging. 'Outsiders' lack a secure base within their social group, and are potential targets for prejudice and attack. Loss – of country, loved one(s), status, health – renders a person doubly vulnerable: first through the psychobiology of bereavement itself, and second because what is lost represents the very person or group to which one would resort at times of loss and unhappiness. Seen developmentally, the lack of an internalised secure base in childhood resonates with the lack of a secure self in adult life. Affect regulation is problematic: there is no one there to help mitigate overwhelming feelings, and one has few positive regulatory experiences from the past on which to draw. When mental pain becomes insupportable, there is no stable internal self to draw on for comfort and soothing.

Shame, emphasised by Schneiderman (1993) in his pioneering studies of the psychodynamics of suicide, is a feeling of being a pariah, unwanted and unacceptable to one's social group. In shame one cannot bear to be seen – one's defences are stripped away; one becomes, to return to *King Lear*'s Poor Tom on the heath (a scenario of absolute insecurity), 'the thing itself . . . a poor, bare, forked animal'. People suffering from psychotic depression are often suffused with shame. They feel naked and vulnerable, bereft of the possibility of re-finding the comfort of a secure base. Failure of mentalising – of the ability to see depression-distorted thoughts for what they are – can bring a person to the pseudo-rational, 'altruistic' view that his family would be better off if he were 'out of the way', 'not around'.

An attachment perspective sees suicide, failed suicide and parasuicide/deliberate self-harm (DSH) as lying on a spectrum, rather than distinct entities. In every completed suicide or serious suicide attempt there is still the hope of survival, however minuscule, whether this be after death in the post-death narrative (see below) or a last-minute quirk of fate or spin of the Russian roulette wheel that will pluck life from the jaws of death. There is always the faint hope of the unexpected telephone call, the pills that fail to reach their lethal dose, the noose-knot that slips. Equally, DSH, while often apparently trivial – a handful of pills flung back in the midst of an argument – still *plays* with the idea of death, and, especially if repeated, statistically greatly raises the chances of 'accidental' or semi-accidental death. Clinically, it is wise to assume that all DSH sufferers want at some level to die, and that all 'serious' suicidal people, somewhere in their deepest being, have not entirely given up on hope and life.

DSH is frequently seen disparagingly as 'attention-seeking', which indeed it is, but in a way that attachment theory makes meaningful. When an attachment bond is in jeopardy the care-giver or care-seeker, or sometimes both, react with protest, anger or rage. Protest in the face of separation is healthy: in the Strange Situation securely attached infants complain vigorously when their care-giver leaves them in an unfamiliar room for three minutes, but are smoothly soothed on reunion by a mother sympathetic to her child's angry distress. This provides, as already suggested, a negative reinforcement schedule whose purpose is to re-establish the attachment bond, and discourage future threats to it.

Self-injurious behaviour is an analogue of this healthy protest, but here the insecurely attached sufferer feels unable to direct their anger at the attachment figures for fear of further alienating them. The attack is therefore displaced onto the Self and the body, thereby eliciting care-giving behaviour indirectly. 'Playing dead' (or 'possum') – e.g. going to bed with a sub-lethal dose of tranquillisers – can be a way of staying 'safe' until danger has passed and a care-giver is once more available: the row passed, the partner's arousal sufficiently subsided to return to a care-giving role. After an overdose attempt leading to hospital admission, the estranged parent or partner is not infrequently to be found at the patient's bedside chatting cheerfully, often to the fury of the hospital staff (the client's anger now safely projected into them). The DSH episode has worked its magic and normal attachment relations, including the ability to mentalise, with arousal levels lowered, may well have been restored.

How does the basic attachment typology apply to working with suicidal people?

Suicidal behaviour in 'organised' insecure attachment

Deactivating and hyperactivating attachment strategies are 'organised' in that they represent predictable pathways for maintaining proximity to a sub-optimal care-giver. A deactivating individual tends to have had a parent who, while reliable and 'loving', to a greater or lesser extent rebuffed bids for closeness. By minimising attachment needs, security is achieved, albeit at the price of partial inhibition of freedom of exploration and emotional expression. Such people tend to have a 'dismissing' narrative style clinically and on the AAI. When interviewed following a suicide attempt, they may find it hard to describe in any detail the antecedents of the attempt or what they were feeling at the time: 'Oh, it's all over now, I don't really want to think about it'; 'It just sort of happened, I can't really think why I did it, something must have come over me'. They may well fail follow-up appointments.

The hyperactivating person has had a care-giver, no less loving, who tended to be inconsistent and forgetful. Under these circumstances, a good way to get noticed when stressed, and therefore to feel safe, is to escalate attachment needs, to cling, to make one's presence felt. These individuals tend to have 'preoccupied' narrative styles, to be prolix, to find it hard to tell a coherent story and to leave the interviewer feeling overwhelmed and confused. 'Well, it all goes back to when I was 12 and I went on holiday with my friends and felt really left out and fat . . .'. Post-suicide attempt interviews with such clients may be difficult to terminate, and there may be frequent 'between' session bids for proximity, telephone calls and desperate attempts to contact therapist when another crisis arises.

Compared with deactivation, DSH is more commonly seen in hyperactivating individuals, hypersensitive to inattention, for whom *Sturm und Drang* is emotional small change, and who react with panic and therefore heightened attachment behaviours at slight relational ruptures, misunderstandings or minor rows. Deactivators may be more impervious to relational disruption and therefore less prone to DSH. However, avoidant people can, when faced with loss, sometimes 'flip' into a highly needy state in which long-warded-off vulnerabilities suddenly hit them with full force, leading to an apparently 'out of the blue' serious suicide attempt, sometimes tragically 'successful'.

Disorganised attachment, borderline personality disorder and suicide

Suicidal and self-injurious morbidity is an integral part of the syndrome of borderline personality disorder (BPD). Female borderline sufferers will often have made several overdose attempts, their arms criss-crossed with razor- or scissor-inflicted scars. Their male counterpart may have harmed himself while drunk or drugged, and may have accumulated more violent injuries such as self-inflicted cigarette burns, broken bones and missing body parts. Suicide is a significant cause of premature death in BPD, and reduction in suicidal behaviour is an accepted indication for the success or otherwise of therapeutic strategies (cf. Bateman and Fonagy 2008).

Two suicide-relevant features link disorganised attachment and BPD:

difficulty in affect regulation; problematic mentalising. In disorganised attachment the psychobiological attachment procedures for dealing with arousal are disrupted. A distressed care-seeker has a care-provider who is unable to respond effectively and predictably to her infant's distress. The child is thus left with 'un-mirrored' and potentially overwhelming negative affect. Fonagy et al. (2002) suggest that this un-mirrored negative affect may be experienced as an indwelling, potentially terrifying 'alien' part of the self. The unmentalised child is himself unable to mentalise/visualise his feelings. He withdraws into 'pretend' mode, or is trapped in 'equivalence' mode. He is lost in a nightmare realm of phantasy, or assumes that his perceptions and fears about other people correspond to the real state of affairs. He cannot easily differentiate thoughts and feelings from reality. In both, failure of mentalising is closely linked to difficulty in affect regulation. Overwhelmed with feeling, rational thought is driven out.

Transposing these patterns to adolescent and adult BPD sufferers, suicidal and self-injurious behaviour can be understood in attachment terms. BPD sufferers often have hair-trigger emotional responses, easily tipped into rage or terror by minor stimuli and, in a hyper-aroused state, unable to think clearly about their own and other people's feelings. They operate on the 'equivalence' assumption that whatever they feel, *is*. The 'alien' self may be experienced as an inner voice or demon, urging the sufferer towards self-harm. This injunction feels utterly 'real', and only with difficulty can be seen as part of the self – perhaps an angry abused, outraged vengeful aspect.

An important feature of serious suicide attempts is the period of calm that survivors describe as arising once the decision to kill oneself has been taken. Out of an affray of chaotic feelings, a clear pathway suddenly becomes visible. Death becomes the 'strange attractor' (Gleick 1987) that finally enables unbearable arousal to subside. The fragmented Self suddenly coalesces around the suicide project. A solution to the insoluble problem of living with un-mirrored pain suddenly emerges. Acknowledging the pull of suicide in this way is an important part of working therapeutically with BPD suicide survivors.

Therapeutic strategies with suicidal borderline clients

As argued in the previous chapter, each of the three components – attachment, meaning-making and change-promotion – of successful therapy is problematic for the suicidal borderline client. Attachment needs in people suffering from BPD are highly aroused but difficult to assuage. Therapists and other mental health workers are often viewed by their BPD clients as unconcerned, abandoning, hostile or intrusive. Watts and Morgan (1994) found that prior to suicide in hospitalised patients there is an escalating premonitory period of 'malignant alienation' in which client–staff relationships deteriorate. Feeling misunderstood, the client may make a suicide attempt in a desperate attempt to get staff to grasp the depths of his or her despair. The idea of change itself is threatening. Less self-defeating, healthy alternatives appear to offer little more than a void or an impossible dream.

In BPD sufferers arousal is often so overwhelming that it inhibits fragile mentalisation capacities; this is what underlies much of the relational turbulence so typical of this diagnostic group. Suicidal behaviour is most likely to emerge when arousal is at its height, and may, in a perverse way, serve to regulate unbearable affect. Therapeutic strategies need both to incorporate mentalising skills training, both formal and opportunistic, and to help sufferers with self-soothing and other strategies needed to reduce arousal. Examples include states of emotional arousal or upheaval, for example when the client is upset by something that happens in the therapeutic environment and immediately flares up or threatens to walk out. Staff can help by asking the client to 'press the pause button' (cf. Bateman and Fonagy 2004), and collaboratively try to think about what has happened (including staff acknowledging their own contribution to the client's distress), before making any hasty decisions. The mindfulness exercises that are part of Linehan's dialectical behaviour therapy programme similarly aim to instil affect regulatory habits that can then be deployed when the going gets rough or hot.

The psychoanalytic notion of 'attacks on linking' (Bion 1967) as a feature of severe psychological disturbance is consistent with these current attachment views on mentalising. When in a state of arousal the BPD sufferer is cut off from his thinking capabilities. Psychotherapy offers (which is not the same as saying the offer can always be taken up) to help its clients move to a more coherent inner life, in which feelings and thinking work in concert, in the context of an enduring link with a care-giving other. Therapy offers the possibility of a secure base – albeit one that will inevitably at times be compromised and whose repeated repair will form a vital part of the therapeutic process – out of which more coherent, organised forms of relating both to oneself and others can emerge.

The diagnosis of BPD encompasses a wide range of difficulties and severity; no single treatment is appropriate to the generality of clients. Below, I arbitrarily divide my comments into therapeutic strategies appropriate for three 'types' of client: (a) the 'high-functioning' borderline who can be contained within the normal parameters of out-patient psychotherapy, whether privately or publicly funded; (b) the severe borderline suitable for intensive therapy within an defined 'programme'; and (c) the 'treatment as usual' client unsuitable for, or unwilling to undergo, intensive treatment, for whom avoiding iatrogenesis is the main therapeutic aim. I shall give illustrative clinical examples in each case.

Out-patient psychoanalytic psychotherapy with suicidal clients

The more suicidal and disturbed the client, the more shared-care is desirable. Alongside the therapist, the client needs a key worker whose job it is to manage suicidal episodes, including, if necessary, arranging hospital admission. The therapist needs to feel that it is someone else's job to keep the client alive, while her role is not primarily life-saving but rather helping the client to *understand* why he or she does not wish to live, and to mobilise the life-affirming aspects of the Self that do want to survive.

Early formulations of indications and contraindications for brief dynamic psychotherapy (e.g. Malan 1979) listed suicidality as a contra-indication to psychotherapy. The nostrum that 'there's no such thing as emergency psychotherapy' still applies. If psychotherapy is about mentalising, and if high arousal drives out mentalising, then the anxiety associated with acute suicidality means that low-key listening, flexibility and 'management' rather than formal therapy are what is needed at this early stage. In the immediate aftermath of an acute trauma, the evidence suggests that counselling and therapy may make things worse.

It is wise, however, to assume that each and every psychotherapy client is potentially suicidal. A medical school history-taking rubric is relevant here. To the question 'Do you beat your wife?' the answer is likely to be 'No, of course not, how could you imagine such a thing?'. On the other hand the probe 'How often do you beat your wife?' might elicit the reply 'Oh, only twice a week'!

'What part does suicide play in your thinking?' or 'How near to suicide have you been and are you now?' are questions that every depressed, sad or bereaved person needs to be asked, even if the expectable answer is 'I couldn't do it to my children' or 'I think about it a lot but haven't got the courage'. Indeed, it may be a mark of narcissism never to have at least contemplated suicide; conversely, to be able to mentalise one's suicidality can be an indicator of psychological health. Therapists should be 'acquainted with death', comfortable (if that is the right word) with the reality that when people feel awful or psychotic they do sometimes kill themselves, and able to broach the subject without qualms, although also without prurience.

Implicit in the message of this chapter is the incompatibility of full mentalising and a suicidal act. Even in the absence of formal psychiatric illness, the balance of a suicidally acting person's mind is from this point of view *always* disturbed. To mentalise is to be aware that thoughts are 'just' thoughts, and that the intrinsic fluidity of the mind and of objective reality means that alternative possibilities and outcomes are always feasible.

In suicidal states, one of the three pre-mentalising states of mind outlined in Chapter 2 is likely to hold sway. Many acts of deliberate self-harm can be seen as 'if/then', telelogically-driven: 'If I cut my wrist, I know I'll feel better'.

Swallowing pills or acts of self-destruction become incorporated into a behavioural regime in response to threat or stress, in which the mind is bypassed in the rush to the temporary physiological relief of the 'pathological secure base' (Holmes 2001). Bateman and Fonagy's (2004) prescription 'push the pause button' attempts to halt this process and help the sufferer to think about the feelings that subsume the actions and to contemplate possible alternative outcomes.

Unlike in teleological thinking, in 'equivalence mode' suicidal people are conscious of their thoughts, but take their insufferable mental pain and no-way-out viewpoint for the only possible reality. Gustafson (1986) recommends tapping into clients' 'best and worst moments': therapists working with equivalence mode clients will intuitively help them get in touch with memories of good times as well as bad. The meditation strategies integral to dialectical behaviour therapy and cognitive therapy for depression aim, through calm detachment, to help people distance themselves from their miserable thoughts. For psychoanalytic therapists, an interpretation, if non-dogmatically delivered, is intrinsically mentalising in that it offers another possible perspective on the client's sense of a hopeless cul-de-sac, embedding it in a wider set of meanings (to stay with the metaphor – moving 'upwards' into a vertical dimension is an escape route from a two-dimensional dead-end).

Logical Celia, in Chapter 8, equated security with having a boyfriend; having a boyfriend with sex; being unable to have sex as inevitably losing her boyfriend; being on her own as equivalent to death; thus suicide as the preferred option. Being helped to see that she was confused in her mind between security and sex, and linking this with a frightened/withdrawn mother in childhood, with consequent role reversal in which she became estranged from her own vulnerability, helped reframe her suicidality as the search for security.

In 'pretend mode' reality is radically abandoned. The sufferer withdraws into a world of make-believe where anything is possible. The pre-suicide period of calm supervenes in which the sufferer, after a period of tortured confusion, suddenly and chillingly 'realises' that there *is* a way out – into the arms of death. Everything falls into place, the miserable messiness of real life is finally outflanked: 'I will be out of pain, my poor family will be rid of me, the psychiatric services will have me off their backs', thinks the suicidal person.

Working with such states of mind requires the therapist to have one foot in the world of fantasy, one firmly planted in reality's camp. The importance of fantasy is acknowledged and played with. In the 'post-suicide narrative' we ask: who would attend the funeral? Who would be most, who least, upset? What music would be played? How would the world move on? Such probing will gradually uncover the deep wishes that lie beneath the suicidal act – the longing not just for oblivion and escape from pain, but to be recognised, cared-for, valued, reconciled, to be helpful and generous and loving, to overcome bitterness and hate.

All this may be played out within the therapy itself. A suicidal act between sessions may look like retaliation for the feeling that 'You are just doing your job; you don't really give a damn whether I live or die'. Within that is the wish that the suicidal act will at last force the therapist to care, or to understand the extent of the client's mental torment. There may be a feeling that the therapist, with her imagined happy family and economic security, doesn't and can't really know what it is like to suffer. The suicide attempt becomes a last-ditch attempt to get the therapist to know what it is like to feel a failure, to be overwhelmed with a sense of loss and emptiness and futility. The therapist must be able to see all this while still holding onto her knowledge that the consequences of suicide for the survivors are invariably those of multiplied rather than extinguished misery.

A practical point concerns frequency of therapy, and the impact of breaks in working with suicidal people. Mentalising is a means by which separation and loss are endured, a bridge across the inevitable fractures and ruptures intrinsic to intimacy. Secure attachment makes the insecurity of detachment bearable. But the mental representation of security fades without reinforcement. Absence makes the heart grow fonder – but only for a while; out of sight, out of mind all too easily takes over. Therapists need to have a sense of how long a suicidal client can survive without contact, and to be aware that this may vary depending on circumstances.

The 'good breast'/secure base of therapy may naturally wane or be mentally obliterated by the client who feels abandoned at the end of a session, just as they themselves were abandoned by an absent, distracted, abusive or intoxicated parent. If holding a secure base in mind lasts only 24 hours, then daily therapy is needed, and support over weekends needs to be thought about and planned for. If a week is too long, another therapeutic contact, with a GP or community key worker, needs to be organised between sessions. Similarly holiday breaks need to be covered by a co-therapist. Attending to the transferential meaning of an absence and its consequences for the client is necessary but insufficient; 'mastery' is needed too, seeing the limits of therapy and its place in the overall context of the client's life – and potential death (for a tragic instance of the failure of this precept, see Holmes 1997).

Intensive mentalisation-based therapy for selected suicidal borderline clients

Managing suicidal risk is a key task for psychiatric services. For the reasons outlined, general psychiatric services are not well geared to meet the needs of borderline clients, and indeed often exacerbate their difficulties, by either 'over'- or 'under'-involvement, echoing adverse developmental experiences of this client group. A specialist personality disorder clinic can help redress this,

offering assessment for 'difficult' clients, either followed by specialist treatment in selected cases or helping to maintain and diminishing iatrogenesis
in others. The following example, already briefly mentioned in Chapter 2,
comes from an assessment interview carried out in such a service for people
suffering from BPD. Towards the end of the interview mentalising capacities
emerged that were a positive indication for specialist therapy.

Peter's nemesis

Peter was an in-patient on an acute psychiatric admission ward. The ward
staff were at their wits' end about how to help him. Some thought he was
manipulative and destructively dependent and should be discharged; others
thought he needed a lot of help, but didn't know how to get through to him.
He had been detained in hospital for several months thanks to his tendency
to gouge his arms repeatedly with knives, especially when drunk. He was 26
and had been in and out of hospital for eight years or so. His main 'career'
had been as a psychiatric patient, diagnosed as suffering from alcoholism,
depression and borderline personality disorder.

Peter was referred to the clinic to see if there was anything that could be
done to break this cycle of self-harm and prolonged hospital admissions, and
no real sense of progress.

He was a rather engaging young man with a nice smile, who, it turned out,
was a good guitarist and in his teens used to have his own band (I routinely
try to tap into client's strengths as well as difficulties). But he conveyed a
sense of defeatedness and despair as well. He couldn't see a way forward, and
was acutely aware of the difference between his state and that of the average
28-year-old. He seemed rather proud in a 'macho' way of his ability to drink
vast amounts of cider, and to tolerate the pain he inflicted on himself when he
punched walls and cut his arms.

At assessment he described a typical episode. He was on the ward and
wanted some pills (he took a lot of drugs, both prescribed and illicit). He
asked a staff member for some 'as required' medication, but his request was
refused. He felt an upsurge of rage, got into an altercation and stormed off
the ward and out of the hospital. As he walked down the road he found
himself crying and feeling utterly miserable and desolate. Then a suicidal idea
formed in his mind. He felt calm at last. He went to the nearest shop, bought
some razor blades, made for the public toilets, where he locked himself in and
cut his wrists. Eventually the police, who had been alerted to his disappear-
ance, found him and he was returned to hospital.

I reflected his story back to him as follows: 'You want something badly,
relief from tension; you can't get it; you fly into a rage with your depriver;
beneath the rage you feel utterly alone and abandoned; then your anger
focuses in on yourself and your body, the only thing that seems to be within
your control; you go somewhere where you are alone, a place of primitive

bodily needs; finally your plight is recognised, at least partially, and you are rescued'. (This droning monologue flatly contradicted the dictum that interventions, especially with borderline patients, should be short and to the point – tabloid headlines, not a broadsheet editorial; Bateman 2000, personal communication).

A faint, semi-triumphant smile flickered across Peter's face, almost as though he had been 'found out', caught red-handed putting his hand in the till of his own life. 'Yep, that just about sums it up' he replied laconically, as if to say 'You clever people may try to "understand" me in your own way, but it's not going to make the slightest difference to me'. The response to this 'interpretation' illustrates how, in a non-mentalising state, therapeutic efforts can be experienced by the client as irrelevant or 'mad'. The client seems impervious to understanding, and yet understanding is what, above all else, is needed.

Peter had told us earlier about his parent's dreadful rows throughout his childhood and how he used to steal away up to his room, and cover his ears with the pillow in order to block out the screams.

I went on: 'Perhaps that lonely public toilet is reminiscent of you alone in your bedroom with the rows going on all around you. Cutting yourself is an attempt to block out mental pain and helplessness by inflicting physical pain on yourself.'

I asked him if he felt that anyone on the ward understood him. No one, he insisted.

'What about your "key-worker"?' (whom I knew to be an excellent nurse), I asked.

'Oh, she just thinks I'm a waste of space like everyone else', he replied.

'Do you really mean that?'

'Well, I don't suppose she really does; it's just the way I feel about it most of the time.'

This illustrates the combination of empathy and challenge that is needed to foster mentalising – in this case perhaps no more than a brief glimpse of it – in borderline patients. Neither on its own is sufficient. The patient needs to feel secure: that he is being listened to, non-judged and understood. Only then is he in a position to reflect on his affective experience. Challenge in therapy implies close involvement with clients, not letting them evade painful topics, holding them so that they can begin to face the implications of their behaviour. None of this is likely to be successful in the absence of secure attachment, which lowers physiological arousal. Mentalising requires tolerance of vulnerability – feeling safe enough to risk the possibility that one might get things wrong, recognising that emotion can drive out reason. Peter's response to our interventions at assessment gave us sufficient hope to refer him for the intensive day programme for such clients.

Being supportive while avoiding iatrogenesis in 'treatment as usual' clients

In our own service, out of 49 borderline clients followed for two years, about a third were thought suitable for specialist treatment; the remainder were contained within existing 'treatment as usual' services (Chiesa et al. 2004). The latter group are often people entrenched in dysfunctional relationships, including with the psychiatric team, for whom DSH is a way of life when faced with emotional or practical difficulties. In response to my routine question about whom they would turn to in a crisis, or if they found themselves in hospital, say, after an accident, they might typically reply 'Oh, I'd contact my key worker/the ward/my psychiatrist/the hospital' – a sure sign that, for good or ill, they are deeply enmeshed in the healthcare system. What follows is a typical, if extreme, example. It also illustrates the attempt to remain supportive in the face of onslaught, and of the therapist's self-mentalising as a route to survival with difficult clients.

Susan's masks

It is Friday evening, around 5 p.m. I'm in my car, on my way home at the end of a long week. My cell-phone goes off. It is the hospital switchboard.

'Dr Holmes?'

'Yes.'

'Are you the duty doctor this weekend?'

Reluctantly I am forced to admit that this is the case.

'The out-of-hours social worker would like a word with you.' I draw into a lay-by.

'It's about Susan X.' Already my heart sinks a little. I know Susan well. She takes time, and patience.

'Her friend came into the office today saying she was very worried about her. Susan has sold all her belongings, given away her cats, says she's moving out of her flat. She may well be suicidal. I think we ought to do an assessment.'

'How soon can you get there?', I ask.

'Not for a couple of hours I'm afraid. We're very busy this evening.'

'OK. I'll go straight there. Come when you can. If I can persuade her to be admitted voluntarily I'll ring you. We better line up the police. Susan doesn't take kindly to being forced to do things against her will.'

I've known Susan for some time. She doesn't like me much. I suppose the feeling is mutual, to an extent. She frequently comes to consultations drunk or drugged. She has a way of getting me to do things for her, often against my better judgement: write letters to the council about her accommodation, arrange for the health authority to pay for expensive therapies that in my view don't seem to change things much and prescribe large amounts of medication which I don't really believe in.

Perceptions of her vary. Some people see her in a much more positive light. She is certainly intelligent and resourceful, and she has had a hard life. She was sexually assaulted in her teens. She has an eating disorder, and her weight swings wildly between being pretty huge and absolute starvation. She has made numerous suicidal overdose attempts, as well as frequently cutting her wrists.

I am rather feeble in my dealings with her, and tend to pander to her by misguidedly 'rewarding' bad behaviour, for the sake of a quiet life: a short-term benefit that only makes for trouble later.

I arrive at her house. She answers the door, her face conveying a curious mixture of fear, cunning, triumph and disgust. I explain why I have come, that 'we' are worried she might be suicidal, and feel we should 'do a mental health assessment', talk to her and see if we can help in any way. All this is a bit false, since she knows, and I know, and she knows I know, that when the sweet-talking is over I have the power to make her come into hospital against her will in order to save her life. She also knows that she can 'get' me to do this, making her into the victim, me into the aggressor.

She invites me in. The flat is orderly, tidy, quite tastefully decorated. Hoping to gain her trust, I compliment her on her artistic sense. She is composed and seems quite 'normal'. She offers me a cup of tea, which I decline, although I realise it may seem churlish to her.

I ask her if it is true that she is planning to move away, and has got rid of her beloved cats.

'So what if I have?', she responds defiantly.

'What's going on? Why have you suddenly decided to up sticks?' (using a metaphor makes the comment less persecutory perhaps).

'There's no future for me in this town.'

It is all a bit vague. I feel I am being blocked at every turn.

I raise the 'S' word: 'Are you feeling suicidal? Does life seem worth living? Perhaps you are thinking of doing away with yourself.'

'What if I am? It's a free country.'

Now it becomes my duty to decide if she is 'mentally ill'. Only if she is a danger to herself or others, and is suffering from a mental illness, have we the legal right to detain her against her wishes.

She doesn't seem all that depressed – but, I think to myself, maybe she really is depressed but pretending to be normal. But if she can do that, doesn't it mean she *is* normal? – like Joseph Heller's *Catch-22* in reverse, where if airmen could simulate madness in order to avoid lethal flying missions in the Second World War, they were by definition sane.

I ask about her sleep pattern, appetite, powers of concentration, whether she is feeling miserable.

'You know damn well I feel miserable. I've felt like this for years!', she snaps.

I decide to appeal to her better nature. 'Look, why don't you come into hospital so we can have time to think about all this' (using mentalising as an ethical principle here).

'No way am I going into hospital. No chance. Why don't you leave me alone and let me lead my own life?'

'Or death?', I think to myself. Outwardly calm (I hope), I am inwardly confused and frustrated. I keep thinking there must be some way to persuade Susan to come into hospital voluntarily, thus giving us a chance to evaluate her suicidality, and give her a breathing space. Surely I can persuade her, thereby avoiding the unpleasant business of police and social workers and getting a GP to come and all of us signing the 'Section' papers? That way she will become involved in her own care – surely a good thing. Not to mention that I will inevitably be late home. Anyway, where is that social worker?

But at this moment it is Susan's will pitted against mine, and she is pretty determined to get her way, which, it is becoming clear, is to get us to Section her. Then she will be a victim and will be able to disown the part she has played in creating this situation in the first place. We will have in a sense 'raped' her. I remind myself of one of my psychiatric dictums – in the last analysis, 'the patient always wins: it's their life that is at stake, only our job' (I note the 'them and us' language, the polarisation that I feel Susan has forced me into).

Now I begin to see how I am subtly becoming more and more unsympathetic and hostile to Susan, confirming all her prejudices about psychiatry. It is as though we are being shaped by two unconsciousnesses, over which neither of us has much control. In her case she will have created a situation in which those who are supposed to be helping end up insensitively controlling her – she can then turn round and say 'There you are, you see, no one gives a damn about me; all they want is to bang me up, and tick their risk assessment boxes'. In my case I must face the possibility that behind my desire to help and be a 'good doctor' there is aggression, a need for a payback for my previous feeble pandering, and to impose my will on the situation.

While all this is going through my mind I find myself scanning the walls of her room. Suddenly I notice that they are covered with masks in all shapes and sizes, mostly African.

'I like your masks', I venture.

'Been collecting them for a long time. What of it?' Susan defiantly replies, but I sense that her mood has slightly lightened by the diversion.

'They are helping me to understand what is going on here. I see you as a woman of masks. There is your "Section me if you dare" mask, your "I am a competent and independent woman so why don't you just leave me alone?" mask, but I wonder if there isn't a "I feel miserable and helpless, and just don't know if I can bear to go on living" mask beneath all the others, which isn't a mask at all but how you are really feeling right now.'

This did seem to hit home a bit. Tears came into Susan's eyes, and at least I had momentarily manoeuvred us away from hostility and battle.

Just then the doorbell rang. It was of course the social worker, the GP and two very young-looking police-people. Susan retreated to her bedroom and despite the police's valiant efforts to persuade her to 'come quietly', the upshot was that she was in the end 'Sectioned', since we didn't think it would be right to leave her on her own over the weekend in such a vulnerable state.

As I had feared would happen, she remained in hospital for several months before more suitable placement for her in a hostel could be arranged.

This was not an outcome to be particularly proud of. But the mask image had been helpful and continued to be so during her hospital stay. Whenever I found myself feeing annoyed I would think of Susan's masks and the simple idea that that what we present to the world is only part of the story, or indeed may be totally divergent from what we are feeling inside. It reminded me that my job is to help people feel better able to *face* the world, and thus to mirror, rather than mask, true feelings (cf. Wright 1991). It helped me to mentalise my own reactions to Susan, even if it didn't help her much. We could be justifiably accused of iatrogenesis – i.e. making a bad situation worse – since by 'manipulating' us into Sectioning her, Susan disowned her own contribution to her difficulties, and enacted rather than mentalised her misery. With such entrenched borderline clients perhaps all that can be hoped for is that staff are aware of their mistakes, rather than blindly making them, which at least gives the chance to learn from them in the future. That is the essence of the value of mentalising.

Conclusions

After her beloved elder brother's death in a drowning accident in 1840, Elizabeth Barrett Browning entered a period of irreconcilable mourning, lightened finally when a friend gave her a spaniel puppy, Flush. The second half of her sonnet, *Grief*, reads:

> . . . express
> Grief for thy dead in silence like to death –
> Most like a monumental statue set
> In everlasting watch and moveless woe
> Till itself crumble to the dust beneath.
> Touch it; the marble eyelids are not wet:
> If it could weep, it could arise and go.

In states of grief, when searching and protest have exhausted themselves then comes the despair so accurately described by Barrett – the stasis of 'moveless woe' and 'everlasting watch'. If 90% of suicide is caused by depressive illness (Lonnqvist 2000), and at least 70% of depression is the sequela of present or childhood loss (Brown and Harris 1978), then loss and grief are key underlying themes in most suicides. The suicidal person has reached the nadir of despair, but is unable to envision and so hope for reconciliation and recovery. Suicide happens when there is no psychic home, no secure base, when one cannot weep and therefore is unable to 'arise and go'.

Bowlby blazed a trail in his account of the psychological consequences of the breaking of affectional bonds (Bowlby 1981). A current loss reawakens an earlier one (perhaps the loss of a parent) that can be seen as a 'narcissistic wound' – a blow to the very fabric of the self. In response, relationship is denied, self-sufficiency sought instead. Unlike the pain of living, death appears to be within one's control. However apparently rational, this is a breakdown of mentalising. Thought is ultimately relational: as we saw in Chapter 6, ideas need to be 'checked out' with others before action, to see if one's perception of reality corresponds with another's (Cavell 2006).

The precondition for suicide is the breakdown of that consensual flux. Attachment bonds have been broken, either in the immediate situation (the row with the loved one) or developmentally (the non-mentalising care-giver whose child cannot therefore self-mentalise). Mentalising is the antithesis of stasis. Thought is always mobile, provisional, subject to 'visions and revisions' (Eliot 1986), expressing points of view, not final versions. Therapy with suicidal people tries to help them to see their all-too-real suicidal thoughts as products of a loss-wracked imagination, suicidal plans as merely possible pictures – not concrete maps of an immutable reality.

Unmentalising, the suicidal person *knows* that death is the answer. He cannot or will not consider other possibilities – that 'this too will pass'. It is the job of a therapy team to build or rebuild the capacity to visualise of a life that could be lived – and/or to keep the patient alive until that becomes feasible. The therapist becomes the Other against whom the suicidal person bounces his suicidal thoughts – a responsive reflexive surface, strong yet sensitive. The patient's hope denied is located temporarily in the therapist – for safe keeping. As a citizen I defend the right of clear-minded individuals to take their own lives; as a therapist I strenuously resist that impulse when manifested in my patients. By entering into a therapeutic dialogue with the suicidal person I maintain the *other point of view* that is the essence of mentalising. Psychiatric folklore maintains 'that where there is depression there is hope': even the worst depressions eventually remit, to some extent at least. By jointly elaborating a suicidal narrative, the ever-shifting dialectic of thought and action is exposed for the sufferer to reconsider. Mutual mentalising with a therapist opens up non-suicidal pathways for enduring and overcoming suffering.

Chapter 12

Dreaming

Psychoanalysis struggles to justify an explanatory system in which many different interpretations of any given clinical phenomenon are possible (cf. Wallerstein 2009). Freud's metaphor for the process of 'condensation' in dreams (Freud 1900) – compressed pack-ice, in which many meanings are somehow jammed together – is attractive but it too needs to be 'unpacked'. As discussed in Chapter 1, given the multiplicity of available psychoanalytic models, the problem of finding the 'right' interpretation in any particular clinical circumstance cannot be glossed over (see Tuckett et al. 2008), fuelling the struggles for authenticity and authority that characterise psycho-analytic politics.

Tuckett et al. advocate Bion's ideas of 'polysemy' (many meanings) and 'unsaturation' (openness to elaboration) as antidotes to dogmatism (cf. Ferro 2006). From an attachment perspective multiple meanings are a mark of secure–autonomous narrative style. Matte-Blanco (1975) speaks of 'the unconscious as infinite sets'. In the *spielraum* of the consulting room, or indeed *any* intimate discourse, dialogic possibilities – stories, images, meta-phors, tropes – are unlimited (cf. Ferro 2006). The more secure the therapeutic base, the more able the patient will be to explore the varieties of experience. Bollas (2009, p. 127) sees the unconscious as 'infinitely questioning':

> it would seem that we are endlessly curious about why we think what we do. Our thoughts and feelings are constantly raising questions, which we proceed to work on, most of the time outside consciousness.

Silence – the space into which that questioning is invited to burgeon – is similarly subject to polysemy: silence as a moment of mutual calm and hold-ing; as terror; as stuckness; as a place for tears rather than words. Zeki (2008, p. 88) argues from the perspective of neuroscience that a characteristic of great art is its capacity to evoke multiple meanings, each of which has a validity and potential representation in the mind. This 'high-level ambiguity' should not be dismissed as equivocation or vagueness but celebrated as the 'certainty of different scenarios'. In the imagination all things are possible.

From an evolutionary perspective the capacity to consider different possibilities enhances the range of possible behavioural responses in any given situation, and in an interpersonal context therefore enables one to put oneself in another's shoes. But there comes a moment when the play has to stop. Choices have to be made, actions performed. Patient and therapist need to know when an interpretation feels 'right', and when it seems irrelevant, or just plain wrong. Therapy, as well as enhancing polysemic and unsaturated discourse, has to be able to help its clients to trust their intuition, their 'gut feelings'.

As argued in Chapter 6, therapist and client 'triangulate' their relationship in search of the truth. The therapist's feelings crystallise into an image characterising the transference/countertransference disposition. The client may implicitly be saying: 'Admire me but nurture me at the same time'; or 'Envy me so that I don't have to feel so envious'; or 'Let me abuse you so that you can know what it feels like to be abused'. The client's inner world is continuously being held up against the therapist's imaginative identification of it for confirmation, disconfirmation, modification and eventual instantiation in dialogue. The client acquires a language for decision-making as well as play-making.

Dreams and dream-interpretation are central to psychoanalysis because they triangulate *both* the playfulness and truth-seeking aspects of therapy. Freud's 'royal road' bypasses evasion, window-dressing, defensiveness, social niceties. When the therapist is at a loss to know 'what is going on', a dream can come to the rescue. The bizarreness and creativity of the dream remind the dreamer of the unexpectedness and resourcefulness of the unconscious. Thinking about dreams, freely associating to them, leads to an interpretation, arising in either the client's unconscious or the therapist's, is checked for its veracity, whether it 'works' or glances off into oblivion.

Often an interpretation will find an entry point to the unconscious via a particular image or word in a dream. For example, Crispin in Chapter 7, struggling with his addiction, finally got himself to an Alcoholics Anonymous meeting. At his next therapy session he described a dream in which he was *on holiday in a 'resort' but one in which the 'infinity pool' had been drained to reveal a tawdry bar*. Without thinking too much, 'Ah,' I said, 'sounds like the last resort'.

There is a spectrum running from a focus on a fragment of material to a stance of evenly suspended attention where the patient's narrative infiltrates the therapist's mind, until his/her intuition/unconscious responds with an image, a word or a thought. In supervision, I call these two approaches the working with the 'minute particulars' (R. Hobson 1985), and 'dreaming the session'. In the former, as supervisor, one may interrupt the therapist's account of her work abruptly to look at a fragment of interaction that 'contains' the whole. (The pianist Imogen Cooper described her first class with the maestro Alfred Brendel – they spent the entire hour working on the opening chord of a Schubert impromptu.) 'Dreaming the session', one remains silent for the whole of a presentation and tracks one's own responses to the material, and, if it is group supervision, encourages group members to come up with theirs, in a species of polysemic 'social dreaming'.

In this brief chapter I look at this interplay between triangulation and unsaturation in thinking about dreams. In the spirit of judicious self-revelation that permeates this book, here is a dream of my own.

Pinot noir

I wake up thinking of *pinot noir*, a good wine grape of course, but the words make me think of something black and poignant. Then I remember my dream.

> *I am at a conference on in-patient psychiatric care. It is being held in a European town. Tall buildings surround a courtyard. There is bunting hanging from upstairs windows and music playing. The atmosphere is light and sunny and happy, but somehow I remain in the shade. A friend, Lenny, has brought his violin and tells me about a therapeutic community for the mentally ill in which patients and doctors work collaboratively and creatively. I find myself wishing I could play the violin and could find a way to make things better for my patients.*

'Why black and poignant?', I ask myself. 'Why am I shaded, overshadowed?'

Then I remember: I am semi-retired. All this is going on without me. I have moved into a different phase of my life. I must come to terms with loss. (As I enter the prostatic era, also perhaps saying 'pee – no!'). Those who lose have to cope with their envy of those who have not lost. The old envy the young, the dead the living, the ill the healthy, the bankrupt the rich, the bereaved those surrounded by their loved ones, the unmusical the talented. Envy homes in on lack, is never about counting one's blessings. As Dickens (1857/1973, p. 505) puts it:

> The worst class of sum worked in the every-day world, is ciphered by the diseased arithmeticians who are always in the rule of Subtraction as to the merits and successes of Others, and never in Addition as to their own.

The capacity to cope with loss, to be able to say goodbye, to move on, is integral to being human. Darwin (bereaved of his mother as a child, and his favourite daughter in mid-life) thought natural selection, for survival's sake, had disposed us to cheerfulness, and therefore inevitably to denial. In Chekov's *The Cherry Orchard* the Ranevskaya family are desperate because their beloved orchard is to be sold to an upstart land-agent, who will cut it down and replace it with holiday bungalows. For most of the play the family are miserable, hysterical, impotently angry. Yet, once the decision to sell is forced on them, and a little time has elapsed, they seem blithely to move on. In the penultimate scene they have forgotten their orchard: they talk casually of it as a white elephant that devoured their scarce capital, well rid of, and are full of plans for new lives. The play ends with Firs, the ancient faithful retainer, left behind and forgotten, hidden away in the gloomy darkness of their abandoned country house. Is this mourning completed leading to new life, or avoidance and denial? Or both? As so often with Chekov, the work is poignantly poised at Zeki's (2008) 'higher level ambiguity'.

As I shall discuss in more detail in the next chapter, bereavement has a psychological logic of its own beyond conscious control or awareness. Denial, anger, numbness, despair and longing may be suppressed for a time, but cannot in the end be avoided when someone or something important passes out of one's life. Coming to terms with loss; envy; moving through pain and misery to new hope; not denying what has to be locked away in the darkness, but being able to let light in on loss – all this is the daily work and life of a psychotherapist.

Returning to my dream, I think to myself, tonight I will open a good bottle of wine to celebrate this realisation. But . . . I don't have good bottles of wine – just random pickups from the supermarket. Then I remember the dream's 'day's residue': a conversation with to my brother-in-law the day before. He has just negotiated a loss, moving into a small flat from a big house where he had lived with my sister for 30 years – taking with him his treasured cases of good wine. I envy his organisation and focus. Perhaps that is how the pinot noir got into my dream. Is this a version of my envy? Am I the jack-of-all-trades psychotherapist longing for the purity of analytic work – the ability to make vintage interpretations rather than makeshift eclecticism? Envy again – the ubiquitous iniquitous persecutor. My job is to come to terms with it. If I can't cope with it myself, how can I expect my patients to do so?

I am grateful to my dream for reminding me of this.

Now let us turn to a patient's dream.

Julie's dream: decimals and digitals

I was in a classroom. There were 10 students. The tutor asked us to write ten short stories and come back in September for criticism.

The dreamer, Julie, gets depressed. She doesn't quite know what to do with her life – whether to give up her day job (teaching) and become a full-time writer. In a similar vein, she has a few boyfriends but can't decide if she wants to settle down and get married.

When I ask her whether anything occurs to her about the dream (my way of asking for 'free associations'), 'nothing' comes to her mind. But in psychotherapy 'nothing never happens'. Absence always denotes a presence.

That brings me to the number 10, which appears twice in the space of a short dream. In binary counting ten is one and nothing, or, as they say here in the rural part of Britain where I live, 'something and nothing'.

That is like Julie's life, I think – a presence and an absence, a wanting and a not wanting. And that makes me think of her ever-present mother and her absent father – they split up when Julie was less than one year old. Or her step-father, who came on the scene when she was seven. He is a good man, but a step-, not a 'real' father – another 'something and nothing'.

I try to convey some of this to Julie. She is unimpressed. Then my free-floating attention alights on the word 'criticism'. I often sense that comments that to me sound neutral or positively helpful seem to come across to her as criticisms. A therapist is indeed some sort of critic. The dictionary definition of a critic is 'one who passes judgement'; my 'criticism' and the criticism referred to in the dream reinforces Julie own excessive self-criticism. She is always running herself down, especially when depressed. She can never quite be the perfect daughter she feels her mother would like her to be.

But a critic is also an interpreter of works of art, a mediator between the particular work and the world of artistic tradition, between the singular world of the artist and the wider one of his or her public, a guardian of what 'works' and what does not work aesthetically.

A therapist is similarly an interpreter – one who finds meaning in a dream or a symptom; a mediator between the unconscious and conscious parts of the patient, helping them to communicate more effectively between them-selves; and also a guardian of reality, encouraging the patient to think through the realistic consequences of decisions – in Julie's case giving up a day job or deciding to get married.

Perhaps as therapist I am indirectly being referred to in the dream. A therapist is another one and zero, a something and nothing, an observer but not a participant. What Julie wants, or thinks she wants, is someone to tell her what to do. A father-figure who is an integer, not an O, one who can be integral to her life. So I am a disappointment. I represent her disappointment in herself, her half-life. And that is true, yet it is not true. It is true because that is what the reality of therapy is, and not true because it is a transference (a carry-over – literally – from her past).

My interpretation of ten as a one and a nought could be completely wrong. 'Ten' could be referring to an age at which something significant happened to Julie, or the Ten Commandments of her Moses-mother by which she is required to live. Or it could mean nothing important at all – my whole approach could be *ten*-dentious. It all depends on triangulation – the therap-ist's instincts and the patient's reactions. Together they search for and create meanings. Those co-constructed meanings are the only therapeutic truths. Julie and I will have go on trying to understand one another.

Dreams and 'imposed meanings'

One of the tasks that dream interpreters have to face is to understand the 'bizarreness' of dreams. If dreams are a message from the unconscious, why is it sent, as it were, in code, rather than more straightforwardly into our waking minds?

Freud's answer to this was that 'we dream in order to sleep'. He believed that when disturbing thoughts rise up from the unconscious, they are prevented from waking us up by being 'disguised' in bizarre ways, rather as a cryptographer scrambles his messages so that they cannot be read by the enemy (in this case the conscious mind).

Modern neurophysiology (Rycroft 1985; Bateman and Holmes 1995) suggests that Freud got it the wrong way round: we sleep in order to dream – dreaming is in some way necessary for normal waking mental activity, perhaps through the need for some sort of 'cleansing' process analogous to cleaning the gummed-up hard disc of a computer.

Wittgenstein (1958) was for different reasons unimpressed by Freud's theory of causative dream-formation. In his view, the human mind has the capacity to make meaning out of anything, however random. He gave the example of 'Kim's game', in which the players are briefly shown a random collection of objects on a tray – a watch, a glass, a sheet of notepaper, a penknife, etc. – and then asked to recall as many of the objects as possible. The best strategy, going back to mediaeval memory techniques, is to make a *story* out of the objects – a man has been murdered with a penknife, at such and such a time noted on the watch, the murderer was thirsty and drank some water and then faked a suicide note on the paper. That way all the objects can be recalled. The story is not 'true' – it bears no relationship to reality – but yet is satisfying and 'meaningful'. Similarly it is possible that the story-making part of the mind, the repository of our personal identity, weaves together a dream 'story' out of a multiplicity of random images from present and past that comprises the neurophysiology of dreaming. This is still compatible with the Freudian approach, since the particular story that someone makes out of their dream images will always be unique to them and their personal preoccupations, conscious and unconscious.

'Semiotic space'

Dream analysis highlights the idea of the 'semiotic space' that client and therapist set up together in their work together. This is only possible when attachment feels so secure that deep exploration becomes possible, comparable perhaps to the combination of profound security and excitement suggested in Chapter 9 as a precondition for satisfying sex.

Working with dreams is always a leap into the unknown – Gombrich's (1979, p. 5) 'groping before grasping'. On first hearing, or at first sight in the mind's eye, a dream may seem utterly baffling. Only by holding onto negative capability, tolerating not-knowing, will the triangulation process work its magic and answers begin to emerge. Even when things begin to fall into place there may be a nagging sense of incompletion. In her pedagogic role, working at the 'zone of proximal development', knowing that with just a little more self-scrutiny meanings *will* reveal themselves, the therapist often has to push the client towards further exploration.

Fran's gaffe

Fran came for help in the throes of a mid-life crisis. Normally cheerful and outgoing, she felt miserable, agoraphobic and paranoid. Without the support of her husband she feared that she would relapse into suicidal depression. Despite having brought up a now successful and happy son, who was soon to get married, and holding down a good job as a company secretary, she felt that her life was a failure. The immediate precipitant of her breakdown had been an injudicious email that she had sent to her fellow board members concerning salaries. She had been strongly criticised for this and had resigned from her post. She had also lost money on the stock exchange, and although her husband had a good job and they were in reality fairly financially secure, she felt irrationally worried about money matters and was preoccupied with the possibility of financial ruin.

We contracted for ten weekly sessions. Within a few weeks of starting both therapy and antidepressants she was feeling much better. She decided to put her past woes behind her and think about the future and was applying for new jobs, and looking forward to a more balanced life in which she concentrated on hobbies such as painting and gardening rather than being obsessed with her work. At the eighth session, feeling worried that we hadn't really got to the bottom of the precipitating email debacle, I posed my standard prophylactic end-of-therapy query: 'What would have to happen for you to get ill again?'. Initially she dismissed this, saying that the main thing was that her depressive ruminations about all that had lifted. I tried to challenge this deactivating avoidance: 'but what was that email business all about, do you think?'.

'Well I don't know', came the reply, 'but I did have an interesting dream you might like to hear about. *I dreamed I rammed my car into a huge bank. When I got out there was a bicycle leaning nearby. I just got onto it and rode off.*'

Fran's reaction to the dream was that she was no longer so 'driven', that she had been enjoying gentle rides on her bike along country lanes, and that symbolised her new-found attitude to life.

She then mentioned that she had forgotten her cheque book and wouldn't be able to pay this week. Perhaps prompted by my countertransferential feeling that she was comparing my financial situation with hers, I mused: 'But what about the "bank": could that be the fiscal rather than earthen variety?'.

'Oh, that reminds me of my step-father – he was a bank manager', came the response. She then went on to describe how, fatherless until she was seven, she had lived in happy poverty with her unmarried mother and grandparents until her mother married the local bank manager. This led to a radical change in social status. They moved into a large house and had all that money could buy – except love and security. Her step-father resented her; her mother became preoccupied with her rapidly arriving half-siblings. She was on her own, and was determined to make her own way in the world, and show her plutocratic step-father that she could do without him. She would have loved to lead a smash-and-grab raid on his miserable bank. That led to the unravelling of the email issue: we decided that she was in effect saying to the board, representing her resented step-dad: 'For all your self-important salaries, I don't want or need you' – 'and don't bank on me . . .?', I added. Out of an infinite (in Bollas' and Matte-Blanco's sense) range of possibilities we had the found one that fitted, made sense.

Further analysis of the dream concentrated on the 'bi'-cycle, and, with embarrassment but courage, she began to talk about a period in her teens where she wondered if she was lesbian. She had become depressed and withdrawn until she met her husband and had felt his reassuring appreciation of her femininity and heterosexuality.

We see here a dream's unique capacity to push the balance between polysemic possibility and triangulated truth beyond the confines of ordinary conversation. Therapeutic space provides security; mentalising is the meeting of minds that generates meaning in the innermost 'language of thought'. Secure attachment facilitates imaginative unboundedness. Guided by language's specificity and infinite variety, joint exploration establishes the irreducible emotional facts that underpin the dream narrative.

Chapter 13

Ending

This book is nearing its conclusion. A good starting-point for thinking about endings in therapy is *Analysis terminable and interminable* (Freud 1937), written two years before the author's death at the age of 82. As Pedder (1988) points out, the German title might more accurately have been translated as *Psychoanalysis finite or infinite*, the very different linguistic harmonics of that road not taken steering therapists away from the abortive or guillotine-like implications of 'termination' and the irritable ones of interminability. Pedder's translation suggests instead themes of separation, death, the timelessness of the unconscious, and the infinity of irreversible loss.

There are several obvious questions surrounding termination. *When* should one end – when the analyst decides, when the patient decides, or when a fixed term is 'up'? *How* should one end – abruptly, or with a gradual winding down of frequency of sessions; with or without allowances for follow-up, and 'top-ups'? *Why* should one end – what is the theoretical justification for an ending, how does one know that the job is done, how does a decision to end emerge? *In what way* can one discern if an ending is good enough (analogous perhaps to a 'good death'), premature (as in the Dora case, Freud 1905) or overdue (as with the Wolf Man, Freud 1918)?

While the questions, theoretical and practical, surrounding termination are clear, answers are less certain. Novick (1997, p. 145) argues that, with honourable exceptions (e.g. Balint 1968), 'neither Freud nor his followers paid much attention to termination as a phase of treatment' and that 'for almost 75 years psychoanalysts have been unable to conceive of the idea of a terminal phase'.

Three possible reasons for this dearth seem relevant. First, ending a therapy, as with starting treatment, is a real event, an 'enactment' going beyond the bounds of transference and the imagination. The departing patient is not just deconstructing a transference; she or he is disengaging from a fellow human being with whom many hours of close proximity and intimate affect-laden conversation have been spent (cf. Rycroft 1985). Attachment theory assumes that the therapist and the therapeutic setting provide a real secure base, whose function is to enable the client to explore playfully the 'unreality', yet validity, of her transferential and other imaginings. Relinquishing that connection, especially after many years of therapeutic intimacy, is no mean task. Theorising that separation goes beyond the bounds of normal psycho-analytic thinking.

Second, a fundamental problem for psychoanalysts in relation to ending is that they themselves rarely undergo fully the process of disengagement that awaits the average analysand. The analyst retains her fundamental belief in the potency and importance of psychoanalysis; is likely to have continuing contact with the analytic world, including her own analyst, through her pro-fessional life; and not infrequently undergoes second or even third analyses. If ending analysis is an analogue of 'leaving home' (Haley 1980), an analyst continues to retain a foothold in the parental mansion. It is worth remember-ing, however, that Bowlby emphasised the normality and healthiness of 'mature dependency' through life, including presumably dependency on one's analytic beliefs and collegiate contacts.

Third, the question of termination overlaps, sometimes in confusing ways, with the issue of the aims and objectives of analytic therapy and what a 'good outcome' might be. Removal of symptoms, diminished splitting and greater integration of the personality, strengthening of the ego, overcoming of ambivalence towards the breast, achieving genital primacy formed the mantra of the early literature. More recently, as character disorders rather than neurosis have come to form the bulk of analytic practice, and subtle research methods for studying outcome have become available, earlier ideal-ised views of analytic outcome have been tempered with reality. A more nuanced view of what can and cannot be achieved in analysis is beginning to emerge, in which the prime aim of therapy is to equip patients with new interpersonal and intrapsychic skills, and to help push psychic equilibrium in a more positive direction. The analyst needs to know when 'enough is enough', and to guard against imposing his or her own narcissistic wishes, or colluding with those of the client, for a perfect outcome.

Brief dynamic therapy: Foregrounding termination

The rationale informing brief dynamic therapies (e.g. Gustafson 1986) begins and ends with termination. A time limit is implicit from the first moment of therapy. The therapist will 'count down', usually starting each session by announcing 'this is our seventh session' or, 'we've another three sessions to go'. Termination hangs over the therapy from the start – conspicuous either by its absence (the client 'pretending' it does not exist, sometimes collusively with the therapist) or by its inhibitory presence ('what's the point of going into all this, I'm only going to be seeing you another six times?'), but always grist to the mentalising mill (e.g. 'I wonder if the fact that you know you are going to lose me means that you cannot fully make use of me, rather as you never really let your weekends-only Dad know how angry you were with him for leaving your Mum').

Different varieties of brief dynamic therapy handle endings in different ways. Balint (1968) realised that for psychoanalytic psychotherapy to reach out from the ivory couches of Hampstead to the masses, it must perforce abbreviate itself, suggesting that at the end of therapy the patient should feel both very much better and very much worse, and that what mattered was that this could be acknowledged. Mann's 12-session take-it-or-leave-it approach (Mann 1973) is justified as an analogue of the existential irreversibility of death. If the pain of loss can be experienced it can be transcended; follow-ups and interminable therapies are simply attempts to evade the reality of irreversible separation. Ryle's (1990) CAT therapists provide a goodbye letter, a memento that can mitigate absence, thereby activating an internalised good object imago comparable to the tennis ace Jimmy Connors' letter from his grandmother, kept in the sole of his shoes and taken out and read at crucial moments in his matches.

Ending and attachment

The contribution of attachment to thinking about termination can be considered under four headings: theorising loss in relation to secure and insecure attachments; termination as co-construction; disillusion and dissolution of the secure base; and mentalising in relation to endings.

Theorising separation and loss

The reality of the secure base provided by the therapist provides the backdrop against which the client's transferential distortions, misguided expectations, unconscious wishes and impulses can be observed and made meaningful. Setting up a therapeutic relationship is an inescapable 'enactment' on the part of therapist and client: an action that is 'real', observable, performed rather than merely imagined, phantasised about or desired. As therapy, or indeed an individual session proceeds, the *meaning* of actions and their psychological reverberations become grist for exploration, but a vital precondition is the alleviation of attachment insecurity.

If establishing an attachment relationship is a real event, so too is its ending. For Bowlby (1973), separation is the inescapable counterpart of attachment: the very purpose of attachment behaviours, on the part of both care-seeker and care-giver, is to mitigate loss. Crying, proximity-seeking, responsiveness and soothing all work to ensure that an individual when vulnerable – whether through physical immaturity, illness or trauma – gains and maintains access to protection and succour.

When separation is irreversible – i.e. at an ending – Bowlby and his followers (notably Parkes 2006) identified the now familiar constellation of reactions and feelings: denial, angry protest, searching, despair, and finally recovery leading to the establishment of new attachments. Subsequent research on grief and mourning – both normal and pathological – have fleshed out, and to some extent modified, Bowlby's original formulations on separation and loss.

First, a key issue in reactions to separations is not so much the continuous presence, but the continuing *availability* when needed of the attachment figure. As physical proximity, especially in older children, becomes less salient, what matters is knowing that a helper will be there when called upon. This 'sense of availability' can even transcend the total separation implicit in a death and make grieving bearable (Shaver and Fraley 2008). Sources of comfort helping with bereavement include: thinking what the lost loved one would have done in such and such a situation; conferring with photographs or letters; imagining or even hallucinatorily hearing the dead loved-one's voice; Proustian remembrance of times past.

Second, as might be expected, attachment styles have a significant bearing on reactions to loss. There are two main patterns of pathological mourning: denial accompanied by chronic depression of mood on one hand; and inconsolable preoccupation with the lost loved one on the other. These map well onto our two familiar principal patterns of insecure attachment, deactivation of separation-protest, and hyperactivation and inconsolability. In one case there is a denial that the absence of the lost one 'matters', while physiological and psychological exploration reveal otherwise. In the other there is a doomed and unassuagable effort to recover the lost loved one.

Third, Bowlby's somewhat pessimistic perspective on reactions to loss has been modified in the light of the findings that, under favourable conditions, mourning can be negotiated successfully, and that persistent despair is relatively uncommon. The 'transactional model of attachment' (Sroufe 2005) suggests a dynamic interplay between attachment style and current relationships that accounts for variable outcomes in loss. A supportive context – family, friends, belief system, social group, church or therapist – eases the passage from grief to recovery; its absence adds to the burden of loss.

Finally, contemporary views on bereavement (Klass et al. 1996) emphasise the role of post-loss 'continuing bonds'. To repeat, Bowlby was critical of the idea of maturation as a process of increasing distancing from the primary object, in which atomised autonomy replaces adherence and dependency. His view was that (Bowlby 1981, p. 399) 'the resolution of grief is not to sever bonds but to establish a *changed bond* with the dead person' (emphasis in original). As Andreas-Salome (2003, p. 27) put it in her obituary of her lover Rilke:

> Death entails not merely a disappearance but rather a transformation in a new realm of visibility. Something is not just taken away, but is gained ... In the moment when the flowing lines of a figure's constant change and effect become paralysed for us, we are imbued for the first

time with its essence: something which is never captured or fully realized in the normal course of lived existence.

How do these ideas and findings apply to therapy termination as a bereavement analogue? Separation and loss are integral to psychotherapy, punctuated as it is by repeated separations, mostly planned and expectable, but also by occasional traumatic interruptions. The former include the end of each analytic hour, weekend and holiday breaks; the latter, therapist's and client's illness, and rupture enactments on the part of therapist or client such as changing or forgetting sessions, double booking, muddles over times, turning up on the wrong day. These, while regrettable, are also grist to the mentalising mill.

Ending therapy is a real loss: a significant aspect of the client's life is no longer there. A secure space and time where distressing events and feelings can be digested is now empty. A person who focuses her attention and sensitivity on one's inner world is now absent. One is on one's own with one's story, feelings and life-history. But, like every aspect of psychotherapy, an ending is 'polysemic'. Depending on mood and perspective, the meaning of an ending can be a death, a bereavement, a completion, a liberation; less a funeral (with or without a convivial wake) than a joyful moment of maturation and autonomy-enhancing 'leaving home'.

Ending brings gains as well as loss: the time and money invested in therapy are now available for other projects; the client no longer feels so 'dependent'; autonomy and maturity are reinforced; he or she feels more psychologically robust, more able to provide security for others and less in need of it himself/ herself. Just as the bereaved are sometimes said to have 'earned' their widowhood or widowerhood, the discharged therapy client likewise may feel she has earned her liberation from the obligations, mysteries and miseries of therapy, without having to deny its now absent comforts and gifts. The point at which ending enters the therapeutic frame is when the balance-sheet of benefit and obligation shifts away from the former towards the latter, the investment begins to outweigh the return.

These attachment-informed perspectives have a number of clinical implications. First, therapists must bear in mind the client's predominant attachment style. Deactivating clients may well appear to take an ending in their stride, apparently seeing it as inevitable, natural and appropriate, presenting themselves as eager to move onto the challenges of 'real life' now that their symptoms have diminished and their feel stronger. Regret, doubt, anger and disappointment may be conspicuous by their absence, gratitude superficial and conventional rather than deep-rooted. The therapist should direct the client's attention to these possibilities as manifest in dreams, missed appointments, seeking other forms of treatment, or in manic cheerfulness, fulsome gratitude or Pollyanna-ishness. Premature ending is a not infrequent occurrence with such clients. It is always worth pushing hard for at least one final goodbye session, in which disappointments and resentments can be aired, rather than simply letting a disgruntled client slip away.

Clinical folklore holds that as the end of therapy approaches, the client's symptoms, even if alleviated during the course of therapy, may reappear. This is perhaps particularly likely for hyperactivating clients who may overestimate the negative impact of ending. The therapist may be tempted by this into premature offers of further therapy, or suggesting an alternative therapist or therapy modality (such as a group). Mentalising self-scrutiny is needed to differentiate countertransference-induced guilt from the client's clinical need. Some post-therapy arrangements may well be appropriate, but should not be allowed to divert therapeutic focus from working through the ending.

Second, the client's social context should be taken into account when deciding on either offering time-limited therapy or finding an appropriate moment to conclude open-ended treatment. Time-limited therapy is much more likely to succeed when the client has a good social and emotional network to which they can 'return' once therapy is over. For more disturbed clients in long-term therapy, if treatment has not managed to facilitate the capacity to generate outside attachments, post-therapy relapse is likely. Such clients may need further therapeutic arrangements such as group therapy or key-worker support, and the reality of this needs to be discussed as a period of intensive individual analytic therapy draws to its close.

Third, the therapist needs to consider the meaning of 'availability' and 'continuing bonds' as conditions for secure attachment – the latter being a key outcome goal for therapy. Pointers may well have arisen during the course of therapy.

David's emails

David, who had experienced traumatic separation from both parents at the age of eight when he was in hospital for a year with tuberculous osteo-myelitis, asked at the start of once-weekly therapy, 'Can I email you between sessions if there are things that crop up during the week?'. Aware of my tendency to overlook boundary crossings, my rather rigid response was to say 'On the whole I would prefer that we contain issues within the sessions, and that email is used for practical things like changes of time'. It was only after some months of therapy that he felt safe enough to reveal how put down, rejected and angry he had felt by my response, and to be able to explore how this had evoked echoes of his childhood feelings of emptiness and terror when cut off from his parents when in hospital.

The same client was keen that we should have a follow-up session six months after our one-year period of therapy came to an end. For him, such an actualising manifestation of availability seemed needed, and it would have been churlish to refuse. Other clients are able to tolerate complete separation from therapy, continuing to draw on its benefits when needed, imagining what their therapist might have said, or having fully internalised a mentalising capacity. Attenuated therapy (winding down from intensive work to fortnightly or monthly sessions for a while), or offering an occasional limited series of sessions if a crisis arises in the client's life, are other examples of helping the client to maintain a live sense of an available attachment figure.

Responses to ending can be theorised by bringing together the Bowlbian perspective with Kleinian ideas of working through loss (Klein 1940). Klein's starting point is Freud's paper 'Mourning and melancholia' (Freud 1917), which is usually seen as the germ from which object relations grew. Freud (1917) describes the ego as a 'precipitate of abandoned cathexes' – i.e. the developmental process involves internalising what were previously 'external' relationships with significant Others. For this to happen the bereavement process has to run its course, coming to terms with ambivalent feelings towards an object on which one is dependent. Need and the possibility of abandonment go hand in hand. *Odi et Amo*: love and hate coexist; only once ambivalence is mentalised and acknowledged is full 'reinstatement of the lost object' in the ego possible. Only when that mature state is reached is unambiguous gratitude possible.

Therapists, especially when working in a time-limited way, need to be aware of how this inevitable ambivalence colours reactions to ending. I suspect that my client who asked for a follow-up wanted to be reassured that his hatred of me and my relative unavailability would not have killed me off in his absence. This is not, as I see it, an argument against various forms of attenuated ending, but more a reminder that the meaning of such arrangements must always be thought about and discussed.

Termination as co-construction

The relational approach takes it as axiomatic that the clinician's as well as the client's states of mind need to be taken into account if clinical phenomena are to be fully explored and understood. At first glance this viewpoint seems to equate to object relations theory (ORT), which moved beyond Freud's original intrapsychic account to an interpsychic one in which the therapist's emotional responses to the client were, via projective identification, included in the therapeutic mix. But here the ORT clinician's own projects and personality remain in the background; her main role is as a reflexive receptacle for the client's projections. Relational and attachment approaches go two steps further. First, by reviving Freud's (see Bollas 2007) throwaway remark that analysis at its best involves the direct communication of one unconscious (the patient's) with another (the analyst's), the role of the analyst's implicit character and belief system is acknowledged. Second, and flowing from this, comes the idea of the 'analytic third' (Ogden 1987; Benjamin 2004), the unique relational structure of any given therapy, built from the differing contributions of clinician and client but directly derivable from neither.

A given client will have a different therapeutic experience with different therapists, and particular therapists establish very different therapeutic relationships with different clients (Diamond et al. 2003). It should be noted, however, in contradiction of an absolutist relational viewpoint, that (a) 'difficult' clients tend to do badly by whomsoever they are treated, and (b) excellent clinicians tend to make most of their clients better (Beutler et al. 2004). In the latter case it may be the very flexibility and capacity to accept differing 'analytic thirds' that contributes to the success of these 'super-therapists'.

Attachment research contributes some empirical data in support of these general considerations. Dozier et al. (2008) measured clinicians' as well as their clients' attachment styles, looking specifically at the interactions between them. They found that the therapeutic process differed markedly for secure and insecure clinicians in ways relevant to endings. Insecure therapists tended to reinforce their clients' patterns of insecurity; secure ones to 'redress the balance', pushing against the client's insecure attachment strategies.

If we assume that there is a 'right' time to end therapy, and that there will be an unconscious pull towards either premature or overdue endings, this can be understood in terms of the 'fit' between patient and therapist (cf. Holmes 2001). With an avoidant/deactivating patient and an insecure analyst whose attachment style led her to overemphasise interpretations and intellectual formulation, the ending might be 'too early'. Conversely, with a hyperactivating client and an analyst with a tendency to overvalue support and affective resonance, the therapy might become protracted and the ending 'too late'. Secure therapists will question premature ending with a deactivating client, and push for a definite date with a hyperactivating one.

The moral is, yet again, mentalising: 'clinician know thyself'. Therapists need to allow for their own attachment styles if they are to offer mutative rather than collusive treatments. Each analyst will have her or his unique 'termination style', evoked to some extent by any given patient, but also manifesting his or her own attachment history and predilections. The lineaments of an ending are co-constructed. The task is not so much to get it 'right' as to use the ending as a powerful exemplar from which the client can learn how his unconscious shapes the way he handles, and has handled, loss and separation. For this to happen the therapist must be able to abstract her own attachment style from the therapeutic equation in order to see the client's for what it is.

Dissolution or disillusion?

Why should the ending of a therapy 'matter'? After all, the ending of other professional relationships – a builder whose job is finally done, a banking or legal relationship concluded – is usually a relief. In contrast, the therapist and therapeutic relationship are invested – 'cathected' – in a way that makes them affectively salient. The therapist has become an attachment figure, a person with the properties of a secure base, the loss of whom evokes the attachment constellation of pain, protest, despair and recovery already described.

The question of how an attachment relationship, as opposed to other connections such as friendship, colleagueship and professionalism, is established or disestablished is not entirely clear. Bowlby (1956, quoted in Cassidy 2008, p. 12) put it well:

> To complain because a child does not welcome being comforted by a kind but strange woman is as foolish as to complain that a young man deeply in love is not enthusiastic about some other good looking girl.

An attachment relationship is one that permeates or 'penetrates' (Hinde's term, 1979) every aspect of a person's life in ways that mark it off from others. The more that this is true for a therapeutic relationship, the greater is the significance of its ending.

In classical psychoanalysis, negotiating the oedipal situation entails renouncing the breast, coming to accept the inevitable discrepancy between wish and reality. In the neo-Kleinian model of Oedipus, the child who can tolerate parental intercourse and his own ambivalent feelings is liberated – able to think for himself, and to identify with, or turn towards, the father and through him the outer world, as he or she moves away from maternal dependency (Britton et al. 1989).

Winnicott's (1971) transitional space model introduces a third term between the nirvana-like world of unbridled need and wish, and the harsh, brutish brevity of reality. In transitional space, wish and reality overlap so that the baby's hallucinatory illusion of the breast is matched by the mother's *actual* provision of it. This real, albeit short-lived, blissful 'fit' becomes the basis for later play, creativity and hope. In the Winnicott model there are also repeated failures of fit – a mother is, can, and should only be 'good enough'. There is a necessary 'dis-illusionment' with the breast if the child is to move towards independence and new attachments, and to avoid the narcissism that finds intolerable the inevitable discrepancy between wish and reality.

Resistance to termination can be seen as impediments to these developmental processes. The therapist and therapy are invested with indispensability, an illusory and anachronistic carry-over of infantile needs and wishes into the present. Because the therapist fails to meet the client's overweening need she cannot be relinquished. The therapist may be able to provide only the 'maternal' half of the parental imago, and so be unable to point the client towards independence. Hatred and need might be so stark that they cannot be brought together into the depressive position. 'Failure' (in the sense of 'good-enoughness', and in the terms of this book positive rupture/ repair cycles) is bearable only if balanced by a sufficient bank of success. As Novick (1988, p. 312) puts it:

Seldom mentioned in the literature is the necessity for disillusionment in order to begin the process of giving up and mourning the omnipotent mother–child dyad. To a certain extent, the analyst must be experienced as a failure for the patient to respond fully to the treatment as a success.

An attachment relationship is one in which needs are actually met by the Other – to a greater (in secure attachment) or lesser (insecure attachment) extent. It seems likely that an effective therapist offers analogous responsiveness, sensitivity and attunement to that of the security-producing care-giver. For good-enough therapy there needs to have been sufficient accumulation of 'moments of meeting' (Stern 2004). The therapist's understanding needs to have sufficiently accurately mirrored the client's affective state in ways analogous to the advent of the breast at the moment of its hallucination.

But as well as 'being there' the therapist is also, albeit in a regular and predictable way, *not* there. Indeed it is possible that it is precisely the nature of this absence that marks out someone with secure base properties from, to use Bowlby's phrases, a 'kind but strange' or some 'other good looking' person. During separations, a secure base figure holds the care-seeker in mind, *and* stays in the mind of the care-seeker. A client has the right to expect her therapist to hold her in mind between sessions, and to refer back to things said and felt in previous sessions. As the salience of therapy becomes established, the sessions and the person of the therapist enter the patient's stream of consciousness and unconsciousness (dreams of the therapist, slips about the therapist's name, intrusions of therapeutic vocabulary into the client's 'idiolect' etc.).

Weekly therapy patients often report in the early stages of therapy: 'What we were discussing last week stayed in my mind for a couple of days afterwards and then seemed to fade'. As suggested in discussing suicide, the appropriate frequency of sessions could almost be dictated by the time it takes for these memories to fade; the shorter the time, the more frequent sessions are needed. This affective object constancy is the basis for the salience of the therapeutic relationship, which perforce attenuates when therapy come to an end.

The psychoanalytic frame is ideally suited for the investigation of these issues. By apparently offering 'nothing' other than predictability, availability and responsiveness, the analyst enables the wish/reality discrepancies to be explored. Every ending and break is a rupture; the heart may grow fonder – or more enraged. At termination separation solidifies into irreversible loss.

Reich (1950, p. 182) compares the ending of analysis with mourning in a patient who came to her for a second training analysis:

His description of his reaction to the termination of his first analysis was quite revealing: 'I felt as if I was suddenly left alone in the world. It was like the feeling that I had after the death of my mother . . . I tried with effort to find somebody to love, something to be interested in. For months I longed for the analyst and wished to tell him about whatever happened to me. Then slowly, without noticing how it happened, I forgot about him. About two years later, I happened to meet him at a party and thought he was just a nice elderly gentleman and in no way interesting.'

Seen this way, 'transference' becomes more than merely a repetition of past relationships. It is an investment of the therapist with properties of a secure base that reflect not just the wish for an ever-available attuned primary Object, but also the real responsiveness of a fellow-human. The ending of a relationship, including a therapeutic one, entails dis*so*lution as well as dis*ill*usionment, and gratitude for the (albeit professional, and professionally rewarded) love and attention that the analyst has provided.

The 'work' of mourning consists of the dissolution of this investment. The conscious awareness of someone who was once 'everything' begins to fade into the background; eventually all that is left is a scar which, like a healed physical wound, imposes its restrictions, great or small. A lost parent, partner or worst of all a child, inhabits the psyche forever; but as the pain of loss gradually lessens, new investments become to an extent possible. When this process is incomplete there may be an inconsolable effort to replace like with like, eternally in search of what is irretrievably lost, so condemned to everlasting disappointment. Only when this 'transference' from the past onto the potentially new object becomes less compelling are new beginnings possible.

In psychotherapy coming to terms with loss – 'in my beginning is my end' – starts with the establishment of a professional relationship; moves into the all-important transferential investment reactivating past attachments and losses; ends with acceptance of separation, loss and the fading of the transference.

The teddy-bear's tea party

When I retired from my full-time psychiatric practice I decided, among the other rites of passage of separation from a job I had undertaken for 30 years or so, to have a leaving tea party for 'my' patients. All my regular 'clinic' patients were sent an invitation.

These were not 'psychotherapy' patients, but, rather people with severe mental illnesses whom I had got know quite intimately over the years. We had, together, gone through the vicissitudes of psychiatric practice: most had been in-patients, some involuntarily so, incarcerated at the stroke of my pen. Like Susan in Chapter 12, I had prescribed medication for them, written letters about them, helped them to find accommodation and had seen them regularly in my supportive clinic (typically for half and hour or so every eight weeks), so that I knew a lot about their lives (no doubt as much was *not* known). They too had got used to me as 'their' psychiatrist, tolerating me, more or less, warts and all.

As the day of the party drew near I became more and more anxious. Would anyone turn up? Would my guests have anything to say to each other, or would the whole thing be conducted in a funereal silence? I wanted to give my patients a goodbye present. The time was near Easter, so a chocolate egg seemed suitable. I had, *à la* Winnicott, originally thought of a teddy-bear (i.e. prototypical transitional object) for everyone, but the cost was prohibitive, so I settled for a postcard depicting a teddy-bear. On the back I wrote a note of gratitude. The teddy-bear postcard was something of a joke to myself. I once attended a debate between the proponents of psychoanalysis and those who advocated cognitive analytic therapy, which, as mentioned, uses written communications and instructions to patients (Ryle 1990). Although cognitive analytic therapy is for some an excellent brief treatment, I argued in the debate that giving disturbed patients written communications was comparable to offering a hungry crying baby a piece of paper with the word 'milk' written on it and expecting that to assuage their distress.

As it transpired my fears were confounded. The turnout was good, the atmosphere sociable and festive. Music played, food was scoffed, jokes were told and party games were played. I enjoyed myself and so, it seemed, did everyone else. The event was indistinguishable from the outside from any tea party with a group of people who knew each other quite well – in our small town there is a 'subculture' of psychiatric patients in which they help and interact with each other.

The whole event reminded me of a scene from the film version of that painful (for a psychiatrist) cinematic masterpiece *One Flew Over the Cuckoo's Nest*. The 'inmates' on the mental hospital escape for a day and, led by the Jack Nicholson character, hire a boat for a trip on the river. Just as they are setting out they are challenged by the boat owner – 'Who the hell are you, escaped nuts or something?'. There is a terrible moment when the viewer thinks all will be revealed and they will miss their pleasure trip. In a moment of inspiration Nicholson introduces each one as distinguished professors. As the camera pans across the familiar faces, the inmates are miraculously transformed from the emiserated inhabitants of an impoverished and degraded mental hospital world into the distinguished faces of freedom and respectability. Oddness becomes loveable eccentricity and genius. Context and assumption is all.

So too at the party my patients appeared utterly normal and behaved accordingly. What is more, they treated me as though I was one of them: kissing, hugging, gossiping, teasing, enquiring as they might with a friend or colleague.

As I reflected on this moving event afterwards, I realised that the reason a party was needed for both me and my patients was in order to help with the 'dissolution of the transference' (Sarra 2003, personal communication). My patients needed to 'disinvest' me with the power of good and evil, to see me for what I was – a person like them, nearing the end of his working life, frail, flawed, slightly lost without his role and his job, wanting to say goodbye. I needed to be diminished, made vulnerable and ordinary in their eyes, so that they could begin to move on and to invest my successor with the transference that I had carried for all the years we had been working together. Reciprocally, I needed to 'forget' their patienthood and dependency (theirs on me; mine on them), their vulnerability, and to see them, like everyone else, as equals, fellow-sufferers in the vicissitudes of life. All this was sad, and somehow humbling, but also reassuring. Attachment and separation, investment and disinvestment are part of the flux of life, psychiatric as well as 'normal'.

Mentalising termination

To repeat this book's leitmotiv, which in a final chapter is perhaps legitimate, the essence of mentalising is thinking about thinking. It starts from the Kantian perspective that that absolute truth is ungraspable, and that reality is always filtered through a mind (Allen and Fonagy 2006). However, the combination of two minds looking at the same phenomenon means that reality can be at least partially apprehended (Cavell 2006).

This chapter has been informed by two perhaps paradoxical principles. First, that a 'perfect' ending is both impossible and undesirable. There will always be themes and issues left unexplored in any given therapy. Interviewing analytic patients five years post-termination showed that although most were much 'better', the presenting conflicts and themes had not gone away, merely become less dominant and overwhelming (Bachrach et al. 1991). While the evidence suggests that for clients with complex disorders longer therapies have better outcomes, there will always for one reason or another – money, time, geography – come a point when therapy perforce comes to an end. Improvement in therapy takes the form of a negative logarithmic curve (Orlinsky et al. 2004) in which the law of diminishing returns means that it takes more and more time to produce less and less benefit. The search for perfection, on the part of either patient or therapist, is a narcissistic delusion that needs to be examined, mentalised and discussed, rather than negatively 'acted on' (absence of action is itself an action) by interminability.

The second implicit point is that an ending cannot be other than an enactment. A decision is made: we will end on such and such a day, after so many sessions, with this or that follow-up arrangement, or none. Since the aim of therapy is to replace action with thought, ending is in this sense always counter-therapeutic. But never-ending therapy is ultimately equally unhelpful. The mentalising perspective helps resolve this paradox. If the main therapeutic leverage in psychoanalytic therapies is instillation of the capacity to think about thinking, and therefore better to know one's Self and Others, and Self–Other interactions, it is not so much ending as such that matters as the capacity to think about termination, the feelings it engenders, its meaning, antecedents and sequelae.

Janice: Her ending, not mine

Janice, in her early forties, had sought therapy for depression. Her children were leaving home, and her husband seemed preoccupied with his hobbies and career. About a year into therapy she began her session by saying how much better she was now feeling, more ready to lead her own life rather than seek out 'wise men' (including, by implication, her therapist) who she had thought were in possession of the answers she was looking for.

Despite this apparent vote of confidence, I sensed there was an implicit attack in this announcement and that she was somehow angry with, or disappointed in, me. While mulling this over I noticed that a potted plant on my window-sill looked neglected and half-dead for want of watering, thinking to myself that 'I must do something about that before my next patient comes'.

I said 'I wonder if you are trying out in your mind the idea of leaving therapy'. She admitted that this had been in her mind, hurriedly adding 'not immediately, of course . . .'.

I asked when the thought had first arisen. 'I think it was when I was in your toilet after my last session', she replied, 'it seemed so neglected, so full of cobwebs. It reminded me of my husband, with his career obsession – while he neglects all the other parts of his life.'

'You included?' I asked. 'I can hear a story of disillusionment, or disappointment here . . .'.

'No, I don't feel disappointed, sad perhaps. I realise I've made my own choices; what matters to me is my family, the everyday things of life. But now I must let the children go, develop my own interests and choices.'

'And you seem to be feeling that the so-called "wise men", including me, are an illusion, they neglect what's really important to you; the answers lie within yourself', I suggested, adding: 'I have to confess that I was thinking about that plant over there; it looks, like you, as if could have done with some tender loving care'.

'Well, I suppose I do feel angry with you for not transforming me into the perfect person I thought I wanted to be, but also grateful at the same time for the attention and validation you *have* offered me', she said.

As she left she said jokingly, 'I don't need to go to the toilet today!'.

I replied in kind: 'But it's *pristine*, all the cobwebs have been cleared away!'.

We both laughed; the session seemed to end with a good feeling on both sides.

Janice was deciding to end therapy, prematurely perhaps, but no longer depressed and certainly more creative and balanced than when she started. She now knows who she is, and is not. She feels more autonomous. She no longer has to choose between the false alternatives of femininity and autonomy, or to borrow an idealised identity from 'wise men'. Her feeling of having being 'unwatered' as a child is confirmed, via triangulation, with my sense of having neglected my plants. She can see her feelings for what they are – real but not necessarily appropriate to the context she finds himself in. The 'rupture' of the dirty toilet, perhaps a receptacle for her shitty feelings of rage at neglect and lack of care as a child, became a validating moment, moving her from immature dependency (the 'wise men', the high-flying husband, her role as a mother) to mature dependency (more able to lead her own life). By acknowledging that the toilet *was* dirty, while at the same time exploring what a 'dirty toilet' might represent in her inner world, transference and reality could be differentiated. Rupture repaired gave her a sense of validatory empowerment and enabled her to decide to leave therapy at a moment that, on balance, felt right to her.

When the final moment of parting came, she was still, albeit in a joking way, unhappy about my restrained semi-sceptical stance.

'Are you sure by ending now you aren't punishing me for my failure to wreak the transformations you were hoping for?', I asked.

'Hey, where's the "high five", the happy send-off – I really *am* OK; you have done me a good turn. Stop being so curmudgeonly', came the parting shot.

As *Monty Python* might have put it, therapy was dead, over, an ex-treatment. But the patient was very much alive and with luck the residue of therapy remained so in her mind. My inadvertent use of the word 'wreak' contained within it the possibility of 'havoc'. Perhaps she had to leave at this moment for fear of disrupting the fragile balance of her marriage too much.

Janice had entered into therapy in a state of transferential idealisation: I was to be the 'wise man' who would guide her through life to her 'true self'. I neither enacted this guru-like role nor did I 'allow' her entirely immediately to evacuate me. We negotiated a slow withdrawal from therapy, and were able to laugh about the lavatory. Through this she found a more authentic self, no longer in thrall to her unrealistic expectations, playful, exploratory and self-directed.

Conclusion

Yallom (2008) suggests that death anxiety, a fundamental existential issue, tends to be avoided by patients and therapists alike. Addressing the full implications of termination brings one face to face with the transience of life, the distorting impact of trauma on development, the limitations of therapy and the inevitability of suffering. Schopenhauer (1970), the supreme yet unbowed pessimist, introduced to Western philosophy the Buddhist precept that suffering is unavoidable, and that embracing suffering is the first step towards transcending it. He contrasts the 'world as Will', corresponding roughly with Freud's notion of the unconscious, and 'world as idea' with the conscious mind. The Will, like the unconscious, is infinite and timeless, driven by intrinsic energetic forces that predate human existence and will continue once human life has passed from the universe. The world as idea is the familiar world of experience, in which time's winged arrow is always felt at one's back.

Attachment brings a slightly different perspective to this synchronic/ diachronic dichotomy of time: a biologically informed view of a life-cycle with its nodal points. These include in the up-swing: conception, birth, weaning, walking, talking, school-entry, friendship, adolescence, leaving home, finding a sexual partner, occupation, procreation, parenthood. Then follow from the zenith the beginnings of the slow pathway to involution: children leaving home; declining powers, spiritual and temporal; the mitigating pleasures of grandparenthood; diminishing responsibilities and returning freedom to look back on a life's troughs and peaks. Each of these, especially their interruption or perversion by loss and trauma, will play itself out, in its positive and negative aspects, in the therapeutic relationship (cf. Waddell 2006). The therapist needs to tune into the pulse of this underlying biological trajectory, helping patients to understand better where they are on life's journey. Traumatic and tragic interruptions, such as premature death or disability, are viewed against this expectable biological cycle.

To conclude, perhaps as a manically defensive antidote to Schopenhauerian gloom, consider the stage and screen hit *Mamma Mia!*, adapted from the 1968 film *Buona Sera, Mrs Campbell*. The success of the piece depends largely on its sing-along use of music from ABBA, the palindromic Swedish 1970s two-couple pop-group.

The setting is a Greek Island. Sophie, a teenage girl, brought up by a single parent, Donna, running a hotel that has seen better times, is determined to get married. Donna's fiancé, Sky, is a reluctant bridegroom and feels they'd be better off exploring the world (and perhaps each other) before deciding on marriage. Sophie has never known her father; her mother's secret diary suggests three possible candidates. Unbeknown to Donna, Sophie invites all of them to the wedding. But who is her 'real' father? Sophie assumes that she will be able to sense this instantly when she meets them, but to her dismay she discovers the pre-DNA-testing truism that no one can be absolutely sure of who their father is. Which of the three is to give her away? In her confusion she asks each in turn.

The wedding ceremony begins. The presiding Greek-Orthodox priest naively invites 'the father' to 'give away' the bride to her husband – her new attachment figure. All three rise to assume the honour. At first Sophie graciously accepts their blessing, is happy to waive the DNA test and accept a paternal trinity, but then she abruptly announces that she is not ready for marriage and that the wedding is off.

A crisis ensues. At this point one of the three putative fathers, divorced Sam, steps into the breach: 'Why waste a good wedding?' he says, and proposes to the love of his life, Donna, Sophie's wayward, fun-loving mother. She accepts. Sophie and Sky are delighted and relieved and announce that they will embark on an exploratory round-the-world trip. The movie ends happily with Greek feasting and ecstatic dancing.

The attachment reading is that leaving home works best if there is a secure base to return to. Once her mother has a man, Sophie can look after herself rather than play the role of the parentified child looking after her mother. With a secure base in place and available when needed, she is free to explore the world. Successful termination of therapy similarly implies the achievement of internal feelings of security, matched by external 'real' relationships, including at times a continuing relationship with a therapist.

The psychoanalytic implication is that only once an internalised good 'combined parent' is instated is one free to explore one's own emotional and sexual life. Renunciation of oedipal longings to possess the parent, with attendant feelings of sadness and envy overcome, is a necessary developmental step towards psychosexual maturity. Finding a good internal combined ('primal scene') parent; accepting and transcending one's envy and feelings of exclusion and/or desire to control and possess the primary object; and embracing the independence and freedom to manoeuvre: these are the psychoanalytic conditions for termination.

Both perspectives see coming to terms with loss as central. Sophie can leave home and move onto new attachments (from Donna to Sky) secure in the knowledge that Donna, herself now firmly attached to Sam, will be there for her when needed. Donna is securely instated in Sophie's inner world. Sophie no longer needs to push Donna's neediness away, thereby evading her own vulnerability, nor cling adhesively to Sky in ways that inhibit her exploration. Her inner world is intact, neither threatened by her own aggression nor needing a rigid external scaffold to support it. The listener, bathed in nostalgia, is reassured that despite life's unavoidable ruptures – the passage of time, loss, separation (including the dissolution of ABBA as a group and of its members as couples) – through the reparative power of music, continuity is possible.

In the end, there are moments of existential choice as all four principal characters make leaps into the unknown of each other's arms. The story cannot guarantee future happiness or insure against failure for its protagonists, any more than it can for its audience living vicariously in the dreamworld of the drama. But, as in a therapy, it can help them garner the courage and inner security needed to risk exploring life's infinite possibilities.

Chapter 14

Epilogue

I sometimes half-jokingly ask colleagues and friends, out of all the myriad interpretations they have given and received over their long years of analysis and therapy, how many they can now recall. There is a shocked pause while memory files are hurriedly scanned; when the answer does come, it is invariably in single figures. Whatever it is that helps people about psychotherapy in long run, it seems unlikely that specific interpretations can be the whole story. It is the medium, not the message, that lasts, although language remains an indispensable 'fixative' of developmental change. In that spirit, the valedictory summary below lists ten main points that have informed the making of this book, hoping that some at least may endure once the rest has faded.

1   *The attachment typology*. Therapists need diagnostic typologies, including those that differentiate healthy from sub-optimal and unhealthy developmental pathways. The secure and tripartite insecure, organised and disorganised dividing lines are sometimes blurred, and may coexist in one individual, but nevertheless form a useful and evidence-based rubric for thinking about clinical presentations, and appropriate therapeutic strategies.

2   *Mentalising*, or *awareness of awareness of awareness*. An alert dog is aware; an awake human is aware that she is aware. Psychotherapists, or people trying to repair ruptured interpersonal situations, are aware that they are aware that they are aware. Awareness is needed for effective repair-ness. The essence of mentalising is the Kantian distinction between the thing-in-itself and our appreciation of it. The human mind is inherently fallible, especially in terms of understanding itself and others' emotions, wishes and projects. Mentalising factors in that fallibility.

3   *Triangulation*. With the help of an empathically attuned, reflexive, mirroring, responsive other (mother, partner, therapist) we compare our experience of the world with another's experience of our experience and so have a better chance of arriving at emotional truth.

4 *Recursiveness.* Psychoanalytic psychotherapy is a relationship whose object is the relationship itself. A relationship in need of repair needs to be able to look at itself. The therapist's skill lies in the ability both to participate in a relationship and to observe that participation.

5 *Child development as a model for the consulting room.* The scientific basis for psychotherapy is the study of intimate relationships. The most extensive body of this work comes from our understanding of the emotional growth of the infant and child, not extrapolated in the consulting room from couch to cradle, but painstakingly built up in the attachment laboratories of child development researchers. We know that security-promoting parents combine empathy and mastery in equal measure and suspect that the same is true of good therapists.

6 *Polysemy.* Psychoanalytic psychotherapy is centrally concerned with generating meanings. Attachment theory sees secure children basking in an exuberance of meanings. The more secure, the more and better are the meanings. The psychoanalytic framework is a crucible for promoting this 'higher level ambiguity'. Equipped with a wider range of meanings, analysands have enhanced options for negotiating the interpersonal jungle of intimate social life. The aim of psychoanalysis is 'polysemy of phantasy, triangulation of the truth'.

7 *Attachment vs. exploration.* In conditions of attachment insecurity, the exploratory, meaning-seeking drive is inhibited in favour of security. By promoting security, psychotherapy indirectly facilitates exploration. Evolution deals in compromise, finding the best possible adaptation to a changing and potentially hostile environment given a particular genetic endowment. With a sub-optimal care-giver, a measure of a child's exploratory freedom has to be sacrificed for the sake of security. Psychotherapy helps reset archaic compromise-formations in ways that are more adaptive to current circumstances.

8 *The inevitability of loss.* In Buddhist psychology, suffering is the starting point: only by acknowledging suffering can suffering be endured. Attachment and loss are likewise two sides of the same coin. Attachment behaviour evolved as a bulwark against vulnerability to loss. The pain of separation is alleviated by the comfort of the secure base. Healthy protest on separation ensures smooth reunion; secure attachment promotes courageous risk-taking and acceptance of the inevitability of loss.

9 *The relational multiverse.* The artificial separation between inner and outer worlds is a philosophical error. The 'inner' world is relational from its inception; the 'outer' world is a manifestation of the inner worlds of the collectivity of individuals. Psychoanalytic psychotherapy has yet to embrace fully this dual perspective.

10 *New paradigms.* The cutting edge of contemporary psychoanalytic psychotherapy rests in the combination of accurate phenomenological

accounts of what happens in the consulting room with emerging findings from neuroimaging, genetics and child development. Together these offer the possibility of a new paradigm for psychoanalytic psychotherapy as a science of intimate relationships.

References

Abbass, A., Sheldon, A., Gyra, J., and Kalpin, A. (2008). Intensive short-term dynamic psychotherapy for DSM-IV personality disorders: A randomized controlled trial. *Journal of Nervous and Mental Disease, 196*(3), 211–216.

Ainsworth, M., Blehar, M., Waters, E., and Wall, S. (1978). *Patterns of attachment: A psychological study of the strange situation.* Hillsdale, NJ: Lawrence Erlbaum Associates.

Allen, J. (2006). Mentalising in practice. In J. Allen and P. Fonagy (Eds.), *Handbook of mentalisation-based treatment.* Chichester, UK: Wiley.

Allen, J. (2008). Mentalising as a conceptual bridge from psychodynamic to cognitive-behavioural therapies. *European Psychotherapy, 8,* 103–122.

Allen, J., and Fonagy, P. (Eds.) (2006). *Handbook of mentalisation-based treatment.* Chichester, UK: Wiley.

Allen, J., Fonagy, P., and Bateman, A. (2008). *Mentalising in clinical practice.* New York: American Psychiatric Publishing Co.

Alvarez, A. (1973). *The savage God.* London: Penguin.

Andreas-Salome, L. (2003). *You alone are real to me.* Manchester, UK: Carcanet.

Ansbacher, H., and Ansbacher R. (1985). *The individual psychology of Alfred Adler.* New York: Analytic Press.

Aron, L. (2000). Self-reflexivity and the therapeutic action of psychoanalysis. *Psychoanalytic Psychology, 17,* 667–690.

Aron, L. (2008). *Freud, Judaism, anti-Semitism, and the repudiation of femininity.* Lecture given at the William Alanson White Institute, New York, 10 November 2008.

Avdi, E. (2008). Analysing talk in the talking cure: Conversation, discourse, and narrative analysis of psychoanalytic psychotherapy. *European Psychotherapy, 8*(1), 69–88.

Avdi, E., and Georgaca, E. (2007). Narrative research in psychotherapy: A critical review. *Psychology and Psychotherapy: Research and Practice, 78,* 1–14.

Bachrach, H., Galatzer-Levy, R., Skonikoff, A., and Waldron, S. (1991). On the efficacy of psychoanalysis. *Journal of the American Psychoanalytic Association, 39,* 871–911.

Balint, M. (1968). *The basic fault.* London: Tavistock.

Baron-Cohen, S. (1995). *Mindblindness: An essay on autism and theory of mind.* Cambridge, MA: MIT Press.

Bartels, A., and Zeki, S. (2004). The neural correlates of maternal and romantic love. *NeuroImage*, *21*, 1155–1166.

Bateman, A., and Fonagy, P. (2004). *Psychotherapy for borderline personality disorder: Mentalisation based treatment*. Oxford, UK: Oxford University Press.

Bateman, A., and Fonagy, P. (2008). 8-year follow-up of patients treated for borderline personality disorder: Mentalization-based treatment versus treatment as usual. *American Journal of Psychiatry*, *165*, 631–638.

Bateman, A., and Holmes, J. (1995). *Introduction to psychoanalysis: Contemporary theory and practice*. London: Routledge.

Bateson, G. (1972). *Steps towards an ecology of mind*. New York: Ballantine.

Belloc, H. (1907). Jim. *Cautionary tales for children*. London: Duckworth.

Benjamin, J. (2004). Beyond doer and done to: An intersubjective view of thirdness. *Psychoanalytic Quarterly*, *73*, 5–46.

Beutler, L., Malik, M., Alimohamed, S., Harwood, T., Talebi, H., Noble, S., et al. (2004). Therapist variables. In M. Lambert (Ed.), *Bergin and Garfield's handbook of psychotherapy and behaviour change* (pp. 227–306). Chichester, UK: Wiley.

Bion, W. (1962). *Learning from experience*. London: Heinemann.

Bion, W. (1967). *Second thoughts*. New York: Jason Aronson.

Bion, W. (1970). *Attention and interpretation*. London: Tavistock.

Bion, W. (1987). Clinical seminars. In *Clinical seminars and other works*. London: Karnac.

Bion, W. (1988). Notes on memory and desire. In E. Bott-Spillius (Ed.), *Melanie Klein today. Vol. 2: Mainly practice* (pp. 17–21). London: Routledge.

Bleiberg, E., (2006). Enhancing mentalizing through psycho-education. In J. Allen and P. Fonagy (Eds.), *Handbook of mentalisation-based treatment* (pp. 233–248). Chichester, UK: Wiley.

Bollas, C. (1987). *The shadow of the object: Psychoanalysis of the unthought known*. London: Free Association Books.

Bollas, C. (2007). *The Freudian moment*. London: Karnac.

Bollas, C. (2008). Projective invitation. *European Psychotherapy*, *8*(1), 49–52.

Bollas, C. (2009). *The infinite question*. London: Routledge.

Bowlby, J. (1971). *Attachment*. London: Penguin.

Bowlby, J. (1973). *Separation: Anxiety and anger*. London: Penguin.

Bowlby, J. (1981). *Loss: Sadness and depression*. London: Penguin.

Breuer, J., and Freud, S. (1895). Studies on hysteria. *Standard Edition* (Vol. 2). London: Hogarth Press.

Brisch, K. (2002). *Treating attachment disorders*. New York: Guilford.

Britton, R. (2005). Anna O: The first case. In R. Perelberg (Ed.), *Freud: A modern reader* (pp. 31–52). London: Whurr.

Britton, R., Feldman, M., and O'Shaughnessy, E. (1989). *The Oedipus complex today*. London: Karnac.

Brown, G., and Harris, T. (1978). *The social origins of depression*. London: Tavistock.

Budd, S. (2001). No sex please we're British: Sexuality in English and French psychoanalysis. In C. Harding (Ed.), *Sexuality: Psychoanalytic perspectives* (pp. 52–68). Hove, UK: Brunner-Routledge.

Budd, S. (2008). *The use and misuse of transference interpretations*. Lecture given to the qualifying course in psychoanalytic psychotherapy, Department of Psychology, University of Exeter, UK, October 2008.

Busch, F. (2009). Can you push a camel through the eye of a needle? Reflections on how the unconscious speaks to us and its clinical implications. *International Journal of Psychoanalysis*, *90*, 53–68.

Camus, A. (1955). *The myth of Sisyphus*. London: Hamish Hamilton.

Canestri, J. (Ed.) (2006). *Psychoanalysis from practice to theory*. Chichester, UK: Wiley.

Caper, R. (1999). *A mind of one's own*. London: Routledge.

Carter, C. S., Ahnert, L., Grossmann, K. E., Hrdy, S. B., Lamb, M. E., Porges, S. W., et al. (2005) *Attachment and bonding: A new synthesis*. Cambridge, MA: MIT Press.

Casement, P. (1985). *On learning from the patient*. London: Routledge.

Cassidy, J. (2008). The nature of the child's ties. In J. Cassidy and P. Shaver (Eds.), *Handbook of attachment: Theory, research, and clinical applications* (2nd ed., pp. 3–22). New York: Guilford.

Cassidy, J., and Mohr, J. J. (2001). Unsolvable fear, trauma, and psychopathology: Theory, research, and clinical considerations related to disorganized attachment across the life span. *Clinical Psychology: Science and Practice*, *8*, 275–298.

Cassidy, J., and Shaver, P. (Eds.) (2008). *Handbook of attachment: Theory, research, and clinical applications* (2nd ed.). New York: Guilford.

Castonguay, L., and Beutler, L. (2006). *Principles of therapeutic change that work*. Oxford, UK: Oxford University Press.

Cavell, M. (2006). *Becoming a subject*. Oxford, UK: Oxford University Press.

Chambers, W. (1972). *Twentieth century dictionary*. Edinburgh, UK: Chambers.

Cheney, D., and Seyfarth, R. (2007). *Baboon metaphysics*. Chicago: Chicago University Press.

Chiesa, M., Fonagy, P., Holmes, J., and Drahorad, C. (2004). Residential versus community treatment of personality disorders: A comparative study of three treatment programs. *American Journal of Psychiatry*, *161*, 1463–1470.

Choi-Kain, L., and Gunderson, J. (2008). Mentalization: Ontogeny, assessment, and application in the treatment of borderline personality disorder. *American Journal of Psychiatry*, *165*(9), 1127–1135.

Conrad, J. (1904/1963). *Nostromo*. London: Penguin.

Crandell, L., Patrick, M., and Hobson, P. (2003). 'Still face' interactions between mothers with borderline personality disorder and their 2-month infants. *British Journal of Psychiatry*, *183*, 239–249.

Crittenden, P. (1985). Maltreated infants: Vulnerability and resilience. *Journal of Child Psychology and Psychiatry*, *26*, 85–96.

Dalal, F. (2002). *Race, colour and the process of racialization*. Hove, UK: Brunner-Routledge.

Damasio, A. (1994). *Descartes' error*. New York: Jason Aronson.

Dare, C., Eisler, I., Russell, G., Treasure, J., and Dodge, L. (2001). Psychological therapies for adults with anorexia nervosa: Randomised controlled trial of outpatient treatments. *British Journal of Psychiatry*, *178*, 216–221.

Dawkins, R. (1978). *The selfish gene*. London: Penguin.

Denman, C. (2004). *Sexuality: A biopsychosocial approach*. London: Palgrave.

Dennett, D. C. (1987). *The intentional stance*. Cambridge, MA: MIT Press.

Dennett, D. (2006). *Breaking the spell*. London: Allen Lane.

Diamond, D., Stovall-McClough, C., Clarkin, J., and Levy, K. (2003). Patient–therapist attachment in the treatment of borderline personality disorder. *Bulletin of the Menninger Clinic*, *67*, 227–259.

Dickens, C. (1857/1973). *Little Dorrit*. London: Penguin.

Donnet, J.-L. (2001). From the fundamental rule to the analysing situation. *International Journal of Psychoanalysis*, *82*, 129–140.

Dozier, M., Stovall, K., and Albus, K. (2008). Attachment and psychopathology in adulthood. In J. Cassidy and P. Shaver (Eds.), *Handbook of attachment: Theory, research, and clinical applications* (2nd ed., pp. 718–744). New York: Guilford.

Eagle, M. (2007). Attachment and sexuality. In D. Diamond, S. Blatt, and J. Lichtenberg (Eds.), *Attachment and sexuality*. Hillsdale, NJ: Academic Press.

Eagle, M., and Wolitzky, D. (2008). Adult psychotherapy from the perspectives of attachment theory and psychoanalysis. In J. Obegi and E. Berant (Eds.), *Clinical applications of adult attachment theory and research* (pp. 351–378). New York: Guilford.

Eagleton, T. (2007). *How to read a poem*. London: Blackwell.

Eliot, T. S. (1986). *Collected poems*. London: Faber and Faber.

Farber, B., and Metzger, J. (2008). The therapist as secure base. In J. Obegi and E. Berant (Eds.), *Clinical applications of adult psychotherpy and research* (pp. 46–70). New York: Guilford.

Feeney, J. (2008). Adult romantic attachment: Developments in the study of couple relationships. In J. Cassidy and P. Shaver (Eds.), *Handbook of attachment: Theory, research, and clinical applications* (2nd ed., pp. 456–481). New York: Guilford.

Ferro, A. (2006). *Psychoanalysis as therapy and storytelling*. London: Routledge.

Fischer-Mamblona, H. (2000). On the evolution of attachment-disordered behaviour. *Attachment and Human Development*, *4*, 8–21.

Fonagy, P. (2001). *Attachment theory and psychoanalysis*. New York: Other Press.

Fonagy, P. (2006a). The failure of practice to inform theory and the role of implicit theory in bridging the transmission gap. In J. Canestri (Ed.), *Psychoanalysis from practice to theory* (pp. 29–43). Chichester, UK: Wiley.

Fonagy, P. (2006b). The mentalization-focused approach to social development. In J. Allen and P. Fonagy (Eds.), *Handbook of mentalisation-based treatment* (pp. 53–100). Chichester, UK: Wiley.

Fonagy, P., and Bateman, A. (2006). Progress in the treatment of borderline personality disorder. *British Journal of Psychiatry*, *188*, 1–3.

Fonagy, P., Gergely, G., Jurist, E., and Target, M. (2002). *Affect regulation, mentalisation, and the development of the self*. New York: Other Press.

Fonagy, P., Steele, H., and Steele, M. (1991). Maternal representation of attachment during pregnancy predicts the organization of infant–mother attachment at one year of age. *Child Development*, *62*, 891–905.

Fonagy, P., Steele, M., Steele, H., and Target, M. (1997). *Reflective-functioning manual for application to adult attachment interviews, Version 4.1*. London: Psychoanalysis Unit, Sub-Department of Clinical Health Psychology, University College London.

Fonagy, P., and Target, M. (1997). Attachment and reflective function: Their role in self-organization. *Development and Psychopathology*, *9*, 679–700.

Fonagy, P., and Target, M. (2000). Playing with reality 3: The persistence of dual psychic reality in borderline patients. *International Journal of Psychoanalysis*, *81*, 853–874.

Fonagy, P., and Target, M. (2005). *Getting sex back into psychoanalysis*. Paper presented at Day Conference, May 2005, University College London.

Fonagy, P., and Target, M. (2007). The rooting of the mind in the body: New links between attachment theory and psychoanalytic thought. *Journal of the American Psychoanalytic Association*, *55*, 412–456.

Frankl, V. (1978). *The unheard cry for meaning*. New York: Simon and Schuster.

Freud, S. (1895). Project for a scientific psychology. *Standard Edition* (Vol. 1, pp. 295–397). London: Hogarth Press.

Freud, S. (1900). The interpretation of dreams. *Standard Edition* (Vols 4, 5). London: Hogarth Press.

Freud, S. (1905). Fragment of an analysis of a case of hysteria. *Standard Edition* (Vol. 7, pp. 3–122). London: Hogarth Press.

Freud, S. (1911). Formulations on the two principles of mental functioning. *Standard Edition* (Vol. 12, pp. 213–226). London: Hogarth Press.

Freud, S. (1911–1915). Papers on technique. *Standard Edition* (Vol. 12). London: Hogarth Press.

Freud, S. (1912). Recommendations for physicians on the psycho-analytic method of treatment. *Standard Edition* (Vol. 12, pp. 109–120). London: Hogarth Press.

Freud, S. (1914/1958). Remembering, repeating, and working through. *Standard Edition* (Vol. 12, pp. 157–173). London: Hogarth Press.

Freud, S. (1917). Mourning and melancholia. *Standard Edition* (Vol. 14, pp. 243–258). London: Hogarth Press.

Freud, S. (1918). From the history of an infantile neurosis. *Standard Edition* (Vol. 12, pp. 1–122). London: Hogarth Press.

Freud, S. (1921). Group psychology and the analysis of the ego. *Standard Edition* (Vol. 18, pp. 64–144). London: Hogarth Press.

Freud, S. (1937). Analysis terminable and interminable. *Standard Edition* (Vol. 23, pp. 209–253). London: Hogarth Press.

Gabbard, G. (2000). Disguise or consent. *International Journal of Psycho-Analysis*, *81*, 18–29.

Gabbard, G. (2003). Miscarriages of treatment with suicidal patients. *International Journal of Psychoanalysis*, *84*, 249–261.

Gabbard, G. (2005). Major modalities of psychotherapy: Psychodynamic. In G. Gabbard, J. Beck, and J. Holmes (Eds.), *Oxford textbook of psychotherapy*. Oxford, UK: Oxford University Press.

Gabbard, G., Beck, J., and Holmes, J. (Eds.) (2005). *Oxford textbook of psychotherapy*. Oxford, UK: Oxford University Press.

Gabbard, G., Lazar, S., Horngerger, J., and Spiegel, D. (1997). The economic impact of psychotherapy: A review. *American Journal of Psychiatry*, *154*, 147–155.

Gabbard, G., and Westen, D. (2003). Rethinking therapeutic action. *International Journal of Psychoanalysis*, *84*, 823–842.

Gardner H. (Ed.) (1972). *New Oxford book of poetry*. Oxford, UK: Oxford University Press.

George, C., and Solomon J. (Eds.) (1996). *Defining the caregiving system*. New York: Wiley.

Gergely, G. (2007). The social construction of the subjective self. In L. Mayes, P. Fonagy, and M. Target (Eds.), *Developmental science and psychoanalysis* (pp. 45–82). London: Karnac.

Gergely, G., and Watson, J. (1996). The social biofeedback model of parental affect-mirroring. *International Journal of Psychoanalysis*, 77, 1181–1212.

Gleick, J. (1987). *Chaos*. London: Penguin.

Gombrich, E. (1979). *The sense of order*. London: Phaidon.

Green, A. (2005). The illusion of common ground and mythical pluralism. *International Journal of Psychoanalysis*, 86, 627–633.

Green, A., and Kohon, G. (2005). *Love and its vicissitudes*. London: Routledge.

Greenhalgh, T., and Hurwitz, B. (1998). *Narrative based medicine: Dialogue and discourse in clinical practice*. London: BMA Books.

Grossmann, K., Grossmann, K., and Waters, E. (2005). *Attachment from infancy to adulthood: The major longitudinal studies*. New York: Guilford.

Grossmith, G., and Grossmith, W. (1892). *Diary of a nobody*. New York: Oxford University Press, 1998.

Grotstein, J. (2007). *A beam of intense darkness*. London: Karnac.

Gustafson, J. (1986). *The complex secret of brief psychotherapy*. New York: Norton.

Guthrie, E., Creed, F., Dawson, D., and Tomenson, B. (1991). A RCT of psychotherapy in patients with refractory irritable bowel syndrome. *Gastroenterology*, 100, 450–457.

Haley, J. (1980). *Leaving home*. New York: McGraw-Hill.

Hazan, C., and Shaver, P. (1994). Attachment as an organisational framework for research on close relationships. *Psychological Inquiry*, 5, 1–22.

Heard, D., and Lake, B. (1997). *The challenge of attachment for care-giving*. London: Routledge.

Hertsgaard, L., Gunnar, M., Erickson, M., and Nachmias, M. (1995). Adrenocortical response to the strange situation in infants with disorganised/disoriented attachment relationships. *Child Development*, 66, 1100–1106.

Hesse, E. (2008). The Adult Attachment Interview. In J. Cassidy and P. R. Shaver (Eds.), *Handbook of attachment: Theory, research, and clinical applications* (2nd ed., pp. 552–598). New York: Guilford Press.

Hinde, R. (1979). *Towards understanding relationships*. London: Academic Press.

Hinshelwood, R. (1994). *Clinical Klein*. London: Routledge.

Hobson, P. (2002). *The cradle of thought*. London: Macmillan.

Hobson, R. (1985). *The heart of psychotherapy*. London: Routledge.

Holmes, J. (1992). *Between art and science*. London: Routledge.

Holmes, J. (1997). *Attachment, intimacy, autonomy: Using attachment theory in adult psychotherapy*. Northvale, NJ: Jason Aronson.

Holmes, J. (2001). *The search for the secure base: Attachment theory and psychotherapy*. London: Routledge.

Holmes, J. (2003). Borderline personality disorder and the search for meaning – an attachment perspective. *Australian and New Zealand Journal of Psychiatry*, 37, 524–532.

Holmes, J. (2006). Mentalising from a psychoanalytic pespective: What's new? In J. Allen and P. Fonagy (Eds.), *Mentalisation* (pp. 31–50). Chichester, UK: Wiley.

Holmes, J. (2007). Sense and sensuality: Hedonic intersubjectivity and the erotic imagination. In D. Diamond, S. Blatt, and J. Lichtenberg (Eds.), *Attachment & sexuality* (pp. 137–160). Hillsdale, NJ: Academic Press.

Holmes, J. (2008a). Getting it together: From attachment research to clinical practice.

In J. Obegi and E. Berant (Eds.), *Clinical applications of adult attachment*. New York: Guilford.

Holmes, J. (2008b). Mentalisation and metaphor in poetry and psychotherapy. *Advances in Psychiatric Treatment*, *14*, 167–171.

Holmes, J., and Bateman, A. (2002). *Integration in psychotherapy*. Oxford: Oxford University Press.

Holmes, J., and Lindley, R. (1997). *The values of psychotherapy* (2nd ed.). London: Karnac.

Holt, J. (2008). *Stop me if you've heard this: A history and philosophy of jokes*. London: Profile.

Hrdy, S. (1999). *Mother Nature*. London: Penguin.

Jurist, E., and Meehan, K. (2008). Attachment, mentalisation and reflective functioning. In J. Obegi and E. Berant (Eds.), *Clinical applications of adult psychotherapy and research* (pp. 71–93). New York: Guilford.

Klass, D., Silverman, P., and Nickman, S. (Eds.) (1996). *Continuing bonds: New understandings of grief*. Washington, DC: Taylor & Francis.

Klein, M. (1940). Mourning and its relation to manic depressive states. In *The Writings of Melanie Klein, Vol. 1: Love, guilt, and reparation* (pp. 262–289). London: Hogarth Press.

Kuyken, W., Watkins, E. R., and Beck, A. T. (2005). Cognitive-behavioural therapy for mood disorders. In G. Gabbard, J. Beck, and J. Holmes (Eds.), *Oxford textbook of psychotherapy* (pp. 111–126). Oxford, UK: Oxford University Press.

Lacan, J. (1977). *Ecrits: A selection* (trans. A. Sheridan). London: Tavistock.

Lakatos, I. (1970). *Criticism and the growth of knowledge*. London: Butterworth.

Lakoff, G., and Johnson, J. (1980). *The metaphors we live by*. Chicago: University of Chicago Press.

Laplanche, J., and Pontalis, J. B. (1973). *The language of psycho-analysis*. New York: Norton.

Larsen, R. (2009). *The selected works of T.S. Spivet*. London: Waterstones.

Lear, J. (1993). An interpretation of transference. *International Journal of Psychoanalysis*, *74*, 739–755.

Lecours, S., and Bouchard, M.-A. (1997). Dimentions of mentalization: Outlining levels of psychic transformation. *International Journal of Psychoanalysis*, *78*, 855–875.

Leichsenring, F., and Rabung, S. (2008). Effectiveness of long-term psychodynamic psychotherapy: A meta-analysis. *Journal of the American Medical Association*, *300*, 1551–1565.

Leiman, M. (1995). Early development. In A. Ryle (Ed.), *Cognitive analytic therapy: Developments in theory and practice*. Chichester, UK: Wiley.

Lessing, D. (2007). *Nobel lecture*. Available online at http://nobelprize.org/nobel_prizes/literature/laureates/2007/lessing-lecture_en.html (accessed 17 June 2009).

Levy, K. (2008). Psychotherapies and lasting change. *American Journal of Psychiatry*, *165*, 556–559.

Linehan, M. (1993). *Cognitive behavioural treatment of borderline personality disorder*. New York: Guilford.

Linehan, M., Comtois, K., Murray, A., Brown, M. Z., Gallop, R. J., Heard, H. L., et al. (2006). Two-year randomized controlled trial and follow-up of dialectical behavior therapy vs therapy by experts for suicidal behaviors and borderline personality disorder. *Archives of General Psychiatry, 63*, 757–766.

Llosa, M. V. (1983). *Aunt Julia and the scriptwriter*. London: Faber and Faber.

Loewald, H. (1980). *Papers on psychoanalysis*. New Haven, CT: Yale University Press.

Lonnqvist, J. K. (2000). Epidemiology and causes of suicide. In M. Gelder, J. Lopez-Ibor, and N. Andreason (Eds.), *Oxford textbook of psychiatry* (pp. 1043–1055). Oxford, UK: Oxford University Press.

Lorenz, K. (1959). *King Solomon's ring*. London: Butterworth.

Luquet, P. (1981). Le changement dans la mentalisation. *Revue Francais de Psycho-analyse, 45*, 1023–1028.

Lyons-Ruth, K., and the Boston Change Process Study Group (2001). The emergence of new experiences: Relational improvisation, recognition process and non-linear change in psychoanalytic psychotherapy. *Psychologist/Psychoanalyst, 21*, 13–17.

Lyons-Ruth, K., and Jacobvitz, D. (2008). Attachment disorganisation: Genetic factors, parenting contexts, and developmental transformation from infancy to adulthood. In J. Cassidy and P. Shaver (Eds.), *Handbook of attachment: Theory, research, and clinical applications* (2nd ed., pp. 666–697). New York: Guilford.

Mace, C. (2008). *Mindfulness and mental health*. London: Routledge.

Main, M. (1995). Recent studies in attachment: Overview with selected implications for clinical work. In S. Goldberg, R. Muir, and J. Kerr (Eds.), *Attachment theory: Social, developmental and clinical perspectives* (pp. 407–474). Hillsdale, NJ: Analytic Press.

Main, M. (1999). Epilogue. In J. Cassidy and P. Shaver (Eds.), *Handbook of attachment* (pp. 845–888). New York: Guilford.

Main, M., Kaplan, N., and Cassidy, J. (1985). Security in infancy, childhood and adulthood: A move to the level of representation. In I. Bretherton and E. Waters (Eds.), Growing points of attachment theory and research. *Monographs of the Society for Research in Child Development, 50*, 66–104.

Main, M., and Solomon, J. (1986). Discovery of a new, insecure-disorganized disoriented attachment pattern. In T. Brazelton and M. Yogman (Eds.), *Affective development in infancy* (pp. 39–51). Norwood, NJ: Ablex.

Malan, D. (1979). *Individual psychotherapy and the science of psychodynamics*. London: Butterworth.

Malan, D., and Della Selva, P. (2006). *Lives transformed: A revolutionary method of dynamic psychotherapy*. London: Karnac.

Mallinckrodt, B., Porter, M. J., and Kivlighan, D. M. J. (2005). Client attachment to therapist, depth of in-session exploration, and object relations in brief psychotherapy. *Psychotherapy: Theory, Research, Practice, Training, 42*, 85–100.

Mallinckrodt, B., Daly, K., and Wang, C. (2008). An attachment approach to adult psychotherapy. In J. Obegi and E. Berant (Eds.), *Clinical applications of adult psychotherapy and research* (pp. 234–268). New York: Guilford.

Mann, J. (1973). *Time-limited psychotherapy*. Cambridge, MA: Harvard Unversity Press.

Margison, F. (2002). Psychodynamic interpersonal therapy. In J. Holmes and A. Bateman (Eds.), *Integration in psychotherapy* (pp. 107–124). Oxford: Oxford University Press.

Marty, P. (1991). *Mentalization et psychosomatique*. Paris: Laboratoire Delagrange.

Matte-Blanco, I. (1975). *The unconscious as infinite sets*. London: Routledge.

McCluskey, U. (2005). *To be met as a person*. London: Karnac.

McLuhan, M. (1964). *Understanding media: The extensions of man*. New York: McGraw-Hill.

Meins, E. (1999). Sensitivity, security and internal working models: Bridging the transmission gap. *Attachment and Human Development, 3*, 325–342.

Mikulincer, M., and Shaver, P. (2008). Adult attachment and affect regulation. In J. Cassidy and P. Shaver (Eds.), *Handbook of attachment: Theory, research, and clinical applications* (2nd ed., pp. 503–531). New York: Guilford.

Milrod, B., Leon, A. C., Busch, F., Rudden, M., Schwalberg, M., Clarkin, J., et al. (2007). A randomized controlled clinical trial of psychoanalytic psychotherapy for panic disorder. *American Journal of Psychiatry, 164*, 265–272.

Money-Kyrle, R. (1956). Normal counter-transference and some of its deviations. *International Journal of Psychoanalysis, 37*, 360–366.

Novick, J. (1988). The timing of termination. *International Journal of Psychoanalysis, 15*, 307–318.

Novick, J. (1997). Termination conceivable and inconceivable. *Psychoanalytic Psychology, 14*, 145–162.

Obama, B. (2008). *Dreams from my father*. Edinburgh, UK: Canongate.

Obegi, J., and Berant, E. (Eds.) (2008). *Clinical applications of adult attachment theory and research*. New York: Guilford.

Ogden, T. (1987). *The matrix of the mind*. Northvale, NJ: Aronson.

Ogden, T. (1989). *The primitive edge of experience*. London: Karnac.

Ogden, T. (1999). 'The music of what happens' in poetry and psychoanalysis. *International Journal of Psychoanalysis, 80*, 979–994.

Orlinsky, D., Grawe, K., and Parks, B. (2004). Process and outcome in psychotherapy. In M. Lambert (Ed.), *Bergin and Garfield's handbook of psychotherapy and behaviour change* (pp. 270–376). Chichester, UK: Wiley.

O'Neill, S. (2008). The psychotherapy site: Towards a differential theory of therapeutic engagement. *European Psychotherapy, 8*, 53–68.

Parkes, C. (2006). *Love and loss: The roots of grief and its complications*. Washington, DC: Taylor and Francis.

Parry, G., Roth, A., and Kerr, I. (2005). Brief and time-limited therapy. In G. Gabbard, J. Beck, and J. Holmes (Eds.), *Oxford textbook of psychotherapy* (pp. 507–522). Oxford, UK: Oxford University Press.

Pedder, J. (1988). Termination reconsidered. *International Journal of Psychoanalysis, 69*, 495–505.

Piper, W. E., Ogrodniczuk, J. S., Joyce, A. S., McCallum, M., Rosie, J. S., O'Kelly, J. G., et al. (1999). Prediction of dropping out in time-limited, interpretive individual psychotherapy. *Psychotherapy, 36*, 114–122.

Popper, K. (1959). *The logic of scientific discovery*. London: Routledge.

Racker, H. (1968). *Transference and counter-transference*. London: Hogarth Press (reprinted London: Karnac, 1982).

Reich, A. (1950). On the termination of analysis. *International Journal of Psychoanalysis, 31*, 179–183.

Reik, T. (1922). *The inner eye of a psychoanalyst*. London: Allen and Unwin.

Roth, A., and Fonagy, P. (2006). *What works for whom?* (2nd ed.). New York: Guilford.

Roth, A., and Lemma, A. (2008). *The competences required to deliver effective psychoanalytic/psychodynamic psychotherapy*. London: Department of Health. Available online at www.ucl.ac.uk/clinical-psychology/CORE/Psychodynamic_Competences/Background_Paper.pdf (accessed 11 June 2009).

Ruiz, P., Bland, I., Pi, E., and De Zuletta, P. (2005). Cross-cultural psychotherapy. In G. Gabbard, J. Beck, and J. Holmes (Eds.), *Oxford textbook of psychotherapy* (pp. 431–442). Oxford, UK: Oxford University Press.

Rycroft, C. (1985). *Psychoanalysis and beyond*. London: Chatto.

Rycroft, C. (1995). *Critical dictionary of psychoanalysis* (2nd ed.). London: Penguin.

Ryle, A. (1990). *Cognitive analytic therapy*. Chichester, UK: Wiley.

Safran, J., and Muran, J. (2000). *Negotiating the therapeutic alliance: A relational treatment guide*. New York: Guilford.

Safran, J. D., Muran, J. C., Samstag, L. W., and Stevens, C. L. (2001). Repairing alliance ruptures. *Psychotherapy: Theory, Research, Practice, Training*, *38*, 406–412.

Sandell, R., Blomberg, J., Lazar, A., Carlsson, J., Broberg, J., and Rand, H. (2000). Varieties of long-term outcome among patients in psychoanalysis and long-term psychotherapy: A review of findings in the STOPP. *International Journal of Psychoanalysis*, *81*, 921–942.

Santayana, G. (1905). *Life of reason*. London: Butterworth.

Schafer, R. (1983). *The analytic attitude*. New York: Basic Books.

Scharff, J., and Scharff, D. (1998). *Object relations in individual therapy*. Hillsdale, NJ: Aronson.

Schneiderman, E. (1993). *Suicide as psychache: A clinical approach to self destructive behaviour*. Northdale, NJ: Jason Aronson.

Schopenhauer, A. (1970). *Essays and aphorisms* (trans. R. Hollingdale). London: Penguin.

Segal, H. (1991). *Dream, phantasy, art*. London: Routledge.

Seligman, M. (1995). The effectiveness of psychotherapy: The Consumer Reports study. *American Psychologist*, *50*, 965–992.

Sennett, D. (2008). *The craftsman*. London: Allen Lane.

Shapiro, D., Barkham, M., Rees, A., Hardy, G. E., Reynolds, S., and Startup, M. (1994). Effects of treatment duration and severity of depression on the effectiveness of cognitive/behavioural and psychodynamic/interpersonal psychotherapy. *Journal of Consulting and Clinical Psychology*, *63*, 211–236.

Sharpe, E. F. (1940). Psycho-physical problems revealed in language: An examination of metaphor. *International Journal of Psychoanalysis*, *21*, 201–207.

Shaver, P., and Fraley, R. (2008). Attachment, loss, and grief: Bowlby's views and current controversies. In J. Cassidy and P. Shaver (Eds.), *Handbook of attachment: Theory, research, and clinical applications* (2nd ed., pp. 48–77). New York: Guilford.

Shaver, P., and Mikulincer, M. (2008). An overview of attachment theory. In J. Obegi and E. Berant (Eds.), *Clinical applications of adult psychotherapy and research* (pp. 17–45). New York: Guilford.

Slade, A. (2005). Parental reflective functioning: An introduction. *Attachment and Human Development*, *7*, 269–282.

Slade, A. (2008). The implications of attachment theory and research for adult psychotherapy: Research and clinical perspectives. In J. Cassidy and P. Shaver (Eds.), *Handbook of attachment: Theory, research, and clinical applications* (2nd ed., pp. 762–782). New York: Guilford.

Solomon, J., and George, C. (Eds.) (1999). *Attachment disorganization*. New York: Guilford.

Spence, D. (1987). *The Freudian metaphor: Towards paradigm change in psychoanalysis*. New York: Norton.

Sroufe, L. (2005). Attachment and development: A prospective, longitudinal study from birth to adulthood. *Attachment and Human Development*, 7, 349–367.

Steele, H., and Steele, M. (2008). *Clinical applications of the adult attachment interview*. New York: Guilford.

Steiner, J. (1996). The aim of psychoanalysis in theory and practice. *International Journal of Psychoanalysis*, 77, 1073–1083.

Steiner, J. (2002). *Psychic retreats*. London: Routledge

Stern, D. (1985). *The interpersonal world of the infant*. New York: Basic Books.

Stern, D. (2004). *The present moment in psychotherapy and everyday life*. New York: Norton.

Stiles, W. B., Elliott, R., Llewelyn, S. P., Firth-Cozens, J. A., Margison, F. R., Shapiro, D. A., et al. (1990). Assimilation of problematic experiences by clients in psychotherapy. *Psychotherapy*, 27, 411–420.

Stoller, R. (1979). *Sexual excitement: The dynamics of erotic life*. New York: Pantheon.

Strachey, J. (1934). The nature of the therapeutic action of psychoanalysis. *International Journal of Psychoanalysis*, 50, 275–292.

Sulloway, F. (1980). *Freud: Biologist of the mind*. London: Fontana.

Suomi, S. (2008). Attachment in rhesus monkeys. In J. Cassidy and P. Shaver (Eds.), *Handbook of attachment: Theory, research, and clinical applications* (2nd ed., pp. 173–191). New York: Guilford.

Thomas, E. (1971). *Collected poems*. London: Faber & Faber.

Tronic, E. (1998). Dyadically expanded states of consciousness and the process of therapeutic change. *Infant Mental Health Journal*, 19, 290–299.

Tuckett, D., Basile, R., Birksted-Breen, D., Bohm, T., Denis, P., Ferro, A., et al. (2008). *Psychoanalysis comparable and incomparable: The evolution of a method to describe and compare psychoanalytic approaches*. London: Routledge.

Van der Kolk, M. D. (2003). The neurobiology of childhood trauma and abuse. *Child and Adolescent Psychiatric Clinics*, 12, 293–317.

Van Ijzendoorn, M. (1995). Adult attachment representations, parental responsiveness, and infant attachment: A meta-analysis on the predictive validity of the Adult Attachment Interview. *Psychological Bulletin*, 117, 387–403.

Van Ijzendoorn, M., and Sagi-Schwartz, A. (2008). Cross-cultural patterns of attachment: Universal and contextual dimensions. In J. Cassidy and P. Shaver. (Eds.), *Handbook of attachment: Theory, research, and clinical applications* (2nd ed., pp. 880–905). New York: Guilford.

Waddell, M. (2006). *Inside lives: Psychoanalysis and the growth of personality*. London: Karnac.

Wallerstein, R. (1990). Psychoanalysis: The common ground. *International Journal of Psychoanalysis*, 71, 3–20.

Wallerstein, R. (2009). What kind of research in psychoanalytic science? *International Journal of Psychoanalysis*, 90, 109–133.

Wallin, D. (2007). *Attachment in psychotherapy*. New York: Guilford.

Wampold, B. (2001). *The great psychotherapy debate*. New York: Lawrence Erlbaum Associates.

Watts, D., and Morgan, G. (1994). Malignant alienation: Dangers for patients who are hard to like. *British Journal of Psychiatry*, *164*, 697–698.

Welldon, E. (2009). Dancing with death. *British Journal of Psychotherapy*, *25*, 149–182.

Widlocher, D. (2002). *Infantile sexuality and attachment*. New York: The Other Press.

Williams, H. (1994). *Dock leaves*. London: Faber and Faber.

Williams, J., Teasdale, J., Segal, Z., and Soulsby, J. (2000). Mindfulness-based cognitive therapy reduces overgeneral autobiographical memory in formerly depressed patients. *Journal of Abnormal Psychology*, *109*, 150–155.

Winnicott, D. W. (1971). *Playing and reality*. London: Routledge.

Wittgenstein, L. (1958). *Philosophical investigations*. Oxford, UK: Oxford University Press.

Wordsworth, W. (1802). *Lyrical ballads*, preface to 2nd edition. *Oxford dictionary of quotations*. Oxford, UK: Oxford University Press, 1980.

Wright, K. (1991). *Vision and separation*. London: Free Association Books.

Yallom, I. (2008). *Staring at the sun*. London: Piatkus.

Zeal, P. (2008). Listening with many ears. *European Psychotherapy*, *8*, 89–102.

Zeki, S. (2008). *The splendors and miseries of the brain: Love, creativity, and the quest for human happiness*. Chichester, UK: Wiley-Blackwell.

Zizek, S. (2006). *How to read Lacan*. London: Granta.

Index

absence: as a presence 154; suicidality and 143; of the therapist 168; thinking arising out of 17, 95; transferential meaning of 143
acting-out *see* enactment/acting-out
active imagination 87
Adler, A. 67; Oedipus complex 69–70
Adult Attachment Interview (AAI) 4, 10–11, 49, 79, 118–19
affect arousal *see* emotional arousal
affect/emotional expression 33, 35, 138
affect regulation 16–17, 27; contingency, marking and 35; empathic attunement and 36–7; and the linking of disorganised attachment and BPD 138–9; mentalising and 11, 24; mirroring and 36–7; and sexual physiological difficulty 107; therapeutic reawakening of painful affect 46; by the therapist 129; *see also* frustration tolerance
affect withdrawal 37
aggression: difficulty in expressing 'healthy aggression' in sexuality 107; reparation and 95–6, 126; sex and 111–13
Ainsworth, M. 3
alexithymia 19
alliance rupture and repair *see* reparation
alpha elements 17, 18
alpha function 17–18, 19
AMBIANCE (measure of mother–infant communication) 79
ambivalent attachment *see* hyperactivating attachment
analysts/therapists: affect regulation by 129; as attachment figures 6, 167, 168; becoming the Other 150; countertransference *see* countertransference; enactments of 22, 38, 39, 163; non-defensive behaviour 82; role in therapeutic relationship 56; security provided by 6, 37 *see also* therapeutic relationship; termination of therapy and 160, 161
analytic third 57
Andreas-Salome, L. 162–3

anxiety 6, 13–14, 22, 34, 46; attachment anxiety 33, 39, 43, 46, 61, 121; and being misunderstood 37; castration-anxiety 100, 107; death anxiety 173; narcissistic 108; organised insecure attachment and 32–3; and the pressure of paradox 59; as resistance 36; therapeutic acknowledgement and soothing of 38–9; *see also* fear
approach/avoidance dilemma 58–9, 118–19, 128–9
Aron, L. 116
arousal: emotional *see* emotional arousal; proximity and 51; sexual and attachment arousal 102
assimilation model (Stiles et al.) 20
asymmetrical thinking 88
attaching/attachment 31–42; brutal destructions of attachment 70–1; disorganised *see* disorganised attachment; emotional connectedness 34–5; fear of 51; versus infantile sexuality 102–5; insecure *see* insecure attachment; maternal attachment response 12; proximity in *see* proximity; as a psycho-physical phenomenon 51; rupture and repair *see* reparation; secure *see* secure attachment; sexuality and 108; styles *see* attachment styles; termination of therapy and 161–5; theory of *see* attachment theory; in therapeutic relationship *see* therapeutic relationship
attachment anxiety 33, 39, 43, 46, 61, 121
attachment arousal 102
attachment behaviours 31–2; emotional connectedness and 34–5; incompatibility with exploring 31–2, 102, 177
attachment figures: analyst as attachment figure 6, 167, 168; security and 6
attachment relationships 38, 48, 100–1, 123; ending of 161–71; therapeutic relationship *see* therapeutic relationship
attachment styles 3–4, 31–4; deactivating attachment *see* deactivating (avoidant)

Lightning Source UK Ltd.
Milton Keynes UK
UKHW022134051119
352978UK00003B/12/P